MARK HUGHES

LEWIS
HAMILTON
THE FULL STORY

MARK HUGHES

LEWIS HAMILTON

THE FULL STORY

ICON BOOKS

This edition published in the UK in 2008 by
Icon Books Ltd, The Old Dairy,
Brook Road, Thriplow,
Cambridge SG8 7RG
email: info@iconbooks.co.uk
www.iconbooks.co.uk

Originally published in the UK in 2007 by Icon Books Ltd

Sold in the UK, Europe, South Africa and Asia
by Faber & Faber Ltd, 3 Queen Square,
London WC1N 3AU or their agents

Distributed in the UK, Europe, South Africa and Asia
by TBS Ltd, TBS Distribution Centre, Colchester Road
Frating Green, Colchester CO7 7DW

This edition published in Australia in 2008
by Allen & Unwin Pty Ltd,
PO Box 8500, 83 Alexander Street,
Crows Nest, NSW 2065

Distributed in Canada by
Penguin Books Canada,
90 Eglinton Avenue East, Suite 700,
Toronto, Ontario M4P 2YE

ISBN: 978-1840469-41-7

Typeset and designed by Simmons Pugh

Printed in China

CONTENTS

MARK HUGHES is recognised as one of Formula One's top journalists, and his reports and columns for *Autosport* magazine have won him wide acclaim. ITV and Radio 5 Live regularly benefit from his expertise. He has written a number of books on F1, one of which won the 2005 Illustrated Sports Book of the Year.

In the words of *Motor Sport* magazine: 'None have so effectively combined a passion for and understanding of the human and technical sides of the sport, viewed the political machinations with such wry, subversive humour and informed us so well as to how this affects what happens on the track. He's our own beatnik Kerouac taking the best bits from the journalistic greats and raising the bar for everyone.'

INTRODUCTION

The Right Stuff, the Right Place. The Right Dad

Motor racing is not a meritocracy. It likes to think it is, but it's not. It's far too dependent on the quality of the machinery for the best drivers to automatically make it. And machinery costs money, so typically only those with access to large amounts of it – and who can combine this access with some talent – have much of a chance of making it in what is still a very elitist sport.

Lewis Hamilton began without access to large amounts of family money, yet his motor racing career has been set on a sharp upward trajectory since the day he first got his hands on a kart, aged seven. As he stood on the brink of the F1 world championship, aged 22, he could be forgiven for having to pinch himself and ask: 'How in the world did I get here from there?' From an ordinary upbringing in an ordinary British suburb, an ordinary school, ordinary friends. From a life that countless millions of British kids would recognise as very little different from theirs.

Both nature and nurture have been exceptionally kind to

him. In terms of nature, he is blessed, no other word for it, with the right stuff, the necessary magical mix of neurons that determines his inner ear balance and sensitivity, his spatial awareness, his feel for changes in lateral motion that allow him to be keyed into a cornering kart or car, the way he can coordinate this feel with the motor responses of his limbs. The stuff, in short, that makes it easy to drive a vehicle fast, ensuring that it requires only a small proportion of his mental capacity.

Next, such talent needs application, needs the sort of mind that can concentrate on the fine detail that separates competence from excellence. There is footage of a six-year-old Lewis as a guest of British children's TV show *Blue Peter*, totally absorbed in the act of guiding a radio-controlled racing car around a garden, eyes following the action, dextrous fingers on auto-pilot, distractions such as TV cameras or a sense of occasion rendered irrelevant information. Even as he was racing the little model car the interviewer was asking questions and Lewis's responses came straight, clipped, accurate and polite, but all the while concentrating on the car. His mind was wired up perfectly for this.

But such talent and application is next to useless without a supporting competitive personality. In this too his genes have been entirely cooperative. Always, he wants to be better. To be the best he can possibly be, and for that best to be better than anyone else's best. To *really* want it. Badly. Not like a lot of kids who are in love with the *idea* of excelling in their field, but who somehow never summon the relentless energy and focus it requires.

So much for nature. There may have been others of Lewis's age with a similar mix of inbuilt qualities. But how many of them were born in the right part of the world? Many moons ago when Stirling Moss was recognised as the world's greatest driver, he made the point that potentially the best driver in the world may be driving a bus in Calcutta. He could just as easily have said cutting rubber trees, or eking out survival in a corrupt African state, or being damaged by an abusive parent, or left to fend for himself in some ghetto or third-world orphanage. Lack of nurture weeds out a lot of those blessed by nature.

Then, of those with the necessary gift that are born into reasonable circumstances – to caring parents in an affluent society – Britain is about the most advantageous place to have arrived. South-east Britain, in particular. Because Britain is the centre of the motor racing universe, and has been since the late 1950s. Nowhere else has as structured a nursery slope, or offers as much opportunity to put a toe into the motorsport water. This is where attention is focused, where excellence is noticed. Once he has established a foothold in British karting, the young hopeful will then usually have to spread his wings and compete in mainland Europe where the heavy-duty championships are based. But from there, the move into cars brings the focus back to Britain, for most of the top junior formulae car racing teams – as well as most of the F1 teams – are based here. Furthermore, English is the language of motor racing throughout its international echelons. In looking at the perfect circumstances for a would-be racer to be born into, Hamilton's location – actually in Stevenage, Hertfordshire – was pretty much spot-on.

Then there's his father Anthony, in many ways the main thrust of Lewis's story. He was much more than a caring, supportive parent, although he was always that first. He had no interest in or knowledge of motor racing. It was Lewis who stumbled onto something that very quickly became an obsession, but it was Anthony who not only supported this interest but guided and plotted his progress in it. Getting involved in motorsport can be a minefield. There are hundreds of wrong ways of doing it for every right way. There are licensed vultures looking to make commercial gain from naive newcomers. As you progress through the ranks, the cost of competing accelerates almost vertically. It's the perfect environment for shrewd purveyors of hope. They feed on the ego, lack of knowledge and lack of self-awareness of those who arrive cold into the sport. Before you know it, you can blow all the money you have access to, having still not made an impression – regardless of your ability. Anthony Hamilton was pulled into this world by the precocious talent of his son, took a look around, and with a streetwise savvy and a lot of intelligence, sniffed out the scene, bedded himself down in it – and made a series of brilliant calls, learning more as he went along. Had Anthony – a computer programmer with British Rail when Lewis raced his first kart – got any one of dozens, perhaps hundreds, of critical moves wrong, Lewis's career momentum, like those of many gifted drivers before him, could have come to a dead halt. Because the Hamiltons didn't have the money to simply buy their way out of any problems they may have encountered, every move had to be the right one.

Anthony's not everyone's cup of tea. Like Lewis, he's very principled, but some find him a little too cocky, too pernickety, too much hard work. But that's fine. Because pretty much everyone likes Lewis, the genuine sunny spirit, the handsome kid who wraps his total inner confidence with a layer of real grace that comes naturally, unforced. Actually, there's a part of Anthony that's like that too, but it's not so much on display, given the reserve that hard experience has brought, the front needed from someone who is at once Lewis's hustler and his doorman. Given the protection that Anthony has provided, Lewis has been able to afford to relax into his own self, totally natural, confident and likeable. Unlike Anthony, there are no edges to Lewis, the man. But Lewis the competitor, well that's a different matter. Then he's a full-time, full-on walking edge. Then, he is truly formidable, a guy who can walk into the pinnacle of the sport and command instant respect from his rivals, a guy who has left a record-breaking double world champion team-mate gasping, a guy so good that he has created problems for his team.

Yes, he's fantastically gifted and his personality is perfectly suited to supporting that gift. But he's found himself in a fantastic situation too, regardless of the lack of family wealth. And that's almost entirely due to his father. You may think there's an elephant in the room in the story so far, in that we haven't mentioned his colour. How much has that had to do with his relentless rise? How much of a sponsor's dream has been the first black man to succeed in F1? It maybe has been a wet dream for some marketeers – but they have not been the ones responsible for his career. Motorsport, for all its faults, in Europe at least, is at its core a mini-society impressed only by performance and results. Anyone who did what Lewis did, with the career guidance he's had, and who delivered every time he got behind the wheel the way he has done, would have made it. And if some of the early buzz around him came partly from the curiosity factor of his skin colour, then that was soon left behind as irrelevant when the real test was the stopwatch and the timing beam. Forget race, think only racing: in the history of the sport very few men have ever been able to drive like this. The guy is a phenomenon.

CHAPTER ONE

The Storm That
Sowed A Seed

The storms in Grenada in '55 were bad. They destroyed most
of the nutmeg trees that the island largely made its living
from. Davidson Hamilton could see no immediate future
there, his income from farming the crop in the town of
Grand Roy on the west coast simply switched off. Besides,
recently married, he no longer had just himself to consider.
He had to think of something else – fast. Now 25, his wild
carefree days were in the past – though he still loved to ride
his motorbike like the wind. He had a reputation in town as
the fastest thing on two wheels. The roads that twisted their
way between the hills and towering precipices that overlooked the ocean held no fears for Davidson. 'He once took
just five minutes to ride the three miles between Grand Roy
and the police station in Gouyave, the next town along the
coast,' recalled his close friend Elvis Glean in an interview
with the *Daily Telegraph*. 'He had this enormous BSA and in
those days the roads were much worse than now. He just
loved fast riding. People always used to wonder about him,

about whether he might end up dead. But nothing happened, he never had an accident.'

In fact, most Grenadians will tell you that despite the difficult roads most drive fast there, yet accidents are a rarity. Maybe there's just something in the blood of the people of that island, a speed gene, that makes them suited to going fast. But even by their standards Davidson was fast enough to have a reputation, to mark himself out as a little bit special.

But that reputation wasn't going to find him work. This was during the time of the mass British recruitment drive, when the war had left the country with more vacancies in key sectors such as hospitals and transport than there were takers. Davidson decided he'd try his luck in England and in late '55 he and his wife crossed the ocean and set up home in west London. Davidson got a job on the London Underground.

Interestingly, Davidson's brother stayed in Grenada. He took the storm as an opportunity, not only replanting but buying up the land of other farmers who'd thrown in the towel. In the years to come he would profit handsomely.

In 1963 Davidson's wife gave birth to a son, Anthony, and together they lived in the house in west London. He was a bright boy and determined. He was by no means unusual in being black in that neighbourhood at that time, but England, then as now, had its racial tensions and as he grew up Anthony frequently encountered the vocal minority of racists. But he formed close friendships with white kids and black. This and his strong family grounding helped him develop a well-rounded personality, tough when needed, but smart as a preference, very competitive always.

When he was still a schoolboy, he lost his mother to illness and was naturally devastated. If anything, it seemed to intensify his personality. He'd always been a serious kid but now he was more so. Always thinking ahead, preparation and diligence were very important. He didn't like to leave things to chance and if a job was worth doing, it was worth doing well. He had a temper when roused, but usually it was kept in check. Some found him a little cocky, but that was just part of his competitive drive and it sort of fitted with his trim, compact physique. He became 'Tony' more often than Anthony, though to his father he remained Anthony. Within the tough neighbourhood he was the streetwise, savvy black kid from a good home and with solid family values. A lot of his friends were turning to crime, but it was a path he was never tempted to follow. Partly to give his boy the benefit of a better neighbourhood, maybe partly to leave the house that triggered too many memories of his late wife, Davidson moved them to Stevenage, a 'new town' established in the 1950s in Hertfordshire, one of London's outlying 'home counties'.

In 1980, at age 17, Tony got a job at British Rail, as a clerk. Subsequently he did a night school course in computing and parlayed it into a better-paid job within British Rail, in the computing department. He learned well, received a good grounding in programming and made his way through the organisation. He wasn't management initially, but the job was a step up in status from that of his father's. He was good at his job, naturally. Applied intelligence and diligence always.

In 1983 he married his girlfriend Carmen Larbalestier, a white girl from Stevenage. She worked as a secretary, was pretty, and had a sweet personality, though like Tony she had a fiery side, and as such it wasn't a tranquil relationship, and it worked only for a time. On 7 January 1985 Carmen gave birth to a boy, Lewis Carl, named after the American Olympic gold medallist sprinter Carl Lewis. Together the three of them lived in a respectable end-of-terrace house on the Shephall council estate in Stevenage.

Not long before Lewis's second birthday, Tony and Carmen split up and initiated divorce proceedings. Carmen kept custody of Lewis and remained at the house in Shephall, Tony moved to a nearby apartment convenient for his access to the boy at weekends. It was done in as civilised a way as possible in circumstances that are never easy.

'From where he grew up, having a child at such a young age, it would have been easy for him to pack up and leave,' said Lewis during a *USA Today* interview. 'That's what happened to the parents of most of my close friends. Most people from our area were broke, and they didn't want the responsibility. He was a real man and stuck by us.'

So Lewis grew up living with his mother and her new boyfriend during the week and his father at weekends. Like any kid of that age, he adapted. Both were loving parents; he had plenty of security. He wasn't living in a ghetto, but a Stevenage council estate was not a genteel place. There was plenty of hanging around on the streets, running with the pack. He soon became a streetwise little kid, and with some of his parents' feistiness definitely in his DNA, he could be a handful. But both parents instilled in him politeness and manners.

When the time came he started at the nearby Peartree school. The deputy head there at the time, Carol Perkins, told the *Daily Telegraph* she recalled a boy 'with a bright, smiley face and lovely manners. He seemed very happy. A bright little button, but normal, very normal.'

The deputy head's fondness for Lewis wasn't shared by

the class bully – who made him a target. 'It was when I was about five,' Lewis recalled to the *Daily Mail*'s John McEvoy. 'It was horrible but I told my dad I wanted to start karate so I could protect myself. The bullying stopped and, more importantly, I got real self-confidence.' He would keep up his karate lessons over the years and at the age of 12 become a black belt in the art.

Away from school he was developing a deep interest in cars, had a keen eye for them, knew the difference between models from an early age. When he was six, Tony bought him a battery-powered remote controlled car. 'It was an electric off-roader,' recalled Lewis, 'and I loved it. My dad saw I had good eye-to-hand coordination.' Much of his weekend time at Tony's house would be spent manoeuvring the car around the tight confines of the flat's balcony.

Not long after, Tony took Lewis on holiday to Spain. There was a small fun-kart track near the resort and, not unnaturally, Lewis wanted a try. 'It was a really, really small track with three corners,' Lewis later recalled. 'It may have covered about 200 feet. It was so, so short it was incredible, but I loved it. I just had this feeling getting the kart back up to power and everything that it just felt natural.'

Once back home, it was back to the radio-controlled toy, which he'd bring religiously with him on his weekend visits to his father. He used it so much that Tony's weekends seemed to consist of constantly recharging batteries. This led to a chain of thought that was to have profound consequences for both of them. He'd been a little concerned at the most recent school parents' evening to hear the teacher say that Lewis really needed to work a little harder. It was probably the sort of thing that the vast majority of parents of kids that age heard. But for Tony, who placed such devout faith in effort and preparation, it was a little unsettling.

Tony recalled: 'I thought, "What if I enrolled him at a club for radio-controlled cars as a reward for trying harder at school?"' A bit of research quickly established that there was such a club nearby, at Hertford. 'I said to him, "OK. On Sundays we go there and you race and that's it." Within three months he was leading the championship.'

The miniature cars are controlled from a transmitter panel with joysticks for throttle and steering, which send variable pulses to electric motors that power the wheels and move the steering. Moving up from the simple toy that so delighted Lewis, there are specialised racing models with adjustment in the suspension and steering. There are regional and national championships, and some idea of how competitive it all gets can be gained from the warning in a club's website that 'any driver or his/her representative using foul or abusive language will be excluded from the meeting'.

Lewis was an absolute natural at it. The hand-eye coordination, the motor responses in his hands, were brilliant. Tony's ethics of preparation and effort extended to Lewis's new pastime and he made sure his boy had the right kit. There were only two other kids in the club; Lewis was racing in the main against adults. But he won the championship. There was another class for the more complex petrol-powered cars, still radio-controlled but with tiny petrol engines in place of the electric motor. They are generally considered more difficult to control. Tony asked Lewis if he fancied a go at that too. Lewis didn't need to be asked twice. He finished runner-up in that championship. It's 1991 and the cute six-year-old black kid is standing among the line of adults, all concentrating intensely on their buzzing projec-

tiles, a joyous Tony picking up his boy in celebration afterwards. Lewis was a competitor. He loved it – and so did Tony.

Tony was never one to let things take their own course.
With his competitive juices flowing, even if one step
removed, he looked to get some media coverage for his boy.
He got in touch with BBC kids' TV programme *Blue Peter*, the
producers of which were taken by the storyline of the kid
beating all the adults and invited him to the *Blue Peter* garden
to show his prowess. He duly won the display race, his off-
roader jumping spectacularly over the bridge across the
stream, Lewis answering the presenter's questions as he
moved the joysticks, eyes on the car the whole time. The
relationship with the programme was to last several years as
they made regular updates of his karting progress. But the
most significant thing was that it had cast Tony in the role of
hustler for his boy. Articulate, bright and just the charming
side of pushy, Tony was going to make a brilliant agent. Even
if he didn't quite see it like that yet.

But what to do next? 'I thought you could spend a fortune
competing in British or world championships,' he
explained. 'So do we do that to become world champion
model racer, or with whatever skills he has, do we try karting?
We went down to Rye House, sat him in a kart. It was a crap-
py old thing but he was only a couple of seconds off the pace
in it. That encouraged us. He was only seven, not old enough
to race.' Tony himself had a go in a kart that same day – and
Lewis lapped him. Maybe Davidson's speed genes had
skipped a generation, maybe it was just the lighter weight of
the boy compared to the father. But Lewis just had an
instinctive feel for the correct lines through a turn, for how
much speed you could take into a corner, for how late you
could leave it before you braked, for how to control the kart

when it slid, for how to use the brake and throttle to control the kart's attitude through a corner. Because he was blessed.

He would be old enough to race on his next birthday, a couple of months away. 'But the thing was seeing his face when he got out of it,' recalled Anthony. 'That's when I knew I was doing the right thing for him; he was like "Wow, where did that come from?" His eyes would light up when he was doing the radio-controlled cars but this was something else again. He seemed to love it so much that I said I would continue to support him and do extra jobs, whatever it took, so long as he worked harder at school. Also, it was something we could [do] as a family together.'

That family had extended now, for Tony had remarried. At the time of Lewis's first try-out at Rye House, Tony's new wife Linda had not long given birth to a boy, Nicholas. Together they lived in a one-bedroom flat. It wasn't long before it became apparent that Nicholas was suffering from cerebral palsy, a disorder that affects muscle tone, movement and motor skills. There is no cure and it's a condition that Nicholas has coped with admirably – to an extent that has come to inspire Lewis.

Between that first kart test and Lewis's birthday was Christmas Day 1992, and sitting in the flat was a Cadet kart. It wasn't new. Tony had bought it second-hand for £1,200 – three-quarters of his and Linda's combined monthly salary – from a club member at Rye House, stripped it, repainted it, and it looked fantastic. Hard work and preparation: Tony may have been indulging his boy, but he was doing it in such a way that it made him a perfect role model.

As well as the kart, Tony bought a box trailer and a generator. He would hook the trailer up to his old Vauxhall Cavalier and the family – Tony, Lewis, Linda and Nicholas –

would head for the track. Tony would be the mechanic, Lewis would race, Linda and Nicholas would cheer. This was going to be their weekend life for years to come. To help pay for it all, Tony took on any extra part-time work he could find to supplement his modest income with the railways. One of these was erecting signs for an estate agent – at £15 per sign.

CHAPTER TWO

The Prodigy

Rye House is in Hoddesdon, about 15 miles away from Stevenage. It's been upgraded a bit since, but back in '93 it was a God-forsaken place, laid out on a bit of old waste ground beneath some electricity pylons. When the karts aren't running you can hear the constant traffic drone of the M25 motorway. It couldn't be further removed from the glamour of F1, and when you turn up there it can have the effect of making the sport's pinnacle seem further away than ever. But at the same time, like the other kart tracks around the country, it's the primordial soup in which the DNA of champions is formed.

Cadet karting is the entry point of the entire motor racing ladder. A category for 8- to 12-year-olds, the karts use 60cc engines of around 6 horsepower, all to the same specification. Ostensibly. More of which later. On 7 January 1993 – Lewis's eighth birthday – he was there on the Rye House Cadet grid. His racing number – 44 – was in white on a black background. The black denotes you are a novice. Once you have competed in six events to the satisfaction of the race stewards, you graduate to yellow plates, with black numbers. He won the novice class in all six of his black plate races – but more importantly he was often giving the yellow platers a hard time.

Martin Hines is Mr Karting in the UK, a multiple champion driver in the sport in the 1970s and 80s, using his family company's Zip karts. Since retiring as a driver he's expanded the company. Zip karts have for decades been one of the most popular choices in a variety of categories. But he's more than just a kart manufacturer, he's also an entrepreneur and a great self-publicist and he has a scheme called Zip Young Guns whereby, in return for some financial help, a small coterie of karters race under this banner. David Coulthard, Jason Plato and Allan McNish were some of the early beneficiaries of the scheme. As was Martin's son, Luke. Luke just happened to be racing in one of the senior classes that day at Rye House when Lewis was making his Cadet debut, and Martin just happened to be watching that race.

'I noticed this kid on black plates running near the front, fighting it out with the leaders on the yellow plates. Normally novices just don't have the experience to be able to come through the traffic like he had, let alone the pace. He just stood out, for that reason. He finished third overall in the final, way in front of the other black plates, and I assumed he must be near the end of his novice phase. But then his dad told me, "No, this is his first race", and I was stunned. I said, "Cor, you better come and see me." They did and the following week he was in a Zip. It was pretty obvious they had no money, but I could see the kid was very good and I just wanted to help. He had this lovely big smile too.'

It's amazing how many people mention the smile. But you

can see why. His whole face opens, revealing a noticeable gap between his two upper front teeth. He radiates openness, frankness, and is the most natural character you could possibly imagine. According to those who were there, he was always like this. A few years later, Jonny Restrick would become Lewis's mechanic in the JICA category of karting – and he too fell immediately under the spell. 'It's amazing. As soon as you met him, you sort of just fell in and you would do anything in your power to help him – you'd want to help.'

It was an amazingly good break to be spotted by Hines at his first race, but you'd have to say it wasn't down to luck that he was there to be spotted – it was down to Tony's hard work and amazing drive. The fact that Lewis was so personable, confident without cockiness, polite without deferring – just so genuine – that people automatically wanted to help him also reflects well on his parents.

The deal with Hines was just an exploratory one initially. The budget still wasn't there to contest a full season, but the Hamiltons would turn up whenever the pennies allowed, whenever Tony could get enough time off from his various fund-raising jobs. 'It was great at that time,' recalled Tony years later. 'Because we had no aspirations to be professionals. It was just: "When's the next race we can do? Off we go." At first I was using it as the carrot and stick for his school work but actually it became clear at some stage that he really was exceptionally good and it then became very difficult to use it as that.'

They moved further afield to other circuits to give Lewis a broader experience base. His first race on the coveted yellow plates came at the Clay Pigeon track in July 1993 – and he won. He completed another limited Cadet programme in 1994, and again won more often than he didn't – and against older, more experienced boys.

It was during a test session at Rye House in '94 that Tony Purnell of the electronics company PI first noticed Lewis's raw speed. Through his company, Purnell began sponsoring them, helping out with the bills. Purnell was at the time developing a piece of data-logging kit for the Cadet class, and in order to test it was running Adam King, the son of one of the company directors, in the category. 'Adam looked reasonable, so I thought well let's buy him some decent equipment and I bought some really good engines. But about halfway through that year it became apparent that he still needed time to learn and the engines were a bit wasted on him. So I approached Tony and gave him four of these engines and he was over the moon. And that's where it started.'

The engines Purnell donated had been built by Leon Lerego of Soixante Racing, one of the top tuners in the category. An ace biker in his day, Lerego knew all about how to get the best from a two-stroke engine and had got back into it when his son Leon Jnr began karting. Eventually he began building motors for others too. The business was still quite young when Purnell had bought his batch. Thereafter Purnell would pay Lerego for Hamilton's rebuilds.

This was the year in which Lewis's hero Ayrton Senna was killed in the San Marino Grand Prix. As a nine-year-old it made an impact on him, but not one that had any real resonance. His was a very different world to F1, for all that it still had its perils. 'Actually, I don't think my parents truly understood how dangerous it could be at first. I had one big crash where I went off and ploughed into a wall. I bashed my head and had a nosebleed, but I just told dad to fix the kart. I raced the next day and won.'

You can't really compare drivers from different eras, but Hines says he can see similarities between Senna and Hamilton – and he's seen both men in action at close quarters. 'I'd say there's five key factors in making a great racing driver and it's very rare you find a driver with all five, even in F1. One is an overwhelming desire to be the absolute best. Two is focus – to know 100 per cent where you're going and not let anything distract you. Three, unquestionable talent. Four, a strong supportive family. Five, a feel that allows you to jump into any new machine and instinctively be able to drive it to its limit almost immediately. I saw it in Ayrton when he came to Europe at 16 to race karts against my two drivers, who I rated as the best in the world. Ayrton had more passion for motorsport than anyone I've ever known. Lewis has that unerring, not to be deflected focus. But they both had all the qualities. Lewis is definitely one of those special talents like Ayrton, Michael Schumacher or Fernando Alonso.'

But all that was still to come. Promising though he looked, at the end of '94 all he'd done were a couple of part-seasons in Cadets. For '95, with increased backing from Hines and incorporation into the 'Young Guns' scheme, Lewis was to contest the full season. But, as a little indicator of how Anthony was determined to retain control of his son's career, Lewis would not run out of the Hines awning, like the other Young Guns. He would still be run from the box trailer on the back of Anthony's Cavalier.

Anthony had picked up some invaluable backing too from Martin Howell of Playscape, a company that specialised in the tamer indoor kart racing – typically catering to 'fun days' for birthday parties, corporate days or 'works nights out' – rather than the more serious stuff of the 'real' karting world.

'But it was very advantageous for me to have a presence in each of the categories of mainstream karting in terms of having the name around,' explains Howell of his sponsoring of key drivers by way of supplying them with tyres. Because of the large fleet of karts he prepared for his business, he could get a good discount on tyres anyway. 'I'd been helping a driver called Nicky Hopkins in Cadets, but he was moving up into the next category so I needed someone else in Cadets and it was Nicky's father John who suggested "Take a look at this kid Lewis". I met his dad and we did a deal where basically I paid for his tyres in exchange for him being a Playscape driver, with the decals on his overalls, helmet and kart and him coming to corporate events etc. He was a very good ambassador for Playscape, he was very likeable and worked very hard. It all came very naturally to him.'

'That was an enormous help,' recalled Anthony. 'A set of tyres for the weekend would cost £200–£300 – which was more money than I was making at the time. Martin Howell provided those free of charge. I also got help from John Button who did our engines that year on very favourable terms. Good people. Without people like that I don't think we'd ever have got Lewis off the bottom rung of the karting ladder, let alone F1.'

John Button is the father of current F1 ace Jenson. Six years older than Lewis, Jenson at the time was competing in the more senior JICA category and John had decided it was time to step back from his son's career, this after preparing and running his kart since Jenson's Cadet days. 'It had come to the stage where Jenson and I were starting to argue a lot,' he recalls, 'and I didn't want our relationship spoilt, so I got someone else in to run him. Then I thought "Well, what do I do?" and I started to run Cadet kids out of the same awning and I prepared our own engines and we won championships. Then Tony approached me and asked if I could I help out. I knew the lad was quick so I said yes.'

There was no dissatisfaction with the Soixante Racing engines that had been used through '94; it was simply that Soixante, at this young stage in its history, couldn't afford to supply them free. It's quite usual in karting for engine, chassis and other trade suppliers to provide subsidised or even free kit to fast drivers. The ensuing results are a good advertisement for their wares – and Button clearly saw Lewis as someone who would enhance the reputation of his engines. 'Anthony came down in his beat-up old car and explained the situation to us,' recalled Lerego. 'With finances the way they were he couldn't turn that opportunity down. There were no hard feelings on our part but at that stage everything had to be paid for.' Here was Anthony the operator again. At the same time he persuaded Purnell to continue his financial backing, redirecting the money saved on engine rebuilds elsewhere in the programme. 'Anthony would do whatever it took for Lewis to achieve his goals,' recalls Lerego.

As some indication of how competitive the sport is even at this level, consider the many ways engine tuners can get around regulations designed to limit modification and therefore cost. In the Cadet category no extra machining of the engine internals can be made, and there are set manufacturer tolerances of the Comer engines. But what is there to stop anyone buying a whole batch of engines, disassembling them and mixing and matching components to make one engine with the most advantageous set of tolerances? Nothing. What is there to stop the internal machining from being carried out to the very limit of the tolerances, so long as the machined finish is identical to that of a factory original so it can't be detected? Again nothing. It all means that an engine that is dismantled by scrutineers can be found to be perfectly legal, but will still have a significant advantage over a standard factory-supplied item.

It's vitally important, even at this level, to have competitive equipment. Actually it's probably not vitally important for the three-quarters or so of the grid that simply do not have the skills required to run at the front, the ones who have not been blessed. Throughout the motor racing ladder there are drivers spending thousands of pounds on tweaks to their equipment that are worth tenths, maybe merely hundredths, of a second per lap. Yet they fail to address the fact that their driving shortfall may be many times greater than that. Self-deception is rife throughout motor racing; drivers will kid themselves that the only reason they're not winning is that the others have more money, better equipment, are cheating, etc. But if you really are one of the few with real and genuine talent, you desperately do need kit as good as the best. Because there will always be other gifted drivers and if your equipment is not as good as theirs they will invariably beat you.

'Even at the lowest level of karting, success is about so much more than driving,' says Martin Howell. 'Yes, even in Cadets. The nasty question of money comes up and determines whether you can do enough testing, get the best tyres, have the opportunity to get good engines, be run by competent people. And Lewis always had the right people. Yet they had very little money. Anthony was a smart cookie and very hard-working, very conscious of making the right moves. A lot of karting dads – myself included possibly – should take a leaf out of his book.'

Anthony's work rate during this period was astonishing. As well as holding down a full-time and several part-time jobs he was overseeing Lewis's karting, working on the kart, dreaming up ways to raise publicity and funds, and generally networking the karting community, parlaying his son's talent and popularity into help.

If Anthony had ever been ambivalent about devoting his future to his son's racing, he no longer was. He came to realise this himself when, during the school holidays, he asked his employer for yet another day off to go testing. The venue was Larkhall, in Scotland, so he needed two days. His request was for once denied. They told him he must decide what he wanted to do – work at his job or run his son's karting programme. He gave it some thought – and decided to hand in his resignation.

This was clearly a momentous move, a life-changing one as it turned out. The sport had its tentacles around Anthony and he'd been drawn in. This much was clear to Purnell. 'Oh, he was in many ways a typical karting dad in that he had long lost any objectivity about it all and was prepared to do anything to help his boy get on.'

But sometimes objectivity just gets in the way in racing. In this case Anthony's subjective call worked brilliantly in his favour. Setting himself up as an IT contractor, head office had contracted him within a few days of his leaving – and had him doing much the same work as when he was employed by them, but getting paid much better for it! The time flexibility meant he could now build up his hours as he saw fit and create his own spare time for the karting. He was soon earning more than his former salary plus Linda's combined, and Linda took the opportunity of stopping work so she could devote more time to Nicholas. By Anthony's own admission, this would never have happened had it not been for Lewis's karting.

Thus freed from his employee status, Anthony could really knuckle down to the karting now! 'I just saw myself in the dad role,' he said, 'ensuring Lewis didn't lose out any opportunity to further his career.' In this quest he had no qualms about using his boy's ethnicity to generate interest – not too difficult, given the almost total lack of an Afro-Caribbean presence in all of motor racing, let alone karting.

'There always seemed to be film crews around Lewis,' recalls Chris Walker, a karting photographer. 'I don't know whether that was because of Tony's efforts behind the scenes or because of the novelty of the black kid stepping into a white sport.' Almost certainly it was both. Purnell: 'Tony was totally up front about how he knew not just that Lewis was very good but that he was incredibly marketable as the only black kid around. Lewis frankly owes as much to his dad as he does to himself. He was talented but Dad – who is the most ultra-competitive person you'll ever meet – really played it well, and in the deck of cards that he had in Lewis, he definitely wasn't shy about playing the colour one.'

The karting scene generally is not a racist one. 'But you always get the odd one,' points out Walker. 'A couple of times something was said and a situation flared up involving Anthony. But generally Lewis, Anthony and his family were very well liked, very popular people.'

Purnell recalls one occasion of racial abuse towards Anthony by an official. 'It was at a race at Wigan and I've no idea what Tony did, but this bloke laid into him with the most obscene racial abuse. Tony's self-control is not brilliant and he got fairly sideways about it, yet Lewis remained totally composed. Good racers are always in control. And one of the things that Lewis is in control of is his temperament. He has fantastic car control, but also fantastic control of himself.

'There was another time we were racing in Ireland and suddenly Lewis was looking all over the place for this particular jumper he was very fond of. Everyone was looking for it and eventually another boy found it – ripped to shreds and dumped in a litter bin. It had been one of his competitors, trying to knock him off balance. Again, Tony was beside himself with rage but Lewis remained totally calm.'

Coinciding with Lewis's first full season of racing came another significant change in his life: his mother and her partner needed to move to London because of their work. Lewis's karting commitments, not to mention his schooling, meant it was better he remained in Stevenage. As such he moved in full-time with Anthony, Linda and Nicholas.

Lewis had already taken to his stepbrother in a big way, and now their relationship would become yet closer. It's impossible to overstate the influence that Nicholas's condition has had upon Lewis's determination to make the most of his own situation. 'He's a great kid,' insists Lewis, 'and an inspiration not only to me but a lot of other people. Whenever I think I have problems I just think how many problems in life he has. I mean, he can't do half the things that I can do and yet he is always happy. For sure, having him as a brother has had a major effect on the way I think.'

The move was undoubtedly a big wrench for Carmen, but Lewis would still travel down to stay with her whenever possible, and to further soften the blow it was agreed she would come to as many race meetings as possible. Tony Purnell marvels at how close-knit and friendly their family situation was: 'You'd have Tony, Linda, Carmen, Nicholas and Lewis and it all seemed very easy and friendly. In fact, I often wondered at how come Carmen and Tony had ended up divorcing because they all seemed to get along so well.'

With everything in place, Lewis was able to finally contest a full season in the main national Cadet championship – the Super One series. It was 1995 and he was now ten years old. The pre-season favourite was a boy in his final year of the category on account of him turning 12 mid-season, Mike Conway. Experienced, well-funded and quick, Conway duly turned out to be Hamilton's toughest opponent on track, even though they were firm friends off it. However far apart they might be in the random grids of the heats, they would invariably be pitched together in the finals, each having worked their way through the pack, with results from the heats determining grid position for the final.

It all came down to the final round, at Shenington in Oxfordshire. 'Basically he had to beat me to win the championship and I had to beat him,' recalls Conway. 'Just before the start of the final it absolutely lashed it down and everybody had to do a quick change onto wet tyres. I was near the back of the grid and he was up the front so I knew it was going to be tough, but in karting anything is possible, especially in the rain. So as far as I was concerned it was still game on, but as I turned into the second corner on the first lap I lost a front wheel – it hadn't been tightened properly when we changed to wet tyres and I knew then that that was it, I'd lost the championship to Lewis.'

Among those cheering hard with Anthony at the end of the race was John Button. 'I was with my second wife back then and we made him a special jacket – a black bomber jacket done in the team colours of black and yellow, with all the various badges on it. Some time after he'd clinched the championship we presented it to him and he was over the moon. It looked really cool. I just saw Lewis as a straightfor-ward, really uncomplicated kid – very trusting and genuine. You could see he was talented. In F1 and even the categories of car racing below that, all you see is a helmet sticking out of the car, but in karts you see the whole body language, you see him working with the guys, see the way he is thinking. You could actually see if a driver was going to make a go of it, and he always was – the body language was there. I've seen a lot of karting kids come through and one thing I've noticed is that basically a driver doesn't change – he carries the same characteristics with him. Giorgio Pantano is a clas-sic example – very, very quick but did some outrageous things that let him down. But in Lewis I couldn't ever see a fault – and that's what we're seeing now. I knew he was good long before Ron Dennis did!'

In fact it was as a result of winning that title that Lewis got to meet Dennis for the first time. As the Cadet title-winner, Hamilton was invited to collect his trophy at the prestigious McLaren-Autosport awards evening, held in London's Grosvenor Hotel in December. So a tuxedoed ten-year-old Lewis got to stay up way past his bedtime, got to stand up there on stage and receive the trophy in front of a couple of thousand people, got to pose for the photographers and get pictured with the Indy 500 winner and recently confirmed F1 driver Jacques Villeneuve, got a taste of the big-time lime-light that seemed a long way removed from queuing at the burger van at Shenington. But none of this was as significant as a little cameo moment as the guests were still sitting at their tables. Looking around the room wide-eyed at spotting yet another of his heroes, another of the star personalities from that seemingly unreachable other-world of F1, Lewis saw where Dennis was sitting and pointed it out to Anthony.

'Go over and tell him you want to drive for McLaren one day,' instructed Anthony, not jokingly. Lewis may have balked a little – he doesn't remember. But probably he didn't. He had that complete faith in himself and that willingness to do as instructed by his father. So the little boy stood up, walked across the room to where Dennis was sitting, waited politely to catch his attention, then said exactly what he'd been told to say and flashed him that big brown smile, looked him square in the eye. How could Ron not have been charmed? Now a smile spread across Ron's face, enjoying the moment. 'You do? How old are you? Ten. OK, well come back and see me in nine years.' A signed menu with a repeat of the message, a shake of hands and the smiling Lewis dodges the waiters and returns to the table where Anthony's eyes have been following his every move. A two-minute interlude, missed by most of those in the function room awaiting their starters, having their conversations – but now the stuff of motor racing legend. The link, however casual, had been made. And the two would be meeting again much sooner than the nine years Ron had suggested.

Though Anthony may have come into this season still feeling they had no aspirations to be professionals, it wasn't so clear-cut now. For Lewis, there was no question of priorities to answer: this is what he wanted. 'You just watched him in a kart and you could see he wanted it,' says John Button. 'He had that thing of never giving up. This isn't something you can train. You've either got it or you haven't – and he did.' It wasn't a hobby, but a passion.

Anthony's commitment off the track was matched by Lewis's on it. Bill Sisley operates Buckmore Park in Kent, one of the best karting venues. Hamilton caught his eye from the beginning. 'He was always very brave and intelligent, always very aggressive going into a bend – very late on the brakes. The aggression and slight risk typified Lewis.'

'He was a very clever racer right from the start,' says Chris Walker, the karting photographer. 'Cadet karting then was like Formula Ford in the seventies used to be, where you had a mad slipstreaming battle and you really didn't want to be the one leading going into the last lap. You had to be very tactical about how you positioned yourself and he was brilliant at it. Lewis had this ability of being third into the last corner but coming out of it in the lead. I always thought he was destined to go all the way.'

Although the basic desire, the will to win, was inbuilt, the mental attitude necessary to achieve it was something Anthony helped instil. 'I had the attitude that if he wanted to do it and I was going to put in all this effort, do all these extra jobs, then he was bloody well going to do it well,' recalled Anthony years later. He could be hard on the boy, but at no stage was there any question of the father living vicariously through the son and the son not really wanting to be there, as is so often the case. David 'Kid' Jensen watched first-hand some of Lewis's exploits in karting and made the following observation: 'I saw some awful things [in karting]. It would be a normal sight where a six-foot guy would be bending over a three-foot-nothing little kid bellowing insults at the top his voice. Anthony was a great exception, someone who I never saw losing it anywhere. He was one of the ones not living out his own frustrations or vicariously trying to make up for their own failures through his child.

'Lewis did stand out amongst a crop of karters who were very, very good and it was not just for his speed or for his great race craft. Even at 11, he was a pleasure to interview, really interesting and amenable. Lewis just had a natural way about him that was always appealing, never arrogant. He was the star of the show.'

Purnell comments upon the appeal of Lewis's nature too. 'He has the ultimate confidence, and that's been there from the start. But there's not a trace of cockiness, just real self-belief and self-assurance. People who have a good feeling about themselves don't feel the need to constantly tell you how brilliant they are. But it's relatively rare in a racing driver. It makes him the sort of sportsman you automatically want to get behind. I think it's partly to do with the regard in which he has been held by his father. I've seen it with the Buttons too, where the father holds the son in such high regard that the boy's whole inner confidence of "I'm the best" is just reinforced. Both Jenson Button and Lewis Hamilton have that. And they're both from paternalistic-centralistic families. Both men were divorced from the mothers and the dad only had time for the son. Lewis could do no wrong – unless the father said so. No one could ever criticise Lewis, but Tony could – and did.'

'I have been very fortunate having my father's support all the way,' said Lewis earlier this year. 'Mentally, he is very strong. He's had a major influence on my mental preparation.'

When asked what this entailed, Anthony replied: 'The thing I always tried to get through to him was to always be positive, always believe you can do it. Adopt an honest approach to things, and if you stay positive and never give up it's amazing what can be achieved.'

But for all Anthony's honesty and openness, he wouldn't ever be mistaken for an easy touch. He's shrewd and absolutely as ruthless as necessary. In former times these were the qualities required of drivers making their way through the sport. As the starting age of racing has come down because of karting, so those required qualities have shifted onto the parents.

Emphasising his ruthless credentials, Anthony switched engine suppliers for Lewis's final year in Cadet racing despite his '95 success with John Button. For '96 another renowned tuner, John Davies, would be supplying the motors. Button still doesn't know why, and did ask Anthony about it: 'Tony said, "We just felt we needed a change." I asked how come, given that we'd won the championship together, and he replied, "Well, Michael Schumacher has just won the F1 title with Benetton, but he's still going to Ferrari."'

For '96 there would be another assault on the Super One series, and also the *Champions of the Future*, another championship for the same category, one set up by Martin Hines. Graham Smith, secretary of the British Karting Association, gives some of the background to that. 'The Cadet class had started off in '87 when there was a one-off meeting to determine a British Cadet champion. Then for the next couple of years there was a year-long series for the British championship, but then it was felt it was unfair to be putting national championship pressure on young kids, so there was then just the Super One series that didn't have British in its title. But de facto it became the most prestigious series in Cadets. But in '94 Martin Hines persuaded [the British governing body] the MSA to allow the Cadet category in his *Champions of the Future* series to be the MSA-recognised British series and so gradually over a period of a few years that came to be the more prestigious series. But when Lewis did it, Super One was still the more prestigious.'

This time Lewis failed to win the Super One series. It went

instead to a promising Scottish kid, Paul di Resta, and Lewis was only third. 'Yes, he had the number one on his kart and he became a bit of a marked man that year because of that,' recalls Purnell.

But Hamilton did win the *Champions of the Future* series – and for all that it was less prestigious at the time, it had one thing that was massively in its favour: it had been set up by Hines in association with the McLaren F1 team. Hines and McLaren's Ron Dennis had met at one of Martin Howell's Playscape evenings in the early 1990s. 'I had a lot of dealings with Ron. Because I used to host a lot of his team's karting days,' Howell recalls, 'where Ron would hire us and the employees would come down and enjoy racing each other. We would also do a McLaren vs. Williams challenge and I also used to help raise money for Ron's wife Lisa's Tomy's charity for the kids of St Thomas hospital. I was planning a corporate night with Ron once and we wanted a demo by a top guy in a fast kart – because when you see a proper racing kart indoors after watching the normal much slower indoor ones, it looks mind-blowing, really makes people catch their breath. I said to Ron, "What about a really top guy, a world champion?" and when Ron asked who, I said "Martin Hines" and that's how the introduction came about.'

Hines and Dennis formed a good friendship – to the extent that a few years later Hines even got to experience driving a McLaren F1 car on an airfield. Being the operator he is, Hines wasn't slow in dovetailing his interests with Dennis's long-term support of the grass roots of the sport. In 1989 McLaren had launched the McLaren-Autosport Young Driver of the Year award, whereby the outstanding junior car racing driver of the season was awarded a support package that would help him progress to the next stage of his career.

David Coulthard was the inaugural recipient on the strength of his victorious season in junior Formula Ford that year. The award came to gain increasing prestige over the years, but in the meantime the cost of competing even in junior car racing categories was rising fast. Swathes of extremely promising kart racers weren't even able to make the step to the starting rung of car racing. With a bit of encouragement from Hines, Dennis sought to extend downwards his support of the junior racing scene and the *Champions of the Future* karting initiative was launched in 1994.

The McLaren-Mercedes *Champions of the Future* series was a Hines-run, McLaren- and Mercedes-backed scheme whereby there was a British championship for both Cadets (for 8–12-year-olds) and Juniors (for 12–15-year-olds). As recounted, Lewis Hamilton won the 1996 *Champions of the Future* Cadet championship, the third year of its running.

Hines kept Dennis up to date with how it was all going and encouraged Ron to try to get to a meeting, knowing what an impact just the presence of the team principal of one of the top F1 teams would have. Ron didn't actually need persuading, and ever since the initiative had started he would try to attend a meeting at least once a year. In '96 he'd turned up at Kimbolton, helicoptered in with Hines to the sparse former airfield in the middle of the Cambridgeshire countryside. There, he saw once again the likeable little kid who had introduced himself at the awards evening a few months earlier. Photographer Chris Walker was there. 'At that point I hadn't realised they'd already met,' he recalled, 'and I was amused that right from the start Lewis called him "Ron" whereas Anthony called him "Mr Dennis".'

The *Champions of the Future* finals were at Buckmore Park that year, and Dennis made sure he was there – together with his driver David Coulthard. The series was being televised for ITV and so all the cameras were there too. Hines the showman was in his element, demonstrating very clearly to the karting community that were his customers just what a link he was providing to the big time. A few years later he recalled the day well, but what stood out for him was how Lewis seemed not to be affected in the slightest, with all this going on as he was on the verge of clinching his title. 'All these F1 personalities were there. As well as Ron and DC, Martin Brundle and Mark Blundell were there. He was being interviewed on camera and he would have known it was all going out to a national TV audience. The pressure was phenomenal and yet he just dealt with it, this 11-year-old kid. Pressure? He just doesn't seem to feel it. When you think about how he handled his F1 debut you can begin to understand why. He's been living with this kind of attention ever since he started. Most kids don't experience it until much later in their careers.'

Coulthard duly presented Hamilton with the race-winner's prize, and years later Lewis recounted just how gracious David was on that day, and how he gave his many questions about racing and F1 so much time. 'A lot of other F1 drivers I met when I was a kid didn't really give you the time of day,' said Lewis, 'but David was very different. It meant a lot to me.'

Anthony Hamilton now no longer needed to be pushy to talk with Dennis, and the two chatted for a time about how Lewis's career was going. Anthony was greatly encouraged by Dennis's parting shot of 'keep in touch'. There was a rosy glow all round as they drove the old Cavalier back home that night.

CHAPTER THREE

The Deal of a Lifetime

All the Hamiltons needed to do now was not blow it. Against the odds, Anthony had help Lewis discover his talent, was instilling in him the mental approach necessary to make full use of it, had hustled behind the scenes to ensure his boy was always in the right equipment, had ensured there was that vital buzz of hype around Lewis – and had even forged an informal link with one of the biggest teams in F1. As the time came now to leave Cadets and move into the next class of karting, it was crucial they made the right move.

So there were some raised eyebrows in the karting community when they elected to go to Martin Hines's undersubscribed Junior Yamaha class. The move everyone was expecting them to make was to the much more popular equivalent class of Junior TKM, where all the hot-shots graduating from Cadets normally fought it out. Some rivals suggested they were afraid of the more intense competition, were looking just to trophy-hunt their way to an impressive CV. 'I remember saying to Anthony, "Why are you doing this class?"' recalls Graham Smith of the British Karting Association, 'and Anthony replying, "Well, we're with Zip and Martin has supported us, so we're sort of obliged to, really."'

Hines, as recounted, had got the British governing body, the RAC MSA, to recognise his Cadet championship as the official British one. But he couldn't pull off the same feat for the Junior category – and so he simply invented his own, directly in competition with the established Junior TKM category. Just like that formula, Hines's Junior Yamaha class was for 100cc engines of around 15 horsepower – much more powerful than the Cadets Lewis had raced in to date. But although the category was going into its third year as the Hamiltons took delivery of their chassis and engines, there were still very few takers. Whereas the rival Junior TKM races would boast starting fields of up to 30 karts, in Junior Yamaha sometimes the numbers didn't even get into double figures. On a really good day, it might attract 20 starters. The intensity of competition was just not there, and there was a feeling of disappointment that such an exciting prospect as Lewis was 'dropping out' of the racing mainstream.

But that was a parochial view, from deep within the karting community. Anthony was thinking bigger than the British karting world. Given that this is what Hines wanted them to do, given that Hines was providing their equipment, given that Hines had a close relationship to Ron Dennis, why ever would Anthony *not* choose to put Lewis in the category that Hines wanted him in? And if that meant a season of easy victories for Lewis instead of hard-fought ones, then what was the problem? There would surely be plenty more hard-fought ones to come in the seasons ahead. In the meantime Anthony employed a mechanic, Owen

Regan, for the first time, though Anthony didn't entirely relinquish the spannering role.

Lewis was slightly disappointed not to be graduating with most of his rivals from Cadets into where all the attention was. But he understood his father's reasoning, understood it would be better in the long run. Since the meeting with Ron Dennis, it seemed, this was becoming more serious. Inwardly he began thinking that F1 was on the radar, that this was achievable. 'Be positive always, give it 100 per cent' was the mantra Anthony had instilled in him. With his dreams taking on a solid form of reality, Lewis had little trouble adopting that philosophy.

Meanwhile, Anthony's hopes of Lewis becoming a high achiever at school too were falling somewhat short. Now at the John Henry Newman senior school in Stevenage, he remained a slight under-achiever, a pupil who did OK but left his teachers in little doubt that he could do better. Someone so bright and articulate could surely achieve more. But it never really came. 'I did sometimes threaten to sell the kart,' said Anthony recently, 'but increasingly it became a more difficult thing to threaten as it became clear just how good he was in karts. It was a tricky situation.'

For Lewis, school was a respite from the competitive intensity he subjected himself to even as a 12-year-old – as he explained to John McEvoy in the *Daily Mail*. 'Kids at school would say "What you doing at the weekend?" and I'd say "Oh, I'm going karting". They'd say: "Oh, I might see you up there" and I'd just nod because I wanted to keep the extent of my racing quiet. It helped make school feel like an escape if no one knew what I was achieving in racing. School was my time to mess about and have a kid's life – to be normal. But at weekends I never had a chance to go to any of those under-18 clubs or parties. And that affects you because your friendships are not so strong.

'When you say, "I can't go out because I'm racing this weekend", your friends think you're blowing them out. Even [in later years] when I'd tell people at school I was going to Japan for a week to race, they'd look at me blankly. It just didn't click.'

Meanwhile, Lewis's mother Carmen, together with her now-husband Ray Lockhart, moved back to Stevenage. Carmen felt that London was simply too far away, and she yearned for more contact with her boy. He began once again splitting his time between the two households.

Lewis still had his karate to occupy him away from the track and it was during this season that he acquired his black belt. He was also a keen and skilled footballer and was soon on the school team as a midfielder, along with his friend Ashley Young, who played as a striker and early in 2007 joined Aston Villa from Watford for £9.65 million. Hamilton told the *Guardian*'s Oliver Owen that 'I was quicker than Ashley and stronger. But he was very skilled and neat and could dribble the ball around people very nicely. I was the fittest in the team by far because of all the training I used to do for my racing. So I could run up and down all day and if people tackled me I wouldn't just leave it, I'd get them back because I never gave up.'

Just as he didn't on the race track. To no one's great surprise, Hamilton was a dominant champion in the 1997 British Junior Yamaha series, his third national championship in three years of racing, albeit with less credibility than his Cadet successes.

The *Blue Peter* crew caught up with him that year at a race meeting, and the dynamic between Anthony and Lewis is interesting. In the first heat Lewis has been struggling uncharacteristically and has finished only fifth. He climbs out of the kart at the end and Anthony's there, asking what the problem is.

'What's it doing? Is it gripping up?' Lewis is still lost in thought, trying to pinpoint exactly why he can't get the kart to do what he needs it to do, and says nothing, just shakes his head as they continue walking side-by-side back to the paddock.

'I'm unable to do absolutely anything,' says Anthony in desperation, 'because you're not telling me what's happening.' More silent walking.

'So we'll walk down here dead silent, shall we? You want more grip on the front? On the back? You down on power?'

The camera cuts and we then hear from Lewis, clearly some time after. 'My dad's pretty hard on me,' he says. 'And when it's not going to plan he's even harder. But we're a team and we work together.' So far it could be interpreted as the meek kid just doing as he's told. But then the individual leaps out. 'If my dad gave me advice about the track I wouldn't take it because he doesn't know what it's like out there. I hadn't really given dad much advice [about the kart] but I've told him now and I think he's going to try the old settings.'

Making it a fairytale ending for the TV cameras, Lewis then goes out and blitzes the final. Just as expected by his brother Nicholas – who had appeared at the beginning of the piece saying: 'My brother's the best because he's really fast and he'll be in F1 some day.'

The camera catches Anthony as the flag falls: 'Never give up, never say die. That's why he's always up the front and a champion.'

For all that it was not as tough a championship as it might

have been, 1997 stands as an extremely important season in Hamilton's career in that it maintained his winning momentum at a time when he had piqued the interest of Ron Dennis. And there were plans afoot at McLaren that the Hamiltons didn't yet know about. Dennis was keen to further help young talent, and along with Mercedes was devising a 'driver support scheme' whereby promising drivers throughout the motor racing ladder would be given direct financial help, with their progress monitored at the end of the year.

It is the sort of thing that is now common for manufacturers involved in F1, with Renault, BMW and Toyota all operating similar schemes, all trying to find the next big talent. But at the time it was unique – and in one respect still is, in that it was initiated by the F1 team, not the manufacturer. Nick Heidfeld had been selected for McLaren patronage in F3000, Norman Simon in German F3. Obviously Lewis was going to be a shoo-in from the karting categories, given the dialogue that had already been established and the success he had already achieved.

At the McLaren-Autosport prize-giving, Lewis was there to pick up his Junior Yamaha championship award and he again met with Ron Dennis, repeating his intention of one day driving for McLaren. A short time later, Anthony received 'The Call' and was asked to attend a meeting at Woking, home of McLaren. Dennis outlined the intended plan and told how Lewis was going to be a recipient. Anthony tried to stop himself from grinning ear-to-ear, but couldn't entirely. It was all a bit late-notice for the beginning of the season, but that was the intention.

Anthony had already got in place plans for Lewis to contest the British JICA (Junior Intercontinental Category A) category of karting, the main series for 13–16-year-olds.

Featuring 100cc engines that revved to around 17,000rpm and gave as much as 20 horsepower, their greater performance over the Junior Yamaha and TKM karts was enhanced by their stickier tyres. It was a deeply competitive category, and placed Lewis very much back in the mainstream of karting. The main British championship for the category in 1998 was the McLaren-Mercedes *Champions of the Future* series.

The mechanic Owen Regan left the camp during the off-season of 1997–98 and in his place came an enthusiastic Irish engineering student called Jonny Restrick, who had competed in karts himself. Going into the year, the McLaren driver support programme had yet to be confirmed with Anthony. All he had was a promise. As such, he played his cards close to his chest.

'We didn't have a full budget as we went into preparing for the year,' recalls Restrick. 'And we didn't have the best equipment. We had to stay with Zip because they were giving us support but the Tony-Kart which the other top guys had was quicker. Also John Davies had moved up as the engine tuner, but this category was new to him so initially he didn't have the experience of the top tuners like Paul Carr and Ricky Grice, so we were a bit down on power too.

'But before the season had actually started Anthony had the McLaren deal confirmed. Suddenly we no longer had a budget problem, though we were still committed to Zip because of the link between them and McLaren. Anthony called me at eight in the morning to tell me what was happening and I was very excited by it too. We had still been running out of the box trailer on the back of Anthony's Cavalier, but suddenly Mercedes were supplying us a Sprinter van and the local Merc dealer provided Anthony with an A-class to get around in.'

The big time was getting closer, you could sniff it in the air around the Hamiltons now. With the racing support now confirmed, the costs of Lewis's racing were completely covered. Besides, Anthony's business was growing rapidly. No longer just an IT contractor, he now had so much business he had become an IT consultant employing contractors of his own. Soon he needed to employ full-time staff too, to keep up with the logistics and administration. Anthony felt able at last to move the family to a three-bedroom house in Tewin, a village on Stevenage's outskirts, a huge boon after the sacrifice of the small flat. The faithful old Cavalier was pensioned off and the smart black A-class took its place on the drive.

The Hamiltons were there at the official launch of the scheme, together with Ron Dennis, his drivers Mika Hakkinen and David Coulthard, and the other recipients of assistance: Nick Heidfeld, Nicolas Minassian, Ricardo Zonta, Norman Simon and another karting kid who had shown impressive form in regional junior championships, Wesley Graves. Dennis outlined the plans: 'The programme will provide financial and technical backing, as well as sound professional advice, to six up-and-coming racers in karting, F3 and F3000. The driver support programme, which we have put together with Mercedes, has been designed to create genuine support for drivers who, without the commercial horsepower that we can bring, may not have made it on their own. To be in the programme, above all else, you have got to be exceptionally talented, focused and capable of winning races.

'Our programme of support will vary from driver to driver and we will take into consideration the circumstances of each one, giving them what support we feel appropriate for 1998. We will then decide how big or small it should be on a year-by-year basis.'

Heidfeld went on to win the 1999 European F3000 championship, his springboard to graduation to F1 with the Prost team in 2000, but was disappointed to be overlooked for a McLaren drive in 2002 in favour of his junior team-mate at Sauber, Kimi Raikkonen. Zonta went on to sports car success with Mercedes, but his F1 career never really took off. Minassian, Simon and Graves were all released from the scheme after the first year. Hamilton was the only one of the original recipients to stay on the programme long-term.

Staying on the scheme became the preoccupation for the Hamiltons for the next few years. It was their lifeline. 'I will do anything to repay Ron,' Lewis declared at the launch. 'It's a great feeling and things couldn't be much better.'

Even during the short time he'd been with the Hamiltons, Restrick noticed the change in emphasis that came with confirmation of the McLaren deal. 'Once that happened the pressure was really on to keep it up, to keep the momentum of the whole thing. It was no longer about just the next race win. Things got longer-term. There was definitely a pressure, a push to keep getting the results and what was needed to do that. Sometimes it came from Tony. He could be pretty tough on Lewis, we both could. But then Lewis could be pretty tough on us too. Suddenly he'd fire back at us if the kart wasn't right – find me more grip, more power, and you realised who the boss was. It was definitely not just Tony pushing things along; it was Lewis too. There was no room for the niceties. This was serious, they were going somewhere.'

Coming into a class at the bottom of the age group presented Lewis with quite a challenge. 'It really was a big step up from what he'd done before,' maintains Restrick. 'Not only had the 15–16-year-old guys been doing it for two years longer but they were just that bit tougher physically and mentally – as most 16-year-olds are compared to a 13-year-old. These were guys Lewis looked up to when he was in Juniors and Cadets. Yet you would never have known it – it seemed to make no impact on Lewis at all. He was just focused on getting out there, looking forward to the racing. He didn't enjoy testing – but that's normal for kids of that age; it's the racing that excites them. His feedback about what the kart was doing was always good and he was amazing in how he could squeeze everything from the kart – I've never seen anyone before or since who could consistently get so incredibly close to their theoretical best lap, which you work out by taking best sector times and adding them up, then comparing to the best actual lap.'

The pre-season favourite was a 15-year-old called Fraser Sheader, one of the front-runners from the previous season. Hamilton was coming in with a big reputation from the junior series but was not seriously expected to challenge for the title in his rookie season of JICA as a 13-year-old. But those perceptions had to be adjusted after the opening round – held at Larkhall in Scotland.

Rain was falling hard as the final began, with puddles quickly forming around the track. Sheader took an immediate lead from pole, with Hamilton vaulting up to second from the second row, but being elbowed down to third on the opening lap by Russell Parkes. For the next few laps Hamilton attacked Parkes remorselessly, sitting in a ball of spray just inches from his back bumper. All this was playing into the hands of Sheader because as Parkes concentrated on defending from the new kid, the leader was able to eke out his advantage. Hamilton's creed of never giving up was very apparent here and after a few laps, Parkes got off line trying to defend, hit one of the puddles and spun out. With Parkes out of the way, Hamilton began lapping quicker than anyone and closed down on Sheader – with the rest a long way behind. Soon, probably sooner than Sheader was expecting, Hamilton was right there, darting this way and that, diving out of the spray, looking for an opening. Eventually he got a run on him as they came down the straight and took the lead through a right-left sequence at the end. Sheader hung on around the outside of the left but that put him off line for the left-hand hairpin that followed. His right-rear tyre caught the wet painted line, giving him a big twitch before he could even begin turning in – and so Hamilton was clearly through. As the rain came down yet heavier, there was Lewis just dancing his way through the puddles, wonderfully spectacular, kart being rescued from all sorts of angles as his lead stretched. Sheader eventually retired with technical problems and Lewis won by over 15 seconds on his debut.

It had been a sensational performance, but it wasn't a repeatable one in the next few dry races, which Sheader dominated, with Hamilton doing as best he could just to stay in touch. Restrick, though, was never less than totally convinced he was running the best driver in the category. 'He was awesome. The most impressive thing was how he dealt with traffic. I'd be more confident of a win with him starting from the back than from pole; he just seemed magically able to do very special things then. He had no idea how he did it, how he passed five cars on one lap. You'd see him come up to a group and think "This will be tough" but then he does a crazy move, totally unexpected, down the outside into a hairpin say, and it works, almost like people were moving aside for him. I'd say how do you do that? How do you know the gap will be there? And he says I don't know, it just happens.'

It's the sort of spatial awareness and instinctive vision of how other drivers will react, second-guessing where they will place themselves, that would later be seen to such dramatic effect through his car racing career all the way to F1.

His speed was just as natural as his racecraft, and when Lewis was interviewed during the previous season by Michael Eboda, editor of *New Nation*, he'd told him he didn't know why he was quick. He knew only that he would arrive at the corner and the answer just came, that he would accept the answer and just go with it. There were faint overtones of religion in his response.

Hamilton began coming back at Sheader in the second half of the championship, and rattled off a series of victories, including a dramatic win from the back of the grid at Buckmore Park. The title fight would go down to the final round at Rye House. In order to win the championship, Lewis needed to win the final, with Sheader no better than third. These were exactly the positions they were running in until the very last corner when Sheader's team-mate Alex Lloyd, who was running second, pulled over and allowed Sheader through. Lewis won the race but was only runner-up in the championship.

Nonetheless he had done more than enough to remain on the McLaren young driver scheme. Although it had been Ron Dennis's initiative, Ron's deputy Martin Whitmarsh came to have a more active role in its operation, and was the point of McLaren contact for the Hamiltons. Anthony today makes much of the pressure there was to stay on the McLaren programme, about how resolute they had to be in this aim, and how it coloured their every move, how they felt they had to win championships. Whitmarsh concedes the reality: 'As long as Lewis was competitive in his races, and they wanted to stay in the scheme, there was never any real prospect of him being dropped. We were very much taking a long term view of it all, and would take a view at the end of each season – but only really on what the next stage should be, never on whether we wanted to continue with Lewis or not. That was pretty much a given.'

'I got the impression the Hamiltons used the McLaren link to put some self-imposed pressure on themselves,' says Martin Howell. 'I think once they had that McLaren deal in place there was no way Lewis wasn't going to F1 ultimately and there was no way he was going to be dropped. But I don't think they allowed themselves to think that way and preferred to use the pressure of the link to drive them forwards. There are people in karting critical of Anthony and how pushy he was, but let's get real here: he made it all happen for Lewis. How many dads could a) have got that deal in the first place and b) held onto it once they had it? Not many.'

Still only 14 at the beginning of the 1999 season, Lewis was too young to race in the next category of karting, Formula A. But at the same time, Whitmarsh and Anthony together felt there was little point in another season of the British JICA series, where Lewis had been so exceptional in '98. He did the opening round in Britain before then spreading his wings to Europe.

It was a big move, in many ways the end of an era, and of the happy little Hamilton team. For his forays into Italy and Belgium, Lewis would be part of the works Top Kart Comer JICA team, all paid for by McLaren.

Driving for a works team in Europe is a big step up in

approach from contesting the domestic championships in Britain. The driver becomes to all intents and purposes a professional racing driver, representing his team, playing his part in developing the kart. The manufacturer is relying on his results to showcase its own product in order to generate sales to keep it in business. It's very intense and involves a lot of pre-event testing.

As such, it required some reorganisation of the Hamiltons' home life, again in consultation with McLaren. A private tutor was taken on in an effort to compensate for the big chunk of missed school days. Lewis would study with him for an hour each day before school to catch up on missed lessons from testing and race meetings. Anthony still came to Lewis's races, but was no longer running the team and could not afford the time to attend all the testing, especially with the IT business continuing to grow. Accordingly, his mechanic, Kieran Crawley, found himself in the role also of chaperone.

Crawley had been running a kart for the son of a man who sponsored a stunt driver, Terry Grant, who owned a garage in Stevenage and was a friend of both Crawley's and Anthony Hamilton's. Since Restrick had left to finish his degree, Anthony had been having trouble finding a good spanner man he could rely on. On visiting Grant's garage one day, Anthony asked if he knew of anyone good and Grant recommended Crawley. 'I got a call from Tony and he arranged to come round to see me the next day,' Crawley recalls. 'I was in my pyjamas and there was a knock on the door and there was Tony and Lewis, both dressed in very smart suits. They came in and Tony impressed me enormously by how diligent he had been. He'd been in touch with people I'd worked with before and really done his homework. I started the next day.'

Soon his job expanded into more than just working on the kart. 'Because Anthony was trying to run his business too, I ended up taking Lewis to where he needed to be. Quite often he would have to go down to the McLaren factory. One time in particular they had Prince Charles making a royal visit to the place and they had invited Lewis down to meet him. We got there early and so we went to the gym and were doing press-ups and things, trying to beat each other. I was 25 and very fit, he was 14 but he had me covered easily. He was incredibly fit. It sort of developed from there as Tony realised we got on well but being so much older I could keep him on the straight and narrow. Tony was very, very protective of him. He literally wouldn't let him out if I wasn't there with him. And with good reason too. Lewis was a bit of a wild boy. The council estate kid was still very much part of him. It's also why he has the grit that has made him so successful, but there was another lairy side to him at that stage. Like any normal kid of that age he liked the girls, liked a bit of adventure – and Tony knew this. So I'd get a call and it would be Lewis. "Fancy going to the pictures?" he'd say, and I'm like "Oh, I don't know, I've got a lot on," and he'd be saying "Oh come on. I won't be allowed to go if you don't come."'

So as the time came to race in Europe, it became Crawley's role to pick him up from school, arrange his travel, see to it that he kept up to date with his school and tutorial work, be there as a confidant, ensure he stayed away from anything that might deflect a 14-year-old from his racing. He also continued to work on the kart. Significantly, they were both afraid of incurring Anthony's wrath, and so you get the picture of Kieran as the guy in the middle of a delicate father–son dynamic at this stage in their lives.

It was a new phase for Lewis, a very different environment to anything he'd known. The tracks were all new to him and even the karts were not exactly the same, using stickier tyres than their British equivalents and therefore possessing greater performance. He was also up against a different set of drivers. But still, he made his mark. His season was not an outstanding one in terms of results, but it certainly had its moments. He was fourth in both the Belgian and Italian JICA championships. An incident at a round of the Belgian series was recalled by Crawley in an interview with Adam Jones in *Karting* magazine: 'The karts would do a rolling lap, stop on the grid and do a standing start. Lewis was always stalling it but you were allowed to wait by the side of the track with a starter. As they rolled up to the grid I could see Lewis looking for me and I realised he'd stalled it. I got the starter into the sidepod just as the lights turned green. Lewis went off the back of the grid and was already half a lap down. He caught the pack and went through it like a hot knife through butter to finish fourth. He was up against some very good drivers like Randy Bakker and Robert Kubica and he beat them after giving them a half lap headstart!'

Crawley gives more background into Hamilton's problem with the starting techniques of these karts. 'You had to run the engine really slowly and adjust the carburettor as you slowed to a stop and it was quite a tricky thing to do – and Lewis was always stalling it. It would run too rich and oil up the plug. Kubica realised that this was a problem for Lewis and whenever they were at the front of the grid together, Kubica would slow the pace right down to make it extra-difficult, sometimes even looking across at Lewis and laughing. It was a problem so we took the kart to a building site in the evenings near where we were staying in Italy and we spent hour upon hour just practising it – until he got it. After that he was really good at it – and even managed to make Kubica stall once or twice! Anthony really appreciated the extra effort I'd made there.

'It was necessary – and a good illustration of why he need-ed someone with him. Lewis was still pretty hot-headed at that time and sometimes the Italian mechanics would take the mickey out of him and he'd lose his temper with them. And it was like that with his starts. A guy would say some-thing, just to make light of it, and Lewis would react.'

Correlating with Jonny Restrick's observations about Hamilton's performances in adversity, Crawley goes on to say: 'In F1 we haven't seen him come from the back ... That's when he's at his most dangerous. When he makes mistakes, just watch him go. That's when you'll see how good he real-ly is. That's when the grit in him is triggered and it's that that will make him the best. Adversity just brings something very special out in him. I think he will in time show himself to be a better, more complete driver than Michael Schumacher – because Schumacher could crumble with the pressure on, could make panic decisions like trying to take a rival off the track in the heat of the moment. Lewis doesn't get affected like that – there is never any panic, just grit. I've seen it so often in karting: the kids from privileged backgrounds that know they will be racing no matter what don't have the same resilience, don't know how to dig deep and their performances are more up and down. With Lewis, no matter what the problem with the kart, he was always a contender, always a factor.'

The '99 European JICA title was a single event and he finished second in it to Reinhard Kofler, beating the more established hot-shots Nico Rosberg and Robert Kubica. In

October there was a series of races called the Italian Industrials, where the kart manufacturers traditionally make a big push in order to sell more karts for the following season. The series covers several categories, and carries a lot of prestige. Hamilton won the ICA category – essentially for JICA karts but open also to more experienced drivers. It rubber-stamped the authenticity of the reputation he had brought with him from Britain, and established him as a serious force within the heavy-duty European karting scene.

The 1999 season had done everything McLaren had hoped it might, in other words, by broadening Lewis's experience base, giving him a taste of racing internationally and outside the confines of the family. Now for a full-scale assault on that world.

CHAPTER FOUR

Beating the Big Boys

By the end of the 2000 season, 15-year-old Lewis Hamilton was widely considered the world's number one karter.

He had won the European Formula A championship, probably the second most prestigious title in the sport of karting, overshadowed only by the world championship in the same category. But that was a single event, a one-off, not a season-long slog, and as such was not as representative of the true form. Actually, Hamilton had looked well in line for the world title too – until an engine failure intervened.

There are always those prepared to knock any achievements, and those who try to belittle Hamilton's – quite often the parents of beaten rivals – will cite the fact that Lewis has had the best machinery from day one. Whatever the truth of that, it certainly applied in 2000, when he and Nico Rosberg drove for Team MBM.com, a karting 'superteam' run by the sport's maestro team boss, Dino Chiesa, a man with a huge record of success in the sport.

Chiesa had been given carte blanche by McLaren and

Mercedes (hence 'MBM' – Mercedes-Benz/McLaren) to create the best team possible. It had all been initiated by Nico Rosberg's father Keke, the 1982 F1 world champion and former McLaren driver. He had been guiding his son's career in much the same way as Anthony Hamilton was Lewis's. In 1998 and '99 Nico had driven for Chiesa in the European JICA series, with promising results. For the move up to Formula A – still with engines of 100cc but with rotary valve engines that allowed over 20,000rpm and as much as 29 horsepower, and no longer single-supply tyres but a full-on tyre war between Bridgestone, Dunlop and Vega – Keke looked to Mercedes for support. Long after retiring from F1, Keke had made a racing comeback in sports cars and touring car racing – and had driven for Mercedes in the German Touring Car Championship. The relationship had always been good, and now he sought to move it on to the next generation, with the idea of a Mercedes-backed team for Nico in Formula A, run by Chiesa.

Mercedes' motorsport boss Norbert Haug liked the idea but was keen not to do something separate from the McLaren-Mercedes driver support programme. Accordingly, he got Ron Dennis involved and at the 1999 Malaysian Grand Prix, Keke flew out in order to talk about the idea with his former team boss. It didn't make sense to have Mercedes backing one driver and McLaren-Mercedes backing a rival in another team. So it was agreed that Nico Rosberg and Lewis Hamilton would be brought into a joint McLaren-Mercedes programme, with CRG-Parilla karts run by Chiesa. The superteam was born.

Anthony Hamilton hadn't got Lewis this far through being naive. He had understandable reservations about Lewis joining an existing driver/team owner partnership, particularly one where the deal had been initiated by the other driver's father. And to cap it all, here was Nico de facto joining the McLaren support programme. But Anthony of course was in no position to make demands of McLaren. There was an alternative on offer: to remain with Top Kart and graduate to Formula A with them. But there were reservations about just how competitive a kart they could field: Chiesa's team was the one with the track record and that was the decisive factor.

Lewis and Nico had become firm friends during the '99 season and Anthony had come to get on reasonably well with Keke too. But still, friendship has its limits and Anthony was very much on his guard in the early stages of 2000. 'Oh, he was like a tiger stalking me,' laughs Chiesa. 'In the beginning it was not easy. He was thinking, "Hey this team has been set up around Nico, he's been here two years already", he didn't know if he could trust me. But as soon as Lewis started winning, he could see there was no favouritism, and it was OK.'

Chiesa didn't quite know what to expect from his new charge initially. 'I'd not seen a lot of Lewis in '99,' he explains, 'but I knew he had a big reputation in England. I saw him in the Top Kart a couple of times but it wasn't the best kart and he didn't know the tracks so he hadn't looked anything special. But I soon saw in the winter tests he was very fast – immediately just as fast as Nico and I rated Nico very highly. The year before he had been just as fast as Kubica, who was probably the number one guy at the time.'

The partnership got off to an uncertain start, with Lewis not initially figuring at the front. 'You have to take a feeling from a driver,' explains Chiesa. 'When he is young he cannot work out what he needs. So after the first three races I went testing with him for three solid days. So I ran him and got a feel: does he need understeer, oversteer, bottom end power, top end? And then you understand – and then you explain to the driver. And it was like this with Lewis. He likes a lot of oversteer because he pushes a lot into the corner and it's the front wheels that arrive there first! So he needs a front because he's arriving so fast and he can control the back. This is usually a good indication in karts of a guy who is fast. If a driver tells me he has too much response from the front, I know that he's not really fast enough.'

Not only was Lewis more than fast enough, but his racing aggression really marked him out – even in this elite company. 'That was the outstanding thing about him,' agrees Chiesa. 'He was very fast, but then so was Nico. He was a clever driver – but so was Nico. They could both use their brain well. For example, both were very good at preserving the tyres. You'd see in the heats they'd be among the fastest or if they were fastest it was only by a tenth. Then in the final suddenly they were fastest by 0.3 seconds or more, because they had conserved the tyres in the heats. But if there was one thing separating why it was Lewis who finished first and Nico who was runner-up in the championship, it was Lewis's fighting attitude. With him it was always all or nothing – he would take risks to win, risks that could mean he wouldn't finish, whereas Nico would always have an eye on finishing the race.

'He had a character to fight, always, at every corner. He is a very aggressive character in the kart, and you need that in karting more than in cars. But this is something you are born with. You cannot tell a driver to be more aggressive. In F1 you see exactly the same character traits as the same guys had in karting and the way you see Lewis fighting now, the aggressive moves he makes, this is exactly how he was in karting. Lewis will always fight – and he nearly always wins his fight. Even against Alonso, or anyone. If he'd fought Michael Schumacher I'm sure it would have been the same. He fought. Like Senna used to fight.'

That comparison keeps popping up. There is definitely a similarity in the driving and racing styles of the two men: Hamilton and the guy he used to idolise as a kid, Senna. In terms of driving style they both favoured a combination of late braking and geometrically perfect lines through a corner, in contrast to others like Schumacher or Alonso who tended to turn in slightly earlier, loading the front wheels up for longer and balancing the two ends of the car more. The Hamilton/Senna technique places more demands upon the grip of the rear wheels and requires constant steering correction of the more wayward rear end. In their racing styles they each had/have a high-risk, no-compromise attitude. It's a combination that is spectacular to behold in its boldness.

But their outward personalities are very different. Kees van de Grint, Bridgestone's racing manager, came to work closely with Lewis in 2000 and '01 and his overriding impression was how such a competitive force could be combined with such an agreeable personality. 'In his driving style he goes for it just as intensely as Michael [Schumacher] or Senna – all out to win, nothing else will do. A lot of the champions are very aggressive in everything they do. But without the steering wheel Lewis has a much nicer surface than them. He has a very open mind – I still see it now. It's the same open-minded guy sitting in the McLaren garage that would be sitting in the grass at Braga. Away from the car he's the sort of guy you feel you could easily go for a beer with. I struggle to think of any other top guys you could say that about. All the successful people have fans and enemies.

But unless he changes I think Lewis will have only fans. He's an exception.'

Hamilton clinched the European title at Valence, with one round still remaining. The vagaries of the weather throughout the weekend threatened to leave him relying on the final round, as he recalled in *Karting* magazine shortly afterwards. 'We arrived at Thursday lunchtime and had therefore missed Wednesday's testing and three of the sessions on Thursday morning. I had never been to the track before so I had to try and learn it as quickly as possible. The first session was 12 laps and within the first 10 laps I was on the pace. On Friday I made a mistake in qualifying which lost me about 0.1s and put me 12th on the grid. I was to race six heats: five on Saturday, one on Sunday. I won four heats out of the five and was fifth in the other.' That fifth place came in the only wet heat. In the rain the Dunlop tyres proved to be around 2s per lap quicker than the Bridgestones Lewis raced on. The fifth place represented the highest-placed Bridgestone driver. 'For the heat on Sunday it had been raining but the track was beginning to dry,' he related. 'We selected slicks. Unfortunately the track didn't dry out quickly enough [for slick tyres] and I fell back to 14th position. For the first final it rained again and the Dunlop drivers had the advantage. The first four drivers were all on Dunlops, and I was fifth. In the second final the track had dried. I started fifth and by lap two was in the lead.' He won the race by seven seconds, and with it the crown. Of the eight races that comprised the championship Hamilton won five, to take the maximum possible points.

It may seem unusual preparation for a title-deciding event to turn up a day later than most of the others. But that was down to both Anthony and Ron Dennis insisting upon school taking precedence whenever possible. It was some-thing that had impressed van de Grint: 'Yes, I first saw that at a test. Keke had asked if his team could join the tyre test and I had agreed. I arrived at the test and there was Keke and Nico – but no Lewis. I asked why he was not there and got the rather surprising reply that school takes priority. That impressed me a lot. Most parents in this situation are think-ing "My son becomes a star", not knowing what the future holds, and they neglect the schooling. I thought this showed a lot of maturity and responsibility on Anthony's part.'

Lewis did take part in later tyre tests, and his feedback impressed van de Grint. 'There is a lot to learn about tyres after coming in from the lower categories of karting where there is just a control tyre. In Formula A there was the tyre war so we were all trying to get the tyre with the maximum performance – which makes it a more sensitive tyre and eas-ier to damage if you don't use it correctly. A driver has to feel and understand it, to realise that if he turns in too sharply and puts all the weight over the front axle you will pick up tyre graining. You have to learn how to trade off the braking and the cornering to look after the tyre. These skills become very important in F1, but are redundant during most of the junior car racing categories, where you tend to go back to control tyres. I must say he picked these skills up very well, as did Nico. In fact their feedback was so good we began to include them as part of our regular tyre testing team.

'Lewis was always an exciting guy to watch in a kart race. He was always a factor. You could never ignore him. Some of his overtaking moves were very exciting but even more impressive is how he's been able to translate these sort of moves all the way to F1. In his first two Grands Prix he did these fantastic moves at the first corner and made up places.

To have the nerve and courage to do that on your debut against Alonso, a double world champion, was very impressive. But the move itself was not a surprise to me because I've seen him do that many times over the years.'

The world championship was held at Braga in Portugal over a single weekend, with a series of heats and a final. As such it was not as representative of form as the season-long European championship, but its tag ensured it had enormous stature. The 2000 event developed into a classic fight – with Hamilton very much in the middle of it all.

'That final was probably the best kart race I've ever seen,' recalls photographer Chris Walker. 'It was won by Colin Brown but featured a scrap between him, Lewis and Clivio Piccione. Colin looked the least likely of the three to win but I think he left some speed in his equipment through the heats whereas the others took more out of theirs, I believe. But the lead changes were unbelievable and you really couldn't call it.'

Brown led the early going from Hamilton, these two pulling out a gap on the rest, with Hamilton then going past to lead. Several times he made a break for it and looked set to pull away, but each time Brown was able to come back at him. Eventually Piccione got past third-place Loic Duval and in no time at all was up with Hamilton and Brown, joining in their battle. The lead changed between the three of them an average of once a lap for the next ten laps. Hamilton was leading with three laps to go – on the verge of the world title to add to the European one he'd already clinched – when his engine broke a conrod. A picture in *Karting* magazine shows him pulling off onto the grass, both hands off the steering and covering his visor in dismay.

There was some compensation with victory in the 'World

Cup', a one-off event held at Suzuka in Japan. He followed this up with a yet more eye-catching victory in the 'Young Hopefuls' section of the Elf Master Karting competition at the Paris Bercy Exhibition Centre in December 2000. This is an annual karting get-together of the great and good in racing, and pits current karters against former top exponents of the sport. Hamilton's victory came against several drivers further on in their careers, and just rein-forced the racing community's awareness of the gifted McLaren protégé. Kieran Crawley accompanied him there: 'It was quite funny because they supplied you with the kart and your own mechanic, and this guy is sitting there in our area, with his allocated blue tool box – and we just said to him "Why don't you go off and get yourself a cup of coffee and we'll see you later on", and I got to work on the kart. We moved the seat position around, which is very important in a kart as it determines how you move the weight distribution around. I looked across and of the others, David Fore and his guy were doing exactly the same – but none of the others were.'

Afterwards there was a reception for the drivers and Crawley saw first-hand the deference Lewis commanded. 'He was just 15 but was being treated like a superstar. Everyone wanted autographs and to have their picture taken with him. I definitely got the impression that some of the older drivers, further on in their careers than him, got the hump about it all. But he's had that sort of thing almost from the start. He's had an attention on him way beyond what most experience from an earlier age – and I think that's what has led him to compose himself more as he's got older. He learned to deal with adults and to carry himself in a certain way when he was still a kid and that wild, hot-headed kid gradually disappeared. He's still got the fire in him, but it's all directed inside the car now.'

There was some irony in the fact that Lewis Hamilton was European Formula A champion at an age where he was not yet allowed to race Formula A in his homeland of Britain. It was just a statistic of little significance to Hamilton's career but it did highlight a small problem that his precocious success had brought him: he'd achieved all that was necessary in karting to graduate to mainstream single-seater car racing but was not yet felt to be ready to make that move. There was a feeling, both in the Hamilton camp and at McLaren, that he shouldn't be rushed into cars at such an early age – even though there were then emerging new junior championships which allowed it. The most prominent of these was Formula BMW – and that clearly was never going to be an option, given the Mercedes connection.

Instead, McLaren, the Hamiltons and the Rosbergs decided to stay with Chiesa for an ambitious assault on one more category of karting. Formula Super A was not necessarily a traditional part of the career ladder of an ambitious would-be F1 driver. The karts were immensely powerful – 35 horsepower in a kart gives a sensation of acceleration very like that of an F1 car – and tended to be raced by paid professional karting specialists. They built up a huge data-bank over the years of the machines' very specific demands, and to go in with two rookies for the 2001 season was quite a brave move.

Chiesa reckoned it would have worked too. Except for one thing: 'This was the first year the formula had stipulated water-cooled engines,' he explains, 'and our engine partner did not adapt as well to the change as some of the others.' Neither Hamilton nor Rosberg won a single race all year, the first time in Hamilton's career that this had happened.

Vitantonio Liuzzi was the Formula Super A world champion that year using a similar CRG chassis to those initially used by the Chiesa boys, but with an Iama engine rather than their Parillas. Although Chiesa reckons this was the crucial difference, it's probably worth pointing out that this was Liuzzi's fourth year in Super A. The relative inexperience of Hamilton and Rosberg may well have contributed to their struggle. Van de Grint believes so: 'The Super As had very big carburettors and that demanded a completely different driving style from other karting categories. In the other categories you come off the throttle late, get the turn in, then go straight back full on the throttle. If you did that with the Super As, you just flooded the engine and didn't get maximum acceleration. You had to adopt a smoother style, one that changed also how you used the tyres. They were up against some very experienced drivers that knew the game very well and so it didn't really happen for them at first. It wasn't a lack of ability: Lewis was doing lap times the year before in Formula A that would have put him in the first two rows of a Super A grid, but he couldn't repeat them in the Super A, just showing how specialised it was.'

Mid-season, Chiesa ditched the CRG chassis for specially commissioned ones from Parolin. There were still no race wins, but there was a very definite competitive upturn towards the end of the season. 'A lot of people – particularly the engine people – were saying that the CRG chassis used by Liuzzi must be different,' says Chiesa. 'I was telling the engine people the problem wasn't the chassis, but the engine. I changed chassis to Parolin to show them that the problem wasn't the chassis. If Lewis had done another year in Super A, I'm sure we could have won. In fact, had the 2001 world championship still been a single event like it had been, rather than a five-round series, I think we could have been in with a chance, because by the end of the season we had made a lot of progress and were very competitive.'

'I think the fact that they were running at the front at all by the end of the first year shows they had exceptional talent,' says van de Grint, 'because for most people that particular transition takes around two years. By the end of the year they were competing with the best in what was an incredibly specialised formula.'

When the world championship visited the Kerpen track for the final round, there was a very special guest competitor: Michael Schumacher, on the verge of clinching his fourth F1 world championship. This was his home town and he couldn't resist being there. Characteristically, he had prepared for the event intensely, spending hours and hours thrashing round the track, getting used to the kart and the tyres. Liuzzi won both finals, with Schumacher second in the second one. Hamilton, still hampered by a kart that was not fully competitive, was seventh in both. But his style and attack certainly left their mark on Schumacher, who commented: 'He's a quality driver, very strong and only 16. If he keeps this up I'm sure he will reach F1. It's something special to see a kid of his age out on the circuit. He's clearly got the right racing mentality.'

Leaving a category without having won in it went against the grain with the Hamiltons, for all that there might have been very valid technical reasons. Chiesa very much wanted them to stay for another assault on Super A in 2002 and feels confident they would have won it. The Hamiltons initially wanted to stay too – and it was McLaren that was pushing to get Lewis into cars. There was some disagreement in the camp, with Ron Dennis insisting he shouldn't stay too long there 'because karting teaches you bad habits' – a view that left the Hamiltons rather gasping in surprise. But in the end McLaren prevailed: Lewis was going to graduate to cars in the British Formula Renault championship.

The Rosbergs too decided it was time for Nico to try cars, but it was not to be with McLaren-Mercedes backing. Nico left to contest the German Formula BMW championship. It would be fair to say that Keke's wealth meant it was nowhere near so crucial for Nico's career that he stay on the McLaren ladder of opportunity as it was for Lewis. But it would also be fair to say that it was a disappointment to the Rosbergs that Nico was allowed to part from the family while McLaren maintained 100 per cent commitment to Lewis. Lewis and Nico remained firm friends throughout, and Lewis spent much time with the Rosbergs at their Monaco home between kart races. It's a friendship that endures to this day as they both make their way in F1. But the relationship between Anthony and Keke definitely cooled during that time, with the latter feeling distinctly bruised by what he perceived as naked ambition.

You hear a similar story from fathers of rival drivers throughout Lewis's karting career. Sour grapes? Probably some. An element of truth? Probably some. But this is a big boy's game. If Anthony Hamilton trod on a few toes, spiked a few egos as he applied his intensely competitive will into getting the best for his boy – knowing that he couldn't possibly afford to buy his way to the top, that just one missed opportunity could bring the whole thing to a halt – then is that so bad? To believe that Lewis was any less driven and competitive than Anthony would be wrong too. But the off-track stuff could be left to Dad, leaving Lewis just to concentrate on making full use of his God-given gift. He had no need to behave against the grain of his sunny, warm character – because Dad was taking care of business. But had he needed to, be in no doubt that he could have done so. His will to succeed is absolute. Anthony can be a warm, likeable person too. In fact, most of the time he is. But his competitive will has no compunction about putting that to one side for the necessities of the moment. The two aren't as different as they seem. But as two halves of a partnership, they are devastating. And that can leave those around them feeling bruised.

CHAPTER FIVE

From Karts to Cars

John Booth is an impressive character: a tall and tough Yorkshireman, in the late 1970s/early 80s he was a good Formula Ford racer, fitting it in between his occupation as a butcher. But as the years went on, so he made the transition to team owner. His Manor Motorsport team, based in Sheffield, has been one of the top junior formula outfits in British motorsport for several years and has won numerous national titles.

At one point in the early 2000s, his team were seriously interested in acquiring the McLaren-backed West F3000 team that had been set up to run Nick Heidfeld but which was no longer needed. Booth's partner in Manor, David Matthews, a touring car racer back in the 1970s, was friendly with McLaren's Martin Whitmarsh. 'It came to nothing in the end,' says Booth. 'It was a little bit more than we could handle.' But that established a relationship, and when Whitmarsh was thinking about where to place Hamilton in his first foray into car racing, he didn't have to think long.

'Martin called and asked us if we could take a look at this kid, give him a run in a Formula Renault and report back,' says Booth of the October 2001 test at Mallory Park in Leicestershire. Formula Renault is a starter category for cars with slick tyres and downforce-producing wings. They all have the same chassis, tyres and engines – with around 150 horsepower. 'Lewis was only 16 and so hadn't even been driving on the road,' continues Booth. 'He went out and straight away he was hard on it, really pushing hard immediately. It was pretty impressive – but then he binned it on the third lap.' He'd gone off at Gerards, a long, fast, sweeping right-hander taken in top gear. By the time the car had come to rest hard against the tyre barriers, its back end was destroyed.

'So we put a new back end on the car and in the afternoon sent him back out. I was expecting he'd be seriously detuned. You can imagine: a 16-year-old having his first run in a racing car and he crashed it after three laps. He would have every reason to be a bit fazed. But he was exactly the same when he got back in, just as hard on it as before. The accident had absolutely no effect on him – not two laps to warm up or anything, just straight back on it. Later, I came to appreciate that this was very much him – all-out attack from the word go.

'I gave a report back to Martin and it went from there. I actually suggested he spend another year in karting. From what I'd seen the best lads from karting that came through were 18 or more. But I sensed if I pushed too far down that line I'd have missed the deal. So I agreed to run him.'

Booth's preference for a slightly older driver was based very much on the most devastating guy he'd run in Formula Renault to date: Kimi Raikkonen. The Finn had dominated the 2000 British Formula Renault championship for Manor, his only car racing experience before moving straight to F1 the following year, aged 21. 'Kimi had stayed in karts a long time, mainly because he couldn't raise the money to get out of it until the Robertsons [father and son driver/manager team, Dave and Steve Robertson] got involved. That extra bit of time, the difference between 16 and 19 or 20, does make an enormous difference. Drivers of that age just tend to be more complete. There was no way Lewis was ever going to be ready as soon after beginning in cars as Kimi was.

'I'm sure had Lewis stayed in karting until he was 20, then did a season of Renault, he'd have been ready to go straight to F1 too. It's an age thing rather than an experience thing. You almost got the impression with Kimi he found the whole thing quite boring. He was driving that Renault as fast as it would go after half a dozen tests. With Lewis it was a constant progression because he was much younger. He was always very fast but still had progress to make.'

Misgivings about Lewis's age notwithstanding, Booth was excited by his potential. McLaren and Manor duly made their deal, and in preparation for Hamilton's assault on the 2002 British Formula Renault series, he was entered in the few races that comprised the 2001 winter series for the cars in November. In the second race of the first round at Rockingham, he showed the racecraft so familiar from karting – with a late-race, tyre-smoking pass for fourth place. In the second two-race meeting at Donington a week later, the same spirit got him into a bit of trouble. Second into the first corner of the race, at the end of the lap he attacked the chicane extra hard, trying to get a better exit speed than the leader so that he could slipstream ahead of him into the following turn. Instead, he ran wide on the chicane's exit, clattered his car over the grass and severely damaged its floor, this accounting for any chance he had. And that was the winter series. Hamilton hadn't set the world alight, but against older, more experienced drivers he'd made a competitive start – and now had a whole winter of testing to learn more about the cars and get himself fully prepared.

Working for Booth as a driver coach was Marc Hynes, who had won the British F3 championship of 1999 driving for Manor. He recalls: 'I was aware that Lewis was the McLaren boy and stood out from the crowd. You'd see him every year at the Autosport awards picking something up. But you didn't quite know if that was because he was a McLaren boy or whether he was really doing so well. But obviously he was beating some people so must've been doing something. He always seemed like a nice kid. He'd won in European karting, which is bloody tough but the quality of your machinery is very important. So I couldn't gauge his ultimate potential until I started working with him.

'From first meeting someone you have half an idea whether they're going to be a sensible proposition for a racing driver or not, and he was – very intelligent, knew a lot about himself from his karting days. You learn to deal with pressure and how to get the best out of yourself, and he had that. He also had total self-belief, but not in an arrogant way, just a quiet but total confidence. The driving experience of a single-seater car is very different from that of a kart. Lewis came into it at the top of his game from karting and expected to jump in and be bang on the pace and just continue with his success. That ended after those three laps at Mallory Park. But it was obvious he had huge natural ability. He never really struggled with speed at all and developed a very good style naturally.

'But even with someone of his ability, raw speed alone

doesn't get you through. You have to learn a lot of technique. Formula Renault is a great training formula, teaches you the exact drving style needed for F3, which in turn is a similar style to F1, especially in the slow corners. If you can drive a Formula Renault properly, when you jump into F3 it all makes sense. We did a lot of work on that – the slow corner, technical stuff, and he learned very well, was very open to coaching and always asking questions, just loved talking about it all and understanding it. It was a complete contrast to the little bit of coaching I'd done the year before with Kimi, who just didn't really want to analyse anything, just wanted to get in and drive the wheels off it.'

In testing for the first race at Brands Hatch, Hamilton was consistently the fastest, but in qualifying could manage only the outside of the second row and in the race was third. At the second race he was restricted by mechanical problems and at Thruxton for the third round he was fifth. Two of those first three races were won by Danny Watts, who assumed a comfortable championship lead. For Lewis, it just wasn't happening – and he was becoming frustrated. The well-seasoned Booth was less concerned than Hamilton about the lack of immediate success: 'Desire sometimes got the better of him. Numerous times we'd be quick in testing or in the first part of qualifying, we'd put his new tyres on and he'd crash – or go over the top with the driving. New tyres were worth a couple of tenths, but he'd go looking for a full second – which you don't mind. You can see what's happening, you know it's all going to come right in the end.'

Next was Silverstone, where an engine failure in qualifying left him at the back of the grid, in 28th place. He fought up to a tenth place finish, pulling off some spectacular passes, and set fastest lap along the way. With the pressure of being at the front removed, he seemed to free-up and be more instinctive about his racing. It was the trigger for his breakthrough – which came in the following event, at Thruxton on 16 June 2002, the date of Lewis Hamilton's first win in cars. He never even looked like losing, qualifying on pole by the margin of 0.4 seconds, leading from lights to flag and setting fastest lap.

From there and into the second half of the season, Hamilton was frequently the fastest guy out there and was a regular winner. But the dominant man of the early season, Danny Watts, continued to be competitive and as such maintained his points advantage over Hamilton, who ended up battling Watts's team-mate Jamie Green for runner-up spot. He'd left it too late to win the title, but he was certainly producing some eye-catching drives. Hynes increasingly came to realise that he was coaching someone special. 'We came to see that perhaps the most impressive thing of all about him was that he was an awesome racer – the way he could find overtaking spots, the way he could spot a gap even before it appeared, was amazing. I was sitting on the grid at Donington with him and we were discussing passing places because he wasn't on the front row. And he said "What about Old Hairpin?" – which is a very fast and tricky downhill turn. And I said "Yes, on the first lap when the cars are bunched up, you might be able to nick the odd place there." He passed someone there on the first lap and then about three laps in he nailed someone else there too. I've never seen anyone even attempt to overtake there; it's madness. But he did it and got away with it. He is certainly a different league of racer to anyone I've seen. He spots the gap so early – and that's a natural instinctive thing you can't teach.'

Booth pinpoints another talent that allows such moves:

'He brakes unbelievably late and still keeps it under control. He can hit the brake and feel when the downforce is coming off as the car slows, and modulate the pedal pressure. That's the hardest skill of all and he was brilliant at it.'

Although Watts clinched the championship, Hamilton was the dominant man at the final meeting of the year at Donington, winning both races on the road, though being penalised back to fourth for the latter one for jumping the start. This penalty had the effect of handing second in the championship to Jamie Green at Hamilton's expense. In all, it had been a good season for Hamilton, even if not the title-winning one he expected. He had translated his karting skills into the very different discipline of cars – which is not always a given; there have been many supremely skilful kartists who simply could not make that transition, even when they did have the financial backing to make the jump. Importantly for Lewis, he'd done more than enough for McLaren to keep the faith, but while Lewis and Anthony both felt he was ready for the next step, to F3, Whitmarsh and Dennis were adamant that they wanted him to stay put with Booth for another season of Renault. 'We felt it important that he win titles in each of his championships,' said Dennis, 'as I believe that builds a certain confidence and attitude.'

'I'm pretty certain McLaren insisted on that second year to see how he dealt with the pressure of being the favourite,' says Hynes. 'They got it totally spot-on. It was the right thing to do.'

'Absolutely the correct thing to do,' agrees Booth, who remains full of admiration for the McLaren approach to Hamilton's formative years. 'They were as good as gold to work with. I expected a contract about 30 pages long but it was just a sheet of A4. There was absolutely no pressure from them, as such. They would call every two or three races just to keep up to date. Martin Whitmarsh would be the first to tell you that their knowledge of the junior racing scene was limited, so they were being guided by us. Lewis always had the impression that there was pressure there from McLaren, whether that came from Anthony I don't know. But in reality it never came from McLaren. It was just in their minds, consciously or sub-consciously.'

Anthony, as ever, was very ambitious for his boy and it would be fair to say there was a measure of frustration that Lewis wasn't being fast-tracked onto the next step of the ladder. Booth frequently found himself having to calm Anthony's occasional impatience, especially when results weren't forthcoming. 'He wasn't as bad as some racing dads,' says Booth diplomatically, 'and for all his faults Anthony's given very good guidance to Lewis as a person, and both his stepmum and mum are real down-to-earth lovely people, and his mum's husband too. But it is his brother Nicholas who has kept Lewis's feet on the ground more than anything. The whole family appeared to be good pals. That sort of mature approach they had as a family rubbed off on Lewis.

'For a time I was thinking that Lewis would want to get away, loosen the shackles, as we all do when we're 16–17. I thought he was coming up to the age where he'd want to strike out on his own and that it would be a very difficult transition, given how closely Anthony was involved. But as time went on I came to realise how much Lewis depended on Anthony – for the whole thing. Control's not the right word, but discipline. Lewis depends on him for that, and he realises it.'

That distinction between being controlled by someone

and being guided by their discipline is very much in line with what we saw between the Hamiltons in karting. Lewis has never been just a meek kid doing as he's told by a domineering dad. He's a feisty individual in his own right, and has been right from the start, but smart enough to realise that Dad has a lot to bring to the party. This was Lewis's dream, after all, not Anthony's – and he didn't automatically defer, as nicely illustrated by Lewis's road-driving instruction. Only part-way through his Formula Renault season did 17-year-old Lewis get his driving licence. He passed after six driving school lessons: 'I paid for them myself,' he said, grinning, 'because I don't think my dad was the best person to teach me. He thinks he's the best driver and even now when I'm at the wheel I still get instructions on how to do it!' Just like the little kid in the *Blue Peter* karting clip, he's not ready to listen to any advice from Dad about driving. But the rest of the stuff … well, he's got something to contribute there.

'Lewis is a very positive person,' says Hynes, 'and his dad has got a lot to do with that. He's hot on mental discipline and strength and it's absolutely rubbed off on Lewis. But the essential thing about Lewis is how driven he is. He is the most driven person I have ever met in my life – by miles. And that can only come from within you. Your dad can't teach you that. He wants it absolutely desperately, he wants to win every race desperately, every championship, he always desperately wanted to be a McLaren F1 driver. He's also very honest – and that's probably rubbed off from his family's values. That quality really works for Lewis because you don't get yourself into trouble when you're honest and that keeps things very simple. He never lets any bullshit cloud a situation; all he wants to do is get in his car and make it go as quickly as possible. If the car is quick enough, he will win the race. That's how simple he makes it.'

With his driving licence and his own car – an original-shape Mini Cooper – Lewis was at least now able to get out without a chaperone, and was dating a girl he knew from school, Rachel Butterfield. He was also working as a car valet at a Stevenage garage and spent a lot of his downtime playing guitar. Just a regular 17-year-old, still living at home. Except he was the prodigy of one of the sport's top F1 teams who had invested to date around £1 million in him and were poised to spend yet more.

CHAPTER SIX

The Pressure of Delivery

Given Lewis Hamilton's devastating Formula Renault form at the end of 2002, there was no way he was anything but hot favourite for the '03 title. He was a man on a mission, determined to bulldoze aside any opposition – just as he had been coming into the previous season, but with the difference that this time he was armed with the knowledge of how to do it. A year earlier, he didn't know what he didn't know.

So after being quickest at every pre-season test – 'by whole tenths, not merely hundredths,' says John Booth – there was an element of panic in the Hamilton camp when after the fourth round of the 17-round series, Lewis had yet to win a race. 'The whole thing began to get a bit edgy,' recalls Booth. 'Anthony was a little bit concerned we weren't doing the job and the pressure was making Lewis try to compensate by pushing even harder. I think it was made worse by the fact that we weren't doing that well in F3 at the time either; we went OK but we had Derek Hayes and Mark Taylor who were struggling against Takuma Sato and Anthony Davidson at

Carling, so it looked like we were lacking.'

Here was where the pressure of running a prospect as hot as Lewis Hamilton was felt by the team. Anthony's haranguing of McLaren to get his boy out of there and into a 'top' team, to keep that momentum rolling, to keep Lewis on that conveyor belt to F1, can be imagined. It was a very unsettling time for all concerned. Thankfully McLaren kept their cool, stayed in close touch with Booth, and felt reassured that all would come good. It wasn't actually difficult to look past the paucity of results and see that it was just a matter of time. But that's easy to say in hindsight. At the time, in the middle of it all, there was a neurosis around around everything, the big worry that it all might be slipping away.

'At Snetterton for the first round, he was quickest by miles,' says Booth, 'but then threw it off in qualifying. He brought the car back looking like a haystack.' The repaired car was less than perfect for the first race, but he led away and stayed in front until tripping over a backmarker. The resultant ride through the gravel trap handed the win to his old karting rival Mike Conway, who commented: 'It goes to show Lewis isn't superhuman. He can be just as feeble as the rest of us and make mistakes.' The following day Lewis could finish only third.

At Brands Hatch two weeks later, Lewis was pressuring leader Tom Sisley when he went off at Paddock Hill Bend and hit the tyre barriers hard enough to wreck the car and wind himself. At Thruxton he was held back to second by a very defensive James Rossiter. Coming into June, the pre-season favourite had not won a race and the lines of communication between Anthony Hamilton and McLaren were red hot. For the following race at Silverstone, two McLaren F1 engineers were dispatched to observe Booth's team in action. Many team owners may have baulked at this, may have been irritated at the implied finger of suspicion. But Booth readily agreed, feeling certain he'd be vindicated and knowing that this would then get the programme back on an even keel. It just so happened that Hamilton won this race, with a brilliant display of wet weather driving. But of almost equal importance was the fact that the engineers reported back to McLaren giving Manor Motorsport a clean bill of health, having been highly impressed by their professionalism.

The race began in the dry, with Hamilton running an initial fourth. He was just taking second place from Rossiter when the heavens opened, with everyone still on slick tyres. In these conditions Hamilton was the fastest man on the track by an outrageous margin, and he quickly closed down on leader Sisley before passing him around the outside of the hugely fast Bridge Corner. It was a sensational performance. 'We didn't do anything any different to what we'd been doing all along,' says Booth. 'But from then on the confidence came back or his faith in us, whatever it was, and he became pretty much unbeatable. I never got to the bottom of what it was, but it didn't really matter. It had clicked.'

From that day, Lewis was never again beaten in the championship. He took a further nine wins from ten starts, retiring from the one he didn't win after a computer failure left him with gear selection problems. Perhaps his best performance of all came at a race at Croft, near Darlington, in July. He was leading when a rear damper bolt sheared. 'The damper was just flapping about in the wind,' recalls Booth. 'You could see it from the pit wall.' The following Mike Spencer was able to quickly close right up to Hamilton's rear – but could not find a way by. 'Within about three laps Lewis just somehow worked out a different way of driving it – and the lap times he was doing were actually pretty good, even by normal standards! It was quite unbelievable really.'

A watching Hynes was equally impressed. 'If that had happened to anyone else they would have quickly fallen down the field,' he says. 'You get drivers coming in saying the car doesn't feel right – and yet the team can't find anything wrong. That's how sensitive the cars are. Drivers will debate whether to fit a 12mm roll bar or a 15mm. But here's the bloody damper hanging off and he's still winning the race! That's just a different league.'

Booth recounts a little postscript to the incident: 'I went down to see Martin at McLaren two weeks later and Ron Dennis came into the room – one of only two or three times I've met him. I told him the story of the Croft race and Ron was more interested in the grade of bolt and the design rather than the driving feat. That stuck in my mind.'

The Croft performance came as Hamilton was in the midst of his exams at the Cambridge Arts & Sciences college, on a cramming course for the final year of his education. He'd met Jodia Ma there, a fellow student from Hong Kong, and the two began dating shortly afterwards, a relationship that would last four years. Earlier in the year he'd been able to trade up his Mini Cooper for a Mercedes C-class Coupe, this a sponsored car from the garage where he'd been working valeting cars. More than ever there was an air of inevitability about his progress.

Hamilton sewed up the title at Donington in September and in so doing became the championship's youngest-ever winner at 18 years, eight months. There were two races left – but after consultation with McLaren, Hamilton decided not to take part in them. They were already working towards the next step – his F3 debut.

Manor Motorsport was already fielding cars in the British F3 championship, and for the final round – at the Brands Hatch GP circuit – they entered another for Lewis Hamilton, paid for, as always, by McLaren. He had never previously driven the Grand Prix loop, the long, fast section around the back of the Kent track that makes for probably the biggest challenge faced by the F3 drivers all year. He had not driven an F3 car before, and all the others had been with their teams all season. It was a very serious challenge.

At the end of the half-day test beforehand he went fourth fastest, having been fastest of all for quite some time. Rivals were disbelieving, suspecting the car must be running under-weight just to generate headlines, and that, come qualifying, the true picture would be revealed. Early in qualifying he had a big accident at Paddock Hill bend, causing the session to be red-flagged. 'It was heavily damaged,' recalls Booth. 'We dragged it back, stitched a couple of corners on it, got the wheels pointing in roughly the same direction and sent him back out in time for the end of the session. With the car like that he qualified it fourth – but they took our best time from us because he'd caused the red flag and didn't get back to the garage unaided. So that left him further back.' In the race he got involved in an incident caused by a suddenly slowing car and was hit hard into the Clearways tyre wall by his team-mate Tor Graves. It was a very big impact and Hamilton was unconscious in the car. It was a worrying time for the team and Lewis's family as the curtains were erected around the accident scene. Eventually he came around and was found to be suffering from heavy concussion. He was transferred to St Mary's hospital in nearby Sidcup on back boards to prevent movement as a precaution against spinal injury. He stayed on these until around 11.30pm, after which he was X-rayed. He was released the following morning.

'It gave us all a bit of a scare,' says Booth. Just as Lewis had given the F3 establishment a scare with his instant raw speed. They were to get another taste of it a few weeks later as the F3 field gathered at Cheshire's Oulton Park in preparation for the forthcoming Macau Grand Prix, the 'world cup' of F3, held around that Asian city's streets. 'That was unbeliev-able,' says Booth of the test. 'At Oulton he went 1.5 seconds clear of all the regulars in the morning. But again he lost it. He went off at Island, into the barriers backwards at high speed.' Hamilton was unconscious again, though this time suffered no ill effects upon coming round. OK, he crashed. But 1.5s is an enormous margin of superiority in a formula where advantages are considered big if they are measured in tenths of a second rather than hundredths.

On the strength of this performance, Manor entered him for Macau. There, the cream of the British, European and Japanese F3 series would converge. Such is the race's pres-tige that the winner's career is invariably boosted hugely. It was an incongruously major event for anyone's second-ever F3 race, and it's an extremely difficult place to learn, totally unforgiving of errors given that the track is lined by barriers rather than run-off areas.

But Hamilton is not one to take a cautious approach – and he didn't. Instantly he began attacking the course and was among the quickest in practice. But again in qualifying, he had a big accident. He stayed conscious this time, but it left him back in 18th on the grid for the first of the two races, with grid position for the second being determined by race position in the first. These are just the sort of against-the-odds circumstances that bring out his best. He finished the first race fifth after a series of spectacular passes. Marc Hynes was watching the start: 'Down to the first corner there's a sequence of flat-out bends and there are parts where the track suddenly funnels in very narrow. Everybody tows each other down there but it's so long you can then re-tow and get your place back – but it's scary old stuff the way the track is. As the field took off you could just see his car darting in and out, all over the bloody place, picking off cars everywhere. It looked very scary but every move he made was the right one. You might say it was chance were it not for the fact that he does stuff like this in every race he does unless he's already at the front. He will always, always do something spectacular – as we're now seeing in F1.'

In the second race he was up to third place and in the process of taking second when he was clipped by another car that had hit the barrier and bounced back out. This punctured a tyre and damaged the suspension, ending his chances. But he had been on the very verge of finishing on the podium at Macau in just his second F3 event.

The worries about delivering suddenly seemed a long time ago.

CHAPTER SEVEN

Straining at the Leash

A look at Lewis Hamilton's results in F3 in 2004 reveals only moderate success, albeit sprinkled with many typically high-octane moments of excitement. But as an indirect result, the balance of power between the Hamiltons and McLaren changed – and not necessarily in the expected direction. Off-track, this was a very tense year in the career of Lewis Hamilton, when the stakes were upped and bold gambles were made.

The prodigy was 19 now, had completed his formal education, and was free just to concentrate on the sport he loved. Given his recent form, his McLaren backing, the marketing men's enthusiasm for the idea of a gifted, personable, handsome black man breaking into the sport, the racing world saw it as inevitable that Lewis Hamilton had an F1 future ahead of him. This was simply the rest of the world coming around to his way of thinking. 'Even in karting, it was always "When I get to F1", never "if",' says his one-time kart mechanic Jonny Restrick. But first there was some more winning to do, new formulae to conquer.

'The logical thing was a full season of British F3 in 2004,' says Booth, 'and Martin Whitmarsh told us he could get us Mercedes F3 engines. Mercedes agreed to it but the further we went, the more I began to feel they were doing it against their will, that they were being pushed into it by McLaren. So a good compromise seemed to be F3 Euroseries. Mercedes were quite happy with that and we became their third team.'

Manor had not competed in the European F3 championship before, but were confident their meticulous methods would apply just as effectively in mainland Europe as they had in Britain. But after a few tests, Booth was not so sure.

'It soon became clear that this was a definite step up from the British series,' he says. 'It was a combination of things, but essentially the ASM team were a step in front of us in the way they worked. They had technology that we didn't in terms of simulation programmes and had an active programme of aerodynamic development. They were running like a miniature F1 team.' ASM, a French-based team run by Frédéric Vasseur, was the recognised pace-setter of the series. This year it was running Hamilton's former rival in Formula Renault, Jamie Green, as well as the rapid Frenchman Alexandre Prémat. They were also setting up a sister team, ART, to run in the following year's new GP2 category, placed between F3 and F1. Lewis's friend Nico Rosberg was running with his own Team Rosberg car.

'This being Lewis's first full season in the formula, his technical understanding was still a bit raw,' says Booth, 'and we really needed to have been better technically equipped to have helped him with that. I had a feeling it might be quite a challenge. Then on top of all that, in testing for the first race at Hockenheim, Lewis had another big shunt. He lost it coming into the Stadium section and hit the wall hard, backwards. He was unconscious again! We hadn't even started our first F3 season and he'd now been unconscious in one of our F3 cars three times! The other times he bounced straight back, but on this occasion I think there might have been a bit of a hangover. It seemed a few races before he was back to the old Lewis.'

Booth's fears seemed confirmed in the opening two races of the first round, in which Hamilton finished only 11th and sixth respectively, having qualified in the midfield. His old karting team-mate Nico Rosberg won both races. Subsequent races were won by Prémat and his ASM team-mates Green and Eric Salignon, with Hamilton still seemingly struggling to find his feet.

The breakthrough came at the Norisring, where he won the first race from pole and was third in the second race. It came after a successful test at Magny Cours where significant set-up progress was made. 'If I had any criticism at all of him during his Formula Renault time,' says Hynes, 'it was that he wasn't always sure what he wanted in terms of set-up. When he moved into F3 in Europe he learned, but it was a difficult start.' His victory was a classic fighting one, with Prémat putting him under big pressure before passing. 'With anyone else, that would have been it,' said Prémat, 'but with Lewis he always comes back at you.' After a few laps of counter-attack, Hamilton slipstreamed back ahead. Prémat's suspension later broke, allowing Lewis to nurse his fading brakes to the end.

But that was to be his only taste of victory champagne during the season. He finished fifth in the championship, with fewer than half the points of champion Green. In some moments the frustration got to him. 'How much difference can a driver make?' he questioned after qualifying 1.2s off pole at Brno. 'It's not a second a lap, that's for sure.'

After such a relatively disappointing season, McLaren were all for Lewis repeating the year, just as they had done in Formula Renault, and for much the same reasons. Again, the Hamiltons felt he was more than ready to move on and that he wasn't the reason for the disappointing results. 'Martin Whitmarsh was pushing very hard to get him to do a second season in Europe with us,' says Booth, who was confident that with a season's learning of the championship behind them they would be much more competitive in 2005, 'but the relationship seemed to have run its course as far as Anthony was concerned and I said "Look, if it's against anyone's will, why are we doing it?" and that was it.' Well, that wasn't quite it for the Hamilton/Manor relationship – there were still two non-championship F3 events, Macau and Bahrain.

'Ever since we first went to Macau,' says Booth, 'we have had a set-up that works beautifully.' Derek Hayes, a good driver but not a great one, held the F3 lap record there in a Manor car for quite some time. For the 2004 race, Booth had not only Hamilton in one of his cars, but Robert Kubica in the other. This was going to be very interesting. Of all the competitors that Hamilton had ever faced since karting, he rated Kubica as the toughest. In addition, the young Pole had a deserved reputation as a street circuit ace. The two Manor cars duly proved to be the class of the field, and Hamilton seemed on even more of a mission than usual to clinch pole position.

'In the practice sessions they'd go out and on the first lap Lewis would be 2.5s clear of everyone,' recalls Booth. 'Robert would chip away and get close to it by the end of the session.

But every session the same, first lap out of the box, Lewis clear by 2.5s. That's just how he is, every lap of every corner has to be maximum attack. He's still like that now. Kubica ended up on pole – but again because Lewis had gone off. At the end of the first session he was over 1s clear of everyone. In second qualifying he hit the wall and Robert just sneaked in front of him. Everybody improved by over 1s in the second session but Lewis's first session time was so fast he was still able to keep the front row. In the Sunday morning warm-up I was that scared about what he was going to try and do, I pulled him in after three laps and said that'll do. We left Robert out the whole session and that resulted in him doing what's still the fastest time that's ever been done around there – despite being on knackered old tyres. And that still rankles with Lewis a bit, I think, because he knew he could've gone even quicker.'

With the two Manor drivers on the front row, each absolutely determined to beat the other, there was definite tension in the camp as the lights turned green. Kubica used the advantage of his starting slot to get away in the lead, but Hamilton was tucked tight into his slipstream as they headed flat out down to Mandarin Bend and at the last moment ducked out and dived for the outside – an extremely brave move, maybe bordering on crazy. 'It was very scary,' admitted Lewis. 'Robert was covering the inside as I got in the tow, but it wasn't enough to get past him. I hoped that he would have to lift as I went round him – and he did, although I went through the corner sideways.' It was the most fantastically judged and committed manoeuvre imaginable, and he went on to win the race. But this was simply the qualifying race that determined grid slots for the final the next day. In this Hamilton was out-accelerated off the line by Nico Rosberg.

On the next lap, with Hamilton piling on the pressure, Rosberg braked too late and hit the tyre wall, and took Hamilton out with him.

The 2004 contract between McLaren and the Hamiltons had expired before they had agreed on what Lewis should do in 2005. So he was driving in Macau as a free agent. It seemed inconceivable that the Hamiltons might shun McLaren support short of reaching the goal of F1 – but it was very seriously considered, as McLaren were adamant they would not support anything other than another year in F3. Anthony shopped around for GP2 deals and was trying hard to raise the finance to run with David Sears's team. He is also believed to have made it known to rival F1 teams that Lewis might be available, and there was a very serious discussion with a leading team in the American Champcar series. In the meantime, ASM's Frédéric Vasseur was very keen to have Hamilton in his F3 team and was prepared to hold out for him, refusing to finalise deals with other drivers until he knew for certain what Lewis's plans were.

Notwithstanding all this, McLaren showed good faith – or maybe they were just keen to remind Lewis what he might be passing up – by giving him his first run in an F1 McLaren. This came at Silverstone on 1 December and was fitted in around the team's commitment to boost the careers of recent winners of the McLaren-Autosport Young Driver scheme. Jamie Green and Alex Lloyd – the winners in 2002 and '03 respectively – were the recipients, and together with Lewis each got 21 laps in the 2004 McLaren-Mercedes MP4-19. His first drive of an F1 car made it a big day for Hamilton under any circumstances, but given the ongoing negotiations with the team about his future plans, it could have been especially difficult.

The McLaren/Hamilton stand-off was still ongoing as Manor and the Hamiltons set off for the Bahrain Super Prix, a one-off F3 event at the Sakhir circuit that had hosted the inaugural F1 Bahrain Grand Prix earlier in the year. It was to be the venue of a typically incident-packed and exciting Hamilton performance. 'He did about two laps of qualifying before going off and taking the floor off,' relates Booth, smiling. 'That left him 21st on the grid.' Later that day, Anthony was called back to Britain unexpectedly by Martin Whitmarsh as negotiations reached a crisis point. McLaren were playing hardball, just as much as Anthony.

So Anthony wasn't present to see Lewis charge up to 12th place in the first race, this establishing his grid position for the final. From 12th he charged up to third, with a series of characteristically brave passing moves. The two cars ahead of him were too far ahead to catch in the time left – but then came a safety car, allowing Lewis to sit himself right on their tails at the restart. He outfumbled them both with his usual dizzy racecraft – and took a truly spectacular victory. It came at a critical moment.

In the end, McLaren and Lewis Hamilton each had too much invested in the other to walk away from the partnership. Theoretically the terms of its continuance were stacked in McLaren's favour, as the partner with the money. Probably only Anthony Hamilton's failure to generate enough short-notice sponsorship to get Lewis a GP2 drive for 2005 rescued the partnership. McLaren were not prepared to have the terms of their backing dictated to them, and all the signs are that they would have walked. The two parties renewed their contract, but as part of the agreement for Lewis to transfer to ASM for a second season of F3, it's believed that some F1 commitment to Lewis by 2007 was made by McLaren. It's difficult to know if this whole matter was triggered only by a genuine frustration from the Hamiltons at Lewis not being moved up the ladder more quickly, or if it was a disagreement contrived by Anthony as a brilliant but high-stakes strategy of negotiating an F1 commitment. If so, he was being as brave off track as Lewis was on it.

CHAPTER EIGHT

Critical Momentum

'Whichever team Lewis Hamilton drove for in F3 in 2005 was going to win the championship,' says Marc Hynes. 'He was now completely on top of the game and was applying everything he'd learned and combining it with his brilliant talent.' Given that ASM had been the dominant team in the F3 Euroseries for the past two years, the combination of the two looked unstoppable on paper – and that's exactly how it panned out in reality. Together they won 16 races and no one else got a look in.

'I was obviously very impressed by what he had done at Manor the previous year,' says ASM's boss Vasseur. 'The team were new to Europe and he did not have an experienced team-mate to help, yet he was very competitive and sometimes gave us a hard time. Martin Whitmarsh called me in September and asked me if I'd be interested and it didn't take too long to say yes – less than a second! I then just waited for the call from McLaren and once that came we did the deal very fast.

'We went testing, just him and his team-mate Adrian Sutil, and straight away he was very fast. But what really impressed me was the relationship he made straight away with the engineers. I saw that he would be a very good catalyst for the team. He was confident and never nervous. The arrogance is not there, just the confidence. In fact he is the other way around to a lot of drivers in my experience. When he's in the car he's totally convinced he's the best. But when he's out of the car he's able to say "OK, I made a mistake, it's my fault", he's very open. A lot of guys have doubts when they are in the car and then look for excuses when they are out of it and try to pretend they think they are the best.'

Hamilton dominated the opening race at Hockenheim, leading from pole to the chequered flag and setting fastest lap. Team-mate Sutil was second. But the second race the following day threw up a set of circumstances that showcased the fact that Hamilton had more than just raw speed and bravery. The race began on a wet but drying track. Everyone started on dry weather tyres and at the end of the lap Hamilton was pushing James Rossiter for the lead. But he had chosen to run his tyres with high pressures to get them up to temperature quickly in the damp opening laps, and soon they were overheating badly as the track dried quicker than expected. He was being caught quickly by Loic Duval, but instead of defending his place with a hobbled car and allowing the pack behind Duval to catch them both up, he waved Duval through and just concentrated on going fast enough to stay out of reach of the rest of them while nursing his tyres. Had he just done the instinctive thing and fought, he would have slowed himself up enough to be caught by the pack, most of whom could probably have found a way around his compromised car. So he finished third on a day when he could easily have been much further back.

He followed up with double victories at Pau and Spa. His second win at the Belgian track came after passing Sutil around the outside at the hair-raising Eau Rouge corner – a flat-out, down-then-up-hill left-right. What's more, he did it on cold tyres at the start of the race. Even Lewis himself described it as 'hairy'. It may well have been the final conclusive proof to Sutil – a very talented driver who would later join F1 at the same time as Lewis, albeit with a lesser team – that he was against someone pretty special. Lewis himself rated the young German very highly. 'He's the strongest team-mate I've had alongside me,' he said, 'and having someone of Adrian's calibre definitely helps me to dig deeper.'

'I'm not ashamed to be second to Lewis,' said Sutil. 'I see it as an advantage to learn, and to keep me pushing always.'

Adrian was as good as his word at Monaco for the Grand Prix support race. Hamilton was on pole position by 0.6s and was 3.5s clear by the sixth lap, but then a safety car bunched the field up and allowed Sutil a second bite at his team-mate. He pushed him all the way and set fastest lap, but Hamilton took the flag. In the second race Hamilton was again victorious, but he almost succumbed to Sutil's pressure, getting off line while lapping a backmarker and clanging the barriers with the sidewalls of his tyres. The deranged suspension cost him some pace, and as Sutil chased hard he again set the fastest lap, before then crashing at Ste Devote, thereby allowing Hamilton off the hook.

The wins just kept coming, and only if unusual circumstances unfolded was he not first past the flag. He took a commanding victory in the Marlboro Masters race at Zandvoort, a non-championship event that brings together the top runners from the European and British F3 championships. 'For me the most impressive of his wins was at the Nürburgring,' says Vasseur. 'It began dry and he was about 4–5s in the lead. And then the rain came. He was 2–3s per lap quicker than anyone else. Each lap he came around his lead would be massively bigger than last time. We said on the radio "Be careful" you know, but he just said "Don't worry", and he won by over 20s. It was quite remarkable. He was already almost sure to win the title by then but he just really wanted to show the others what he could do.'

No one was now in any doubt about that. It had been a devastating season and the natural progression to the sister ART GP2 team for 2006 was duly made. Running the team with Vasseur was Nicolas Todt, son of the Ferrari F1 team boss Jean Todt. The team had won the '05 championship with Nico Rosberg, who had now moved on to F1 with the Williams team, following in his father's wheeltracks. Staying on for a second year of GP2 with the team was Alexandre Prémat.

Hamilton established immediately that he wasn't intending GP2 to be another two-year programme, as with his Renault and F3 seasons. His first test in the 600-horsepower car was at Jerez in late October, just after finishing his F3 season. 'He did four or five laps on old tyres,' recounts Vasseur, 'then we put on a new set and he immediately did the fastest time of the day. Not much adapting necessary! But I was a little bit nervous because that was on the slick tyres we ran with in '05. For '06 the formula was switching to grooved tyres and I wondered if his advantage would be as big with these. But it was not a problem. He was fast on these too.'

Hamilton's form, in fact, was a bit of a beacon for a team that was going through a difficult time internally. A senior engineer, very much part of the team's fabric, was seriously ill in hospital and would not last the year. Hamilton's attitude and speed kept the team positive in what was a trying period. 'He was the engine of the team,' Vasseur admits, 'and kept everyone motivated.'

He took runner-up to Nelson Piquet Jnr in his debut at Valencia in April, but had to wait until the third round, at the Nürburgring, for his first victory in the formula. In the first of the two races there, he took the lead on the first lap and extended it sometimes by whole seconds, each lap. However, at his mandatory pit stop, he lifted his finger from the pitlane speed limiter fractionally early and was awarded a drive-through penalty for speeding. He'd built up a lead of 17s and such was his superiority that he was able to take his penalty and rejoin in second just behind team-mate Prémat – whom he then passed to win. It was a great demonstration, albeit flattered by problems suffered by his main rival Piquet. In the second race, the reversed grid format for the top eight put him eighth on the grid. Using his stunning ability to brake super-late without quite locking up, he out-braked the cars ahead of him until he was leading and then stroked it home.

He took the championship lead at the next race, Barcelona, but was cursing a poor start that cost him victory in the first race. Although he recovered and led until the final lap, team-mate Prémat launched himself inside at the hairpin and spun Hamilton around. Lewis recovered to fin-ish runner-up to his team-mate. Many were expecting anger from him, not the congratulations he offered Prémat as they got out of their cars. 'He made the point that if he hadn't messed up his start, Alex wouldn't have been near enough to do that, so the mistake was his own,' says Vasseur. 'He has a remarkable ability to analyse his performances honestly. Even if Alex was ever quicker through a corner on the telemetry, Lewis had the capacity to say, "OK, I change my line, try something different" and be able to do the same. Whenever we were behind other teams he would say, "OK, you did a good car before and I'm a good driver so if we put it all together we will be OK." He didn't try a crazy set-up in desperation or crash trying to make the difference, and that very simple, no-bullshit attitude was very positive for the team.'

At Monte Carlo he was devastating. In the opening laps of practice, when everyone else was feeling their way on the unforgiving track, the swashbuckling Hamilton was lapping 4s quicker than anyone else! He took pole by 0.8s, then demolished the opposition in the race – leading by over 3s at the end of the first lap and simply managing the opposition thereafter.

If it were possible, Silverstone was even more impressive. By winning the first race after a brave side-by-side pass on Adam Carroll through Copse corner, he'd consigned himself to his familiar eighth-place start for the following day's event. Once the race started he quickly began making up places, and the partisan Grand Prix crowd began to sense that something special was on the cards. After passing Carroll and Giorgio Pantano, he began closing on Piquet and Clivio Piccione, dicing for second. Getting a faster run than them out of Copse, he closed up fast as they approached the top-gear sweep of Maggotts/Becketts. Piccione and Piquet were already side-by-side on the approach when Lewis towed up to them and darted to their right to make it three-abreast at 170mph – and not enough room for three cars to make it through. Lewis made a dive for the inside kerb of Maggotts,

Piccione had to yield – and Piquet was forced to drive over the grass and through an advertising hoarding! It was a stunningly brave pass, and brought the crowd to their feet. They were cheering like it was Mansell-mania all over again when he then passed leader Felix Porteiro to win.

Talking of the three-abreast pass, he said: 'It just presented itself and I put myself there. I was actually tensed up waiting for the impact, but then I saw I was coming out the other side and I was laughing.' Like he told the interviewer during his karting days, he just arrives at the corner and the answer comes to him. That one move gave his career a bigger boost than even winning the title could ever do. It was one of those very special moments when someone pulls off something apparently impossible, a move that will become legendary and almost mythical in years to come. Suddenly his elevation to F1 seemed unstoppable. There suddenly seemed no justification for keeping this phenomenon out of the sport's top category. As if pre-ordained, Juan Pablo Montoya left the McLaren F1 team before the next GP2 race. A gap seemed to be opening up in front of Hamilton in his career just as surely as it had on the track at Silverstone.

Anthony Hamilton wasn't slow in using the performance to put pressure on McLaren for confirmation of some F1 commitment. Dennis was trying to keep things calm, and said when asked at Silverstone of Hamilton's F1 prospects: 'Wherever he ends up next year – and there is every indication that it should be an F1 car – you need to accept that history shows no driver comes into F1 and has a level of success that would make him a championship contender. There will be one, two, three years of coming to grips with F1.

'So what we will try to do is prepare him best for that first year, and hopefully we will be able to reflect in a couple of years that we have done everything to put him in the best possible position, [to ensure he is] more competitive in his first F1 season than any other driver that has come to it.

'But it is now somewhat premature to say how that will unfold, or with which team. The important thing is to keep his feet on the ground and his father's feet on the ground, and just concentrate on getting the job done.'

'Silverstone was a fantastic race,' allowed Vasseur, 'but the attention it brought I think caught him by surprise and affected his performances for the next couple of races.' At Hockenheim he tagged Carroll's car at the start and had to pit for repairs that left him 19th. At Hungary he crashed on his first dry-weather lap of practice, heavily damaging the car. It was repaired for qualifying – and he did exactly the same again at the same corner! In the meantime, title rival Piquet was notching up the results. Hamilton limited the damage with a second place in the second race, but these were not the assured performances of his season to date. 'Before Silverstone his world had been quite private and he could just do his job with the team,' continued Vasseur. 'But the attention he got after Silverstone was huge and far greater than at any time in his career, and I think it was not so easy to manage, and with Piquet not far behind in the championship he was under pressure. His mind was adapting to a new situation. He's human, not a robot.'

But he put things back on track at Turkey – and how! After finishing runner-up to Piquet in the first race he spun early in the second one, caught out by cold tyres, distracted by a high reading on his temperature gauge. He rejoined 16th and put in a truly mesmerising comeback, yet again displaying an astonishing superiority under braking, sensing where the gaps were going to be and instantly filling them with all his car, not just a nose, yet never locking up. With the race in its late stages he dummied Piquet into defending on the wrong side, then set off after Timo Glock's third place. The pass lasted three laps of virtually side-by-side running, culminating in Hamilton squeezing past with millimetres to spare as Glock eased him towards the pit wall, the two showing superb judgement and complete fairness. A lap later and he picked off Carroll to go second, and only the fall of the chequer prevented him from taking the win. It was a sensational performance, one that he judged 'probably my best ever', eclipsing even his Monaco and Silverstone races.

Just when he thought his day couldn't get any better, upon walking back to the paddock after the podium celebrations, Hamilton was surprised to be stopped by Michael Schumacher. 'He said something to me that I will never forget,' recalled Hamilton. 'He said, "Fantastic race. What you did today was outstanding." He didn't have to say that to me. Other drivers have achieved far less than he did but are much more arrogant.'

There was just one round left – at Monza. Although Piquet could still theoretically take the crown there, the numbers much favoured Hamilton, and Lewis duly sealed it with a third place in the first race, just behind Piquet. The Brazilian's position would have been enough to take the title fight to the following day's race, had winner Giorgio Pantano not lost the extra point for fastest lap for setting it when yellow caution flags were showing, resulting in Hamilton – who had set second fastest lap – getting the point instead. That solitary point was enough to put the title out of Piquet's reach. Lewis Hamilton, 2006 GP2 champion. There was nowhere left to go now but F1.

CHAPTER NINE

F1 Beckons

In the opening seconds of the 2006 American Grand Prix, the final pieces of the jigsaw that would see Lewis Hamilton achieve his dream of racing in F1 with McLaren began to slot into place, even though he was several thousand miles away.

A fiery, impulsive character, Juan Pablo Montoya was experiencing a deeply frustrating season with the team. He'd arrived here the year before from Williams, where his relationship had broken down after an altercation at the 2003 French Grand Prix, where expletives were exchanged over the radio about a pit stop sequence he felt was deliberately favouring his team-mate Ralf Schumacher. Ron Dennis had claimed that McLaren were better than Williams at giving drivers the emotional support they needed, and would be better able to access his huge potential. Pairing him with the equally highly rated incumbent, Kimi Raikkonen, Dennis was sure would be no problem. He had, he pointed out, extensive experience of dealing with South American temperaments, this a reference to his fabulously successful partnership with Ayrton Senna from 1988–93.

But Montoya's relationship with Dennis got off to a rocky start early in 2005, their first season together. On the eve of the third race, Montoya fractured a shoulder blade. He claimed it had been while playing tennis. It was almost certainly done while racing a trials bike. It put Montoya out of action for two events and badly compromised his performances for most of the first half of the season. In the latter half of the year, though, it all began to come right and Montoya was invariably at a similar level of performance to Raikkonen, sometimes even quicker. The Finn, however, was in contention for the world championship and Montoya – because of his injury-compromised first half – was not. As such, Montoya even supported Raikkonen's championship cause, obeying team instructions at critical in- and out-laps to enable Raikkonen to get or remain in front. Montoya even surrendered a likely victory in the Belgian Grand Prix to Raikkonen. Despite this, he won three races for the team, and victory in the final race after a straight fight with Kimi augured well for '06.

For '06, Montoya was determined to take the fight to his team-mate and challenge for the world title that had so far eluded him in an F1 career that had promised much but still not fully delivered. But against all expectations, McLaren-Mercedes gave their drivers a less than fully competitive car. Neither driver was going to be fighting for a world title with the MP4-21. The basic problem was one of understeer, something that neither driver liked, but a characteristic that was particularly devastating to Montoya's less subtle driving style. In race after race Raikkonen would out-qualify and out-race Montoya. Being soundly beaten by someone in the same car was not something the Colombian had ever before experienced, and he found it very difficult to deal with.

At Indianapolis things had gone badly for Montoya in qualifying, specifically during the second session when drivers are competing to make the top ten which will then allow them into the final top-ten run-off where they fight for pole position. For a team of McLaren's status and resource, struggling to make the run-off was rather embarrassing. Raikkonen managed to squeeze through but Montoya, his first attempt ruined by traffic, came in for a fresh set of tyres in readiness for a final attempt. With the seconds ticking away there was confusion over his fuel level, and in the ensuing discussion his new set of tyres, with their heating blankets removed, fell below their operating temperature. When he returned to the track the cooled rubber gave him very little grip and he failed to make the run-off. He was consigned to starting the race from 11th place, two behind Raikkonen. He was angry with the team and didn't hold back with his feelings.

The F1 track at Indy features a right-left sequence as the cars filter in from their grid starts. Seconds after the race began, and into the left-handed part of this sequence, there were three cars line-abreast just behind Raikkonen – those of Montoya, Jenson Button and Nick Heidfeld. Heidfeld, on the right, was squeezing Button, who in turn was squeezing Montoya. Montoya, desperate not to allow any chink of light that might allow another car to get between Raikkonen and him, was trying to get right onto Raikkonen's gearbox. But he did more than that: he actually hit it, this instantly ricocheting him into Button, who in turn interlocked wheels with Heidfeld, sending the latter into a barrel roll. No one was hurt, but both McLarens were out of the race. McLaren's American Grand Prix had lasted precisely seven seconds –

and Montoya was very much seen as the villain of the piece.

It was probably ill-advised of Ron Dennis to berate Montoya when he returned to the pits, but it was understandable. Never one to accept criticism, particularly when he felt the team was partly culpable, even before the race had ended Montoya was on the phone to his former team owner Chip Ganassi to enquire whether he could drive for his NASCAR team in 2007. The two quickly agreed terms, they made an announcement the following week – and Montoya was promptly suspended from McLaren for the rest of the year.

This opened up a McLaren seat for the remainder of 2006 – and also for the following season. Britain's daily newspaper journalists were instantly putting the words 'Lewis Hamilton' into the mouth of Dennis, but he wasn't able to give them the answer they craved. First of all, there was his GP2 season to get out of the way – and there was no way McLaren would consider curtailing that for a short-notice stand-in drive in F1, one that could conceivably damage his career. The immediate vacancy would be filled by the team's lead test driver, the experienced Pedro de la Rosa. Pedro did well on occasion – taking a well-deserved second place in Hungary, for example – but other times was simply not at the same level as Raikkonen. It was an open secret that the Finn was leaving McLaren for Ferrari in 2007, though this had yet to be confirmed to McLaren by Kimi's management. But with Fernando Alonso already signed – he'd been contracted for 2007 a full year earlier – Raikkonen's departure was not as devastating as it might have been. It meant that the seat alongside Alonso for 2007 was potentially available – and given that de la Rosa had not set the world alight, surely Hamilton was in with a very realistic shout.

Through the second half of the season, Anthony Hamilton was pushing hard for an F1 commitment from McLaren, sensing the gathering momentum of events – both Lewis's superb displays in GP2 and the 2007 vacancy in the F1 team. As in the past, Anthony wasn't shy about implying the threat of looking elsewhere if McLaren could not offer them what they wanted. It's believed that, had McLaren not been able to offer Lewis an F1 role once he had clinched the GP2 championship, the contractual option with McLaren was on the side of the Hamiltons – i.e. they would be entitled to go elsewhere if McLaren couldn't offer anything in F1. It was a very delicate line to walk, for Ron Dennis isn't one to be held to ransom, but Lewis's performances were making it easier for both sides to want the same thing.

As recounted, Hamilton sealed his GP2 championship at Monza. What also happened at Monza was that Michael Schumacher announced his retirement, effective from the end of the year, and Raikkonen was confirmed as his replacement at Ferrari. Ron Dennis was formally told of Raikkonen's move only on the eve of the Monza weekend, and though the news was no surprise, the manner and the timing of his being informed did not please him. There were strong words between Dennis and Raikkonen on the matter. It did, however, formally confirm that a 2007 McLaren race seat was up for grabs. Although Hamilton was considered the favourite, de la Rosa had not been totally ruled out at this time – and there was even an outside chance for the team's young tester Gary Paffett.

As Hamilton prepared to get into his car for the second GP2 race at Monza, Dennis said to him: 'I've decided I'm going to give you a chance.' Hamilton recalled this to ITV's Steve Rider. 'I thought, "What the hell does that mean?" but

I knew it could only be a good thing. So I kept a professional front and said "OK", but inside I was in a bit of a whirl.'

In the meantime, the remaining three races on the 2006 F1 calendar – China, Japan and Brazil – were possibilities for trying out Hamilton and/or Paffett. McLaren would not be drawn on whether either would happen. There was a three-week break between the Italian and Chinese races, and during this time Hamilton was given his first serious test run – at Silverstone, the same venue as his brief try-out in the F1 car two years earlier, to date his only F1 experience. The first day was limited to installation laps as the team awaited fresh engines from Mercedes, but on the second day Hamilton completed 60 laps of the Northamptonshire track, and 50 laps on the third day.

Running alongside him in the sister car was de la Rosa. The team were anxious to point out that this wasn't a shoot-out between the two drivers and that each was running different programmes, with different fuel levels and different tyres and set-ups, and so the lap times were not comparable. For what it was worth, Hamilton was marginally quicker than de la Rosa by the end of the final day. On the second day he found 1s of lap time and on the third he improved on that by a further 0.8s. He had a couple of offs during that final day, once through not having got the rear brakes up to temperature, once through getting a wheel onto the dust as he was changing down. The gravel traps saved any damage to the car.

It was an opportunity for the team to get comfortable working with Hamilton and vice versa, the chance for Lewis to begin to operate the many systems and functions on an F1 car and get an understanding for what they allowed him to do with the car.

Ron Dennis was keen to play down the prospects of Lewis making his F1 debut in what remained of the season, though he stopped short of discounting it entirely, saying: 'There are things that need to be second nature to an individual in the car. If we go down the path that will see us using Lewis, why not properly prepare him for that? Why throw anybody in at the deep end? There is always going to be expectation, but this is a hero to zero sport and why put anything at risk? The guy has had a brilliant career so far. He is a completely rounded individual who has got all sorts of pressures that will come to bear on him. I would much rather see him as equipped as he could be if he is given the chance of racing for McLaren in the future. I can't see throwing him in the deep end is a particularly smart thing to do.'

As far as the driving was concerned, the step up to F1 from GP2 posed no problems. 'It was an awesome experience,' Hamilton told autosport.com after his first day's running. 'I just cannot stop smiling. It didn't feel that fast compared to a GP2 car, but the way it turns in is amazing. Actually pulling out of the garage and going down the pitlane, you just absorb and take in that moment. It is a feeling I just keep going back to. But when I get in next time, I know [that feeling] will not be as good as this time. Right now I am living my dream. It is difficult to describe. I am just so pleased I am here. I remember sitting and watching David Coulthard here in his early days with McLaren, when I was about 10 or 11, and now I am here and I am 21. It is my dream. It is quite emotional.' After getting more fully acquainted on the second day, he expanded on his impressions of the car. 'The downforce in high-speed corners is a lot more, but how much I don't know. It feels almost double. The high-speed corners are insane, and the first corner here is flat. You approach it at 192mph to take it flat, and it is just incredible. You need to really hold on to the steering wheel. Into Maggotts and Becketts, which is nearly flat, and you don't touch the brakes. It is ridiculous how you carry the speed through that. In GP2, you do touch the brakes and the cars are a lot slower. The braking is a lot better, and the power, and the engine, feels slightly different. Plus there is the traction control. I have got a lot to learn, I think.'

That last sentence, a little throwaway, was important. As the Hamiltons sat down with Dennis and Whitmarsh back at the factory, there was a consensus between them: none of them felt that Lewis should race in the forthcoming Chinese and Japanese races, held on consecutive weekends. Whitmarsh was reportedly more open to the idea than Dennis, but was swayed by Lewis's own feeling that he wasn't yet at a stage of understanding the car that would allow him to perform to his best. It was a hugely confident call on Lewis's part, not to push for the chance of an F1 debut when it was possibly there for the taking, and it indicated the growing confidence in the Hamilton camp of the messages they were getting about 2007. Two days later, de la Rosa was confirmed for the two Far-Eastern races.

A day later, Lewis was sitting on the sofa at home when Anthony took a call. It was McLaren. Could Lewis and Anthony present themselves tonight at Ron's house? This was it, surely! The moment of truth. The excitement inside the car as the Hamiltons made that familiar drive from Tewin to Woking can only be imagined. 'It was an incredible moment,' Lewis later recalled. 'I sat down opposite Ron and Martin Whitmarsh. We sat there and Ron said: "We have decided you are going to be our driver next year." I had to put a professional front on, and I had a small smile on me, but inside it was overwhelming.'

Within a few days, Lewis had inked a multi-page McLaren deal believed to be worth around £380,000 in basic salary but with bonus money based on success on top of that, and an option for renegotiation if certain targets were met by a pre-determined stage of the season. He was well on his way to his first million – and that was just going to be the start. Before the season was very old, the driver agents were stalking him, looking to take the place of Anthony in the management roll. Steve Robertson, who along with father David manages Kimi Raikkonen, made a claim that they could earn him $100 million per year.

'I said, "You're not smiling much",' Dennis recalled of Lewis's reaction to the news of his drive, 'and he said that he was inside.' For all that Hamilton's sometimes sensational GP2 performances had made the choice easier for Dennis than it might have been, this was still a brave call for Ron. Historically, McLaren had not been a team that employed rookies. 'McLaren aren't here to further the F1 education of young drivers,' Dennis had repeatedly said over the years. 'McLaren is a team a driver comes to when he has complet-ed his education and is ready to win.' Hamilton's confirma-tion went against all that. But it's easy to see why he was an exception. First, there was the emotional – and monetary – investment McLaren had made in Lewis's career. Lewis Hamilton was very much a pet project of Ron's – as he read-ily admitted. 'Yes, there is an element of *My Fair Lady* about the story,' he accepted. The monetary investment through the karting and junior categories has been estimated at around £4 million. It would not have made sense to have provided all that and then allowed another team to reap the benefit – as could have happened if McLaren did not provide some sort of F1 opportunity for Lewis in 2007.

Secondly, there was the fact that Dennis had secured the services of a world champion in the other car. In an interview with Martin Brundle in the *Sunday Times*, Dennis explained how this had offset the risk of running a rookie. He even admitted that when he made the decision he was still not fully convinced about Hamilton's true potential! Brundle had asked at what point had Ron realised that Lewis was the real deal. Ron's reply was illuminating: 'Really, not until he was actually racing in Grands Prix. There are lots of young drivers I've seen do excellent jobs in lower categories but the big test is always the transition from the feeder category into F1. Even in testing you don't have the pressure of a race weekend … but it wasn't as difficult a decision as you might think. Because we had Fernando joining the team so that would always give us the opportunity to win races subject to the competitiveness of our car. Obviously everything that Lewis has brought to the team has been great but it came out of a decision that had a degree of calculated risk about it. That risk was managed through the winter preparatory programme.'

There was a third factor too: namely, that Dennis wasn't that impressed with the alternative candidates. Of the three recognised top-level drivers, Michael Schumacher was retiring, Kimi Raikkonen was leaving McLaren and Fernando Alonso was joining. Outside of that trio, Dennis didn't see anyone outstanding. 'I'm distinctly unimpressed by the majority of drivers in F1,' he said. 'Lewis is well equipped to deal with the drivers who fall into that category.' He added to these comments later in the year when questioned by Brundle. 'The vast majority of Grand Prix drivers do not bring the level of commitment to their futures that 99 per cent of athletes bring that enter the Olympics,' he said. 'There is a sad lack of dedication in many of the people who currently compete in F1. I've been in the privileged position of seeing the commitment and dedication of a double world champion. I felt it was necessary for Lewis to make the same sacrifices and commitment to prepare him for F1 – and he's done that.'

So there we have it: the team that signed possibly the biggest talent to hit F1 in over a decade was not fully convinced of him when they made that commitment. The same could have been said of Michael Schumacher's F1 debut in 1991 when Eddie Jordan used him as a stand-in who brought some money. Only once he had created such a sensation in Jordan's car at Spa did the rest of the F1 world wake up to the phenomenon that was Michael. Now the F1 world waited to see how Hamilton would fare, with the pressure of racing for a front-line team as a rookie – and alongside a guy, Alonso, who was now a double world champion.

The perception in F1 was that Hamilton would be doing well if he could keep Alonso in sight, maybe occasionally outqualify him as a little pointer to his future potential. No one seriously expected a rookie to give a world champion a hard time over a season. No one in F1, at least. But that wasn't necessarily the view of those who had fought Hamilton up close. Mike Conway – his rival from Cadet and Formula A karting, and at the time of Hamilton's confirmation, the British F3 champion – had an inkling the F1 world was about to get a shock. 'I didn't want to say it at the time,' he says now, 'because it might have made me look a bit silly, but when it was confirmed he had the drive I suspected he was going to be quicker than Alonso. That's just how good I believe he is.'

What Lewis had known since mid-September – that he was

to be a McLaren F1 driver in 2007 – wasn't actually announced until 24 November. The team felt the news might get lost in the fuss around both the fight for the championship between Schumacher and Alonso and the fall-out from Schumacher's retirement announcement.

In between the deal's agreement and its announcement, Hamilton was continuing with his F1 testing programme, with a three-day stint at Jerez in Spain, again alongside de la Rosa. This time he went into it knowing he was a pukka F1 driver, even if the rest of the world didn't. There was still a possibility that he could make his debut at the final Grand Prix of the year, in Brazil. Again, a view was taken after the tests and again it was agreed that they would defer his debut. 'You have to be able to change settings without thinking about it,' said Dennis. 'You have to make sure your in- and out-laps are completely on the pace, you need to be able to identify problems and recognise default settings that interrupt the smooth running of the car but aren't going to affect it in any way. I can tell you one thing categorically: if Lewis was given the opportunity to race in Brazil and again in Australia next March, he'd almost certainly go better in Melbourne – not because of driving, just through having put in test mileage and having come to terms with the many parameters of a Grand Prix car that go beyond simply driving it.'

This time, with the 2007 deal in place, not making his debut at the next race was a much easier thing to agree to. On his first serious day of running at the test, Hamilton was fifth quickest, 0.1s slower than de la Rosa. On the final day he was second only to Michael Schumacher and a full 0.5s faster than de la Rosa.

It was to be the only time his F1 career overlapped with

Schumacher's, something of a regret for Hamilton, as he recounted some weeks later. 'When I heard that he was retiring, I said: "Damn, please Michael keep going for another season and we'll have some great races against each other." I met him last year before the Turkish Grand Prix and I was impressed because I'd heard that he was arrogant and not very nice, but he took the time to talk to me and I was really honoured.'

Once the announcement was made, plenty of people had a view on it, among them David Coulthard, the former McLaren driver who had so graciously given his time to the 11-year-old Lewis at Buckmore Park. 'I believe McLaren have given him his break way too soon,' he said. 'He could face a very tough time with Alonso as his team-mate – the first person you are compared to is your team-mate, and if Lewis struggles alongside Fernando, it could destroy his confidence. He would have been better off with a year's testing. He's still only 21 and has plenty of racing years ahead of him. There is no doubting his potential. But he needs time to develop – not just as a driver but also as a man. He would have been better armed to deal with the pressure through the benefit of experience.'

But Hamilton's friend and karting team-mate Nico Rosberg, someone who had seen Hamilton from the closest quarters and who now had a season of F1 experience himself, saw things differently. 'He won't have a problem getting used to the speed. I know that. He's talented and he's a really good driver and even an F1 car is still just a racing car. There are a lot of other things around the racing that you have to learn and pick up and that can be energy-consuming – that's one side which isn't so easy. But driving the car fast will not be a problem for him.'

While the racing world saw only an exciting new talent being given a wonderful opportunity to graduate to F1 with a top team, the world at large saw a black man breaking through into what had always been a white man's sport. Invariably the questions about it came thick and fast. 'The only time I think about colour is when other people raise the issue,' he said. 'I hope my involvement will encourage other ethnic groups to become involved.

'When I wake up every day I don't say, "Oh shoot I'm black",' he said to *Autosport* magazine. 'I don't get treated as if I'm different, maybe occasionally by some people, but by most people I get treated normally, so it never really occurs to me unless someone mentions it. Because of my colour I can probably have an influence on other cultures. That's a big bonus. I'd love to be able to do something for other people and have them say, "Oh yeah, that was him that sort of opened the gateway." That would be great. Everyone wants to be special in some way, whether that's good or bad.'

Dennis had a strong and worthy point to make on the matter. 'His blackness isn't important. I have consistently said to him: "The moment that you exploit your blackness, you are going to have a problem with me." Basically, he has to develop his career purely on his ability to drive a racing car.'

In between the announcement and Hamilton's debut in the 2007 Australian Grand Prix, there would be 9,000km of testing. There would also be an intense McLaren programme of preparation, including more hours on the F1 simulator and with the neuroscientist Dr Kerry Spackman, who had been working with Hamilton on McLaren's behalf since 2003. Spackman entered the orbit of motorsport through an encounter with Jackie Stewart in the 1990s. The articulate Stewart talked about the functioning of a racing driver's mind and Spackman was intrigued at the neuro-science behind what Stewart was describing. He developed a thesis that perhaps the racing driver's mind could be trained to perform at a higher level, and Stewart embraced this belief and had Spackman work with the drivers of Stewart's F1 team of the time, Stewart Grand Prix.

Taking the intuitive, physiologically and psychologically complex process of racing a car, deconstructing it and attempting to make it a science is a hugely ambitious endeavour. And there are many in racing – make that most – who seriously doubt that it can ever be done. But it's exactly the sort of apparently science-driven discipline that was always going to appeal hugely to Ron Dennis, a man who distrusts anything he cannot fully understand, who has an excellent instinctive grasp of anything technical, who can apply himself brilliantly to business and politics, but who struggles sometimes with intuitive human processes. Even the awkward, tortured patterns of his speech reveal the mechanistic way he is wired up. He was highly impressed with Spackman, and in Lewis Hamilton back in 2003 Ron had the perfect blank sheet of paper, a driver not yet fully formed, ready to be programmed 'correctly', like one of the gorgeous high-tech components produced at McLaren's space-age 'technology centre'.

In an interview with the *Guardian*'s Richard Williams in May 2007, Spackman explained his philosophy. He likened driving a racing car to being chased by a tiger, in that it was a life-threatening, emotionally charged and unnatural environment, and that the idea was to train the brain to treat it like a chess grandmaster, playing three steps ahead 'in a state of calm, focussed attention'.

This is what any top driver does automatically – from the moment he steps into a kart as a kid. But Spackman believes that by monitoring brain and body activity, the mind can be trained to enhance the qualities necessary for racing success. 'Lewis obviously has talent,' he accepted, 'but he's a vastly superior driver now because he's learnt how to learn, which most drivers don't do. Every experience has a way of being analysed, understood and filed away. He doesn't just pound around a track, repeating old habits.'

Using the McLaren simulator, Spackman would have Hamilton experience two very different versions of the same experience, easy to distinguish. 'This gives the brain a structure to work from,' he explained to Williams. 'Then you bring them closer together. If you bring them together slowly and provide him with feedback in a learning environment, gradually his brain will start to build circuits that can take these nuances and store them.'

Mmm. Lewis did seem to access his talent better in 2003 – his second year of Formula Renault – than he had in 2002. But any young driver gaining experience does that. Is he a recognisably 'vastly superior' driver now? Beyond having the actual experience of better, faster cars? He has looked a sensational driver since he was a kid. It's true there have been others who failed to convert such potential once they got to F1. But actually the most notable example of this was Jan Magnussen, a driver who looked absolutely brilliant coming up the motorsport ladder, but very ordinary once he'd made it to F1. And Magnussen was a Jackie Stewart employee. That's not to say there's nothing in the doctor's theories, but Anthony Hamilton for one does not believe a word of it and points out that the outstanding features of Lewis's driving now are exactly those that set him apart as a ten-year-old.

Lewis himself is contracted to McLaren – and politely declines to talk about it.

'I guarantee you 100 per cent that Lewis's performance does not have anything to do with a simulator or any artificial training,' claims his friend Nico Rosberg. 'I've heard these claims that he's the first robo-driver – and it's bullshit.' But then Nico, like Lewis, is an intuitive guy with plenty of emotional intelligence. If you need to put things into boxes to understand them, you're never going to make a great racing driver. But you might make a great engineer, scientist – or F1 team principal.

Regardless, if he wasn't testing during the off-season, Lewis was usually in the McLaren Technology Centre – or at the Mercedes engine shop in Brixworth, Northants. 'I told Lewis that when he takes the start at Melbourne, I want him to be the best prepared driver on that grid,' said Dennis. 'I want him to know the rules and regulations better than any other driver, I want him to understand the car better than any other driver. When he changes gear I want him to understand not only that the gear has changed but what the mechanical processes are that have enabled that to happen. He is going to spend time here in the factory understanding exactly what is involved in creating the machine he will race.'

With his new contract signed, Lewis was able to buy an apartment in Woking, near the factory. As well as learning about the construction of the car and its parts, Lewis would spend much of the winter with his allocated race engineer, Phil Prew. Together they would go through the theory of car set-up, fuel strategies, tyre wear, pit stops, safety car procedures, pitlane procedures and the many electronic systems on the car. His allocated trainer Adam Costanzo got his fitness more F1-specific, as he related to *Racing Line*, McLaren's own magazine: 'Lewis was already fit,' he said. 'The GP2 cars are fast and they have no power steering, so he was strong. But there was no real structure to his training programme, so that's one of the biggest areas where we've helped him.' Much work went into strengthening his neck and lower back, ready for the higher and longer-duration forces of an F1 car.

McLaren-Mercedes, with new backing from Vodafone and Spanish banking company Santander, revealed their new car in mid-January. The McLaren-Mercedes MP4-22 had a tough task ahead of it – to launch the team immediately back into the winners' circle after the first season in 11 years in which it had failed to win a single race. Not only that, but to give new drivers Alonso and Hamilton any hope of being involved in a title fight, it needed to match anything from Ferrari and Renault, the two teams that had fought out the '06 season.

There were a couple of key regulation changes for 2007, both of which seemed to help McLaren. For one, engines were to be rev-limited to 19,000rpm after a season in which speeds had climbed inexorably towards 21,000rpm. These super-high engine speeds had given McLaren-Mercedes a major headache in '06. As Mercedes had pushed up their engine speeds in the search for ever-more power, they found they were limited in how far they could go by the airflow to the very small radiators. Other teams had more capacity within their airflow regime to increase the flow over the radiators to keep up with the increase in engine speeds. With the 19,000rpm limitation, it was not an area McLaren any longer needed to catch up on.

The second major change was the end of the tyre war. Michelin, McLaren's tyre supplier of the previous five years, had withdrawn from the sport, leaving only Bridgestone to supply the whole field. Renault had developed a car over the previous few seasons with a very unconventional, rearward-biased weight distribution that worked extremely well with the characteristics of the Michelins. McLaren had always favoured a more forward-biased weight distribution than their rivals, and as such had probably not found quite as much from the French tyres. The Bridgestones, by contrast, worked best with a weight distribution as far forwards as it was possible to get. This suited McLaren's design philosophy perfectly. It also suited Lewis Hamilton perfectly, as would become increasingly clear once the season began. Fernando Alonso had spent the last five years of his career in a Renault on Michelin tyres and had come to develop a very specific driving style that maximised that package. It was a style that was going to be unsuited to a McLaren on Bridgestones. He had a lot of 'unlearning' to do in this respect. Lewis, coming in cold, had nothing to unlearn.

Alonso soon suspected the scale of challenge his team-mate was going to represent, as they each began testing. It was 15 December before the champion was released from Renault and could get his first taste of a McLaren – in this case the old '06 car – at Jerez, Spain. Hamilton had already spent the previous four days blasting round there. But it was still an ominous sign for Alonso that Hamilton's best lap was around 0.25s quicker than his own.

Into the new year, the test programme moved to Valencia – this time with the new car. 'In terms of both the car and the engine, it's definitely a step forward from the old one,' said Hamilton. But Alonso seemed to get to grips with the new machine better than Lewis, recording a best lap a full 0.6s quicker. A day later, pushing to find every last ounce of performance from himself, Hamilton tried pushing the car harder than he'd ever done before through a quick left-hand corner around the back of the circuit. As soon as he turned in he knew he'd overdone it, the car simply going too fast even for its massive downforce to keep it glued to the road. In the blink of an eye, Lewis was heading off track at high speed and although the run-off area slowed him down, he hit the tyre barriers hard enough to wreck the car, one of only two that had so far been built.

Jo Ramirez, a former employee of the team but a few years into his retirement, was at the track that day as an interested guest, not far away from his winter home. He recalls: 'Lewis came back and he was honest enough to admit he'd just been pushing a bit too hard. He's a competitor, he had Alonso there in the other car going quickly, and he needs to measure himself against him, to push himself. He did, and he crashed. But that's a good type of accident – if there can be such a thing. It came as he was pushing to find the limit, and I guess he found it. I told him that it was good that he'd had the big one then rather than in the middle of the season when it would have set him back more. Ideally, he would have been able to get straight back into the spare car so he didn't have time to dwell on it, but there wasn't one at that stage, and he had to wait quite a few days before the team had built another one.'

Nine days later, Lewis was back in the cockpit and proceeded to set the third-fastest time at Jerez. A day after that he was fastest of all – and with a small but clear edge over Alonso. The shunt had obviously had no ill effects. 'I am working very hard,' he told reporters, 'and the hard work really shows in the results. I am at the McLaren Technology Centre every day during the week when I am not testing. I spend as much time as possible with my engineer really studying the data and learning as much as possible, which all seems to be flowing nicely. I am just taking it all step by step and I think that is the best approach.'

These tests and the ones that followed at Bahrain on the eve of the season suggested the fight was very much between Ferrari and McLaren and that Renault had fallen completely from the picture, with a new car not as well suited to the Bridgestone tyres as their two rivals. Hamilton continued to impress everyone with his assured pace, and if he sometimes went down a blind alley in terms of car set-up, the experience of the team was there to guide him back onto a productive path. In general he seemed to suffer a small deficit to Alonso in terms of one-lap pace, but over a race stint simulation he was, if anything, faster – apparently able to make his tyres last better. He also deeply impressed the engineers with his ability to adapt his driving around changing handling characteristics. 'I've never seen anything like it,' said one senior and long-serving man there after the tests, someone who had been at the team back in the days when it ran Senna and Prost, not to mention Mika Hakkinen and Kimi Raikkonen in the years that followed. 'He will tell you that the balance is changing from neutral towards oversteer, but then says, "It's OK, I can drive around it, I'm just letting you know," and when you look at his times, he's still just as fast. I tell you, he is going to be sensational.'

Although it hadn't yet come out, Hamilton's performances had left Alonso feeling slightly vulnerable, paranoid about the treatment his supposed junior team-mate was getting as a Brit in a British team. What's more, a Brit that had been part of the McLaren family for a long time. He saw the way the mechanics and other personnel – people who had watched Lewis grow up – greeted his team-mate. He then looked at the lap time read-outs and telemetry. And he wondered if he might not have to beat more than just Ferrari this season.

Hamilton played the Alonso question perfectly. Totally confident in his own ability, far from overawed at having a double world champion team-mate, fully intending to try to beat him straight from the off, he nonetheless publicly deferred – cleverly shifting the pressure onto Alonso. 'I remember talking to Lewis at the time,' says Ramirez, 'and asking about the pressure on him. And Lewis said "What pressure? I'm a rookie, no one expects anything of me. The pressure's on Fernando, a double champion."' The pressure would be on Alonso only if Hamilton was able to measure up to him, of course. But in Hamilton's mind, that was already a done deal. The world of F1 was on the verge of discovering just what a phenomenon Lewis Hamilton really was.

CHAPTER TEN

The Debut

Friday, 10am at Melbourne's Albert Park, and first practice for the Australian Grand Prix was about to get under way. The track was wet and a light drizzle was still falling. In the McLaren garages the Mercedes engines were being warmed as an overall-clad Lewis Hamilton put in his ear plugs, attached the mandatory *HANS* device that protects against spinal injuries, and pulled on his bright yellow helmet. He was minutes away from taking part in his first F1 Grand Prix weekend, the first day of a life that would be very different to that which he'd experienced so far. He was about to be catapulted into an entirely different orbit of existence.

A set of Bridgestone wet weather tyres were fitted to the car and covered in tyre-warming blankets as Lewis climbed into the cockpit. His only experience of which way the track went came via Playstation. He knew the car well by now, and his winter training programme had got him familiar with the operational aspects of a Grand Prix weekend. So under the glare of a watching world of millions, he had most of the pieces. All he had to do was slot them together. But this is a tricky track, comprising the roads of a public park, more usually host to the traffic of picnicking families. As such it has a public road camber, not ideal for the tiny ride heights of an F1 car, it is dirty without the helpful rubber build-up of a purpose-designed track in regular use – and it is lined by barriers rather than wide open run-off areas. A little mis-judgement can easily snowball into a trip onto the grass and then into the tyre barriers. And to cap it all, now it was wet too, making the white painted lines and kerbs extra slippery. Furthermore, even in testing he had never before tried the extreme wet weather tyres. All his prior running had been in the dry.

He accelerated down the pitlane to meet his new life, engine stuttering against the speed limiter, which he then disengaged as he passed the white line and the green lights to join the circuit, to join the party. His F1 career was finally on in earnest. All those dreams – the eight-year-old kid in his first race at Rye House, the battles fought on the track and off, the sheer slog and determination of Anthony Hamilton – here's the moment they were trying to reach. From now it was all in Lewis's gifted hands. No need to worry about career ladders to fall off, finance to find. Just press the pedals, turn the wheel, flick the gearshift paddles. Just do it better than anyone else.

Watching the McLaren glide around the glistening surface, seeing the high entry speeds and the silky smooth inputs, it was difficult to believe you were witnessing a debut. The car looked beautifully balanced but he was driving it with wonderful assurance. At one point he and Alonso were circulating together, and the distinction between Hamilton's high-momentum smoothness and Alonso's more edgy and aggressive style was particularly noticeable. The session lasted one-and-a-half hours and for most of it Hamilton was lapping slightly faster than his team-mate. Only as the track dried near the end and they each put on a set of dry weather tyres did Fernando go quicker, ending up fastest overall. Hamilton's very first lap on dry weather tyres put him fourth quickest, albeit 1.6s behind. In the afternoon, he was third quickest behind the two Ferraris, his best lap 0.1s quicker than Alonso's. He never so much as put a wheel out of place.

McLaren's Martin Whitmarsh was impressed: 'The first time he had ever driven on an extreme wet tyre coincided with his first lap as a professional F1 driver on a circuit he had never driven. If you get it wrong here, it's quite unforgiving. He progressed from extreme wets to wets, then did one lap on the dry. Look at his times. Bang. Straight away, he was there. Quick. In the second practice session, you had red flags, a bit of drizzle. He dealt with all the issues. I was listening to him on the radio, amazed at how articulate, intelligent and insightful he was.'

On Saturday morning, during the final practice session before qualifying began in the afternoon, he was again third quickest, again slightly quicker than Alonso. But practice times count for nothing. Qualifying in the afternoon was when it mattered. In the first session, the McLarens each did a single flying lap on the slower hard compound tyres, this comfortably giving them enough pace to graduate through to the second session. Hamilton was a couple of hundredths quicker than his team-mate at this point. Into the second session and using the faster softer compound tyres, Hamilton was again slightly quicker – and the two McLarens were comfortably through to the top-ten run-off. So it was a surprise when Alonso went back out, with another new set of the softer tyres, to try for another lap. Aided by the track having rubbered in since his first run, Alonso duly went even faster – and in the process beat Hamilton's time. Hamilton's car stayed firmly in the garage. It appeared for all the world as if Alonso had not wanted to be upstaged by his junior team-mate – that he had sacrificed a new set of soft tyres (and thereby left himself with only one new set for the race) just so that he could be faster in a session that didn't determine their grid position. Alonso was asked afterwards if that was the case: 'No,' he replied. 'I just wanted to compare two different set-ups ready for the third session.' It would later transpire there was more to it than that.

Into the run-off session – the one that determines the top ten grid positions, and in which the cars run with enough fuel to complete the first stint of their race the following day – Alonso qualified second, Hamilton fourth, each on the same fuel load. Lewis might have been on course to challenge Alonso's time but had a brief 'moment' on his final run at turn 12, the exit of the fast chicane. If he was disappointed afterwards, he didn't show it. Second row of the grid on an F1 debut was still pretty satisfactory.

Afterwards, both drivers sat in McLaren's 'meet the team' press briefing. Most of the early questions were directed at Hamilton, as the new guy making the big impression. Alonso's body language suggested he was becoming a bit bored by this. At the back of the room Ron Dennis noted that fact. Having acknowledged the great impression Hamilton had made, the press were then already looking for an angle on the Alonso/Hamilton rivalry within the team. Lewis adopted his time-honoured tactic of shifting the pressure off himself and onto the other guy. 'This is a stepping stone for me,' he reasoned. 'I know my place in the team.

How can I be disappointed being behind a double world champion on my debut?'

There was then an intriguing little moment of power-play between them: Alonso was holding the shared microphone as a question was asked, and instead of answering, he passed the instrument over for Hamilton to answer. Lewis took it but looked surprised, slightly irritated at the presumption. He answered the question, but then made the point of looking at Alonso and saying, 'What do you think?' while putting the microphone back in front of him. If it was a game of power-play tennis, he'd just evened the score to 15-all.

But this was just the easily-triggered competitive zeal of two top sportsmen. Off-track the two were getting along just fine: two relaxed, confident young guys with a shared passion. They were different personalities, and their relationship couldn't be described as close, but it remained informal and friendly. On the Thursday before the race weekend, McLaren had convened for their traditional pre-season press lunch at the Stoke House, a beachside restaurant in Melbourne's St Kilda area. There, the two drivers chatted easily and comfortably before being taken to the outside balcony for a filmed Vodafone interview. Touchingly, Anthony Hamilton was in the background with his video camera, for once able to simply enjoy his son's success. Also included in the interview was a six-year-old actor who had recently played the part of a six-year-old Alonso for a Vodafone ad. After talking with the drivers, the compere thrust the microphone in front of the kid and asked if there was anything he wanted to ask Alonso. The boy froze, dumbfounded. Realising his plight, Lewis bent down and whispered in his ear. The actor was then able to come up with a smart, funny response – and the onlookers laughed, getting the poor child off the hook.

It was just a small intuitive act on Lewis's part, but it told of a grace rare in a young sports star.

There were only a few clouds in the sky on Sunday afternoon, 18 March, as the cars lined up on the Albert Park grid. The sun glinted off the gaudy colours of bodyworks and helmets, the mechanics and hangers-on were cleared from the grid. Ron Dennis leant over Hamilton's cockpit for a final quick word – 'Just try to hold your position at the start and don't do anything stupid' – the helmet nodded. A formation lap, then pull up at the second row grid slot, waiting for the lights. Twenty-two F1 engines scream, one of them right behind Lewis's backbone – but it's incidental noise in there, from somewhere else that has nothing to do with you. Because now you're in the zone, in racing mode, the earlier butterflies gone, just waiting for that trigger. You hear your own breathing, feel your own heart beat. Car in gear, red lights coming on in sequence. At some time between one and five seconds after the last light has gone on, they will all go off – and the race has started.

Kimi Raikkonen's pole position Ferrari easily kept its place as they all burst away from the grid, but behind him things were rather more fluid. Alonso had his hands full fending off the lighter-fuelled – and therefore more accelerative – BMW of Nick Heidfeld, and swerved across to the right trying to dissuade him. Hamilton meanwhile was being forced towards the pit wall by the other BMW of his former karting rival Robert Kubica. Hamilton's split-second instinctive racecraft saw him surrender on that move while there was still time for an alternative, and instead he briefly lifted, swept around the back of Kubica and made a run down the left to the first corner, a right-hander. This took him past not only Kubica but also Alonso, who was still distracted by

Heidfeld on his right and was clearly not expecting Hamilton on the left. Within a few seconds, Hamilton's uncanny ability to always put himself in the right place, his incredibly finely-honed spatial awareness and sense of time and space, had overturned Alonso out-qualifying him. They completed the first lap third and fourth, this becoming second and third as Heidfeld ahead of them came in for his early fuel stop.

Although Raikkonen was able to pull away to a dominant win, the two McLarens circulated nose-to-tail. Having a double world champion fill his mirrors didn't faze Hamilton. But they did eventually swap positions – thanks to a better fuel strategy for Alonso. This is what the champion's apparently pointless extra lap in second qualifying had been about. In any modern Grand Prix, fuel-stop strategy is critical. But teams are not allowed to have more than one pit crew, and this forces their drivers to pit on different laps. Therefore one driver must always be disadvantaged in the timing of his stop, if they are on broadly similar strategies. Teams each have their own way of deciding which of their drivers gets preference, but at McLaren at the start of the season the system was that whichever was quicker in second qualifying got to choose which of the pre-decided options to go for. By going out for a second run in Q2 to beat Hamilton's time, Alonso had not been simply wasting a new set of rubber; he had been guaranteeing himself strategic preference for the race.

He was not pleased he'd had to do this. As far as Alonso was concerned, he'd been given assurances that the team's focus would be on gaining him the world championship. Now here he was having to use up the 'golden lap' of a set of new tyres that would thereby be denied him in the race – just to get strategic preference over his team-mate. He had previously assumed he'd be getting that regardless. What McLaren did and did not promise Alonso before he joined is not known, but it was almost certainly assumed by both the team and Alonso that a rookie would not be fighting for the world title. As such, if any assurances were given, they were probably given quite lightly. This was just the niggly beginning of a point of conflict that would escalate massively during the season. Lewis Hamilton's assured speed was already beginning to trigger internal problems, given the no-compromise personality of the team's other driver.

At the first stops Alonso was brought in first, Hamilton a lap later. But Alonso was fuelled to run two laps longer to the final stops – giving him the strategic advantage he had bought himself the day before. It meant that as Hamilton made his final stop, Alonso would still have two more laps of low-weight running while Hamilton rejoined heavy. This was enough to leapfrog the Spaniard ahead into second place – his cause aided by Hamilton being delayed on his in-lap by a slower car. As in qualifying, Hamilton was simply delighted to have got his F1 career under way with a great result, and appeared not to be niggled about Alonso pipping him. But the strategic conundrum and how it had been resolved was certainly noted in the Hamilton camp.

The drivers sprayed the champagne on the podium, and as Lewis came down the steps his eyes met those of Anthony. They didn't speak, just looked at each other for a second – then each burst out laughing. They'd bloody done it: becoming an overnight sensation had taken 14 years from Rye House cadet race to F1 podium. Fourteen years of hard slog and consistent brilliance.

Later, Lewis was again asked about fighting with Alonso,

and this time was fuller in his response. 'It is truly an honour for me to be given this opportunity to work alongside Fernando in my first year as a Formula One driver. I have a tremendous amount of respect for what he has achieved. The sheer size of the challenge of working with him and competing against him is what is most exciting. All of my former team-mates have been hugely competitive, and the challenge and excitement come from having to find the answers to the most important question: "Just how far do I need to push myself to beat that person and just how far can I go?" With Fernando being a two-time world champion, I know I have to dig deeper than ever before, which is what I love about being a racing driver.'

Because he was last of the front runners to pit, Hamilton did technically lead the race for a couple of laps. 'That was a fantastic feeling,' he said, 'even though it was just a temporary thing. The race was intense, and I was working very hard. I made a few mistakes but nothing major and really enjoyed myself. It's good to get that first race under your belt, over and done with. It gives you a confidence. Now I can go and let my hair down and look forward to the next race.'

A podium on his debut, running nip-and-tuck as quick as his double world champion team-mate all weekend, passing him into the first corner and losing out to him only on strategy: it had been a great weekend's work, one that had brought him into the wider consciousness of the outside world – and he'd impressed the hell out of the inner circle, as Martin Whitmarsh made clear: 'Lewis has come to a team of massive expectations, and the pressure that comes with that is incredible. If he'd have flopped here, we know what the headlines would have been. But Lewis exceeded all our expectations. Great drivers always find a little bit more – I think back to Michael Schumacher's debut at Spa and how impressed we all were when he put it seventh in qualifying. This weekend has been truly remarkable.'

Even his former coach Marc Hynes, watching back home on TV, was impressed: 'I wasn't surprised he was able to give Alonso a hard time – but I was surprised he was able to do it straight away. Albert Park's a tricky place he'd never seen before and I thought we wouldn't really start to see his true form until we got to circuits where he'd been before. I was expecting he'd be around 0.4s off Alonso at the beginning. The first lap was just normal Lewis. It might have surprised the F1 crowd but it didn't those of us who've watched him: pick the spot, sense where the gap's going to be, no thought process, no hesitation, just fill that gap. He always comes out better off because he's always a bit further down than most people would be, and it's up to them then to get out the way. He creates his own space that opens up the corner more.'

The off-track Lewis persona was working its charm too. Stirling Moss: 'He is a very impressive young man, the most impressive young driver I've seen in a long while. He has the car control and he has the calmness when he is driving – but he is also a fighter and has a great manner about him. I have been connected with motor racing for 60 years now and he is certainly the best breath of fresh air we've had. It isn't just that he is a driver – he obviously can drive – he is a racer, he can see a gap and he's in it. But apart from that, he is such a nice bloke. And when you think what he has done on the way up in karts, and GP2: he has won so many things he could be big-headed. But he has none of that, he is good, he is easy to talk to. He is a family man and they come along to the races. I think he's fantastic.'

Another driving great, Jackie Stewart, was equally gushing. 'I think he is the brightest star to have entered F1 – ever!'

Round 1 of 17:
Australian Grand Prix, Melbourne, 18 March 2007

1. Kimi Raikkonen (Ferrari)
2. Fernando Alonso (McLaren-Mercedes)
3. **Lewis Hamilton (McLaren-Mercedes)**
4. Nick Heidfeld (BMWSauber)
5. Giancarlo Fisichella (Renault)
6. Felipe Massa (Ferrari)
7. Nico Rosberg (Williams-Toyota)
8. Ralf Schumacher (Toyota)

Drivers' World Championship

1.	Raikkonen	10 points
2.	Alonso	8
3.	**Hamilton**	**6**
4.	Heidfeld	5
5.	Fisichella	4
6.	Massa	3
7.	Rosberg	2
8.	R. Schumacher	1

CHAPTER ELEVEN

Leading the World

Lewis Hamilton emerged from the three long-haul races that began the season in a joint lead of the drivers' world championship. He did so by dint of a record-breaking run of podium places for a rookie, and although he had yet to stand on the top step of that podium, it was clearly only a matter of time. Following on from his sparkling debut in Australia, the consecutive weekend Grands Prix of Malaysia and Bahrain demonstrated to the world – and to his team-mate Fernando Alonso – that Hamilton was very much a contender for the world championship, rookie or no. The way that Alonso reacted to this new reality, together with just how emboldened it seemed to make Hamilton, suggested that McLaren were going to have quite a job on their hands containing the intra-team competitiveness. As if that were not enough, the opening salvoes of an off-track fight with Ferrari that would come to dominate the season were fired.

In the three-week gap between the Australian and Malaysian Grands Prix, the teams decamped to the Asian track to begin preparations for a four-day test there. Lewis took the opportunity to holiday in Thailand with his former team-mate Adrian Sutil. The following week he flew on to Kuala Lumpur for the test. Under new regulations aimed at controlling costs, each team could run only one car. The experience of tester Pedro de la Rosa was used to give McLaren a baseline on the first day, and in the three subsequent days Hamilton drove the car, enabling him to learn the Sepang track, another venue at which he had never before driven, but even more importantly to get his body attuned to the incredible humidity of the place. The air temperature is regularly 35°C or more, but when combined with up to 50 per cent humidity it makes for an extremely tiring environment. Drivers lose as much as 10kg during the course of a race in these conditions.

This was not something Hamilton had ever had to deal with before – and he and his trainer were concerned, given that he tended to sweat more than most drivers. Fluid intake was monitored very carefully in the weeks leading up to the race. After the test concluded, Hamilton flew to Hong Kong to meet up with girlfriend Jodia Ma and together they holidayed in Bali. She had returned to Hong Kong from Britain a couple of months earlier, resigned to the fact that Lewis's F1 career would mean he wouldn't be in the UK very often, and had taken a job as a reception manager at a fashionable restaurant. A devout Buddhist, friends revealed that she prayed at a local temple each time Lewis was racing. Lewis would joke with her and credit any race track success to Buddha. After their holiday they parted, Jodia returning to Hong Kong, Lewis to Kuala Lumpur for the race.

Through the practices Hamilton showed he had made good use of the test, and was again regularly matching

Alonso. It also became clear that this time the McLarens were much closer to the pace of the Ferraris than had been the case in Melbourne. Partly it was to do with the Ferraris' cooling being very marginal in these conditions – meaning they had to cut extra cooling slats and holes into their body-work, thus losing them aerodynamic performance. They also restricted their engine revs, running to just 17,500rpm instead of the permitted 19,000 in order to keep the heat rejection within manageable limits. It may also have had something to do with an amendment that the governing body had made to the regulations since Australia, concerning the rigidity test of the cars' floors. Allowing the floors to bend could confer a serious aerodynamic advantage, and McLaren believed that Ferrari were getting around the static rigidity test by means of a trick sprung fastener that allowed the floor to bend to confer an aerodynamic advantage at speed but which returned to its original shape when static. During the Australian GP weekend McLaren had applied to the FIA (the sport's governing body) for permission to run a similar system in future, and had produced sketches outling the principle, based upon how they believed the Ferrari system worked. The FIA denied permission and instead came up with a tougher flexibility test – something that McLaren were hoping for all along.

Although the difference the new ruling made to the Ferraris' performance was reckoned to be relatively small – most of the Ferraris' lost performance relative to McLaren in Malaysia compared to Australia could be accounted for by the bodywork and engine restrictions needed on the Ferrari – McLaren's actions behind the scenes would turn out to be hugely significant later in the season.

Apparently unknown to McLaren senior management,

the team's chief designer Mike Coughlan was in contact with Ferrari's disaffected chief mechanic Nigel Stepney. The two had worked together in the past, and now Stepney was disappointed that he had not been given the job he was expecting in a recent Ferrari reorganisation. He had apparently revealed to Coughlan how the Ferrari floor system worked, as well as details about the Italian car's rear wing fixing and braking system. Coughlan had outlined these to the appropriate member of McLaren's engineering team, Paddy Lowe, who had then prepared the request to the FIA. He also questioned the rear wing fastening system but received a response that this was legal. These were the opening shots of what became known as 'Spygate', an industrial espionage affair that would come to dominate McLaren's year and threaten the title chances of the team and its drivers.

Three days after the Australian race, de la Rosa – who knew Coughlan well from working with him at the Arrows team in 2000 – e-mailed Coughlan to enquire whether he knew the Ferrari's weight distribution, as he was due to go in the McLaren simulator the next day and was keen to see how a similar set-up might work on their car. Coughlan text-replied with a figure, precise to two decimal points, information apparently gleaned from Stepney. De la Rosa's e-mail – and those relaying this information to Alonso, and telling Fernando that it came from Stepney – would later be used as key evidence in the espionage case against McLaren.

But that was all still to come. At Sepang, Alonso and Hamilton again qualified second and fourth respectively, with Felipe Massa's Ferrari in pole position this time, albeit by a narrow margin. Hamilton's chances of out-qualifying his team-mate were compromised by a heavier fuel load and rain part-way through his final run. This time Alonso had been significantly faster than Hamilton in second qualifying, so earning himself first call on strategy, without having to use an extra set of tyres to do it. Despite their compromised configuration, the Ferraris still looked slightly stronger, in first and third on the grid. But that was overturned within seconds of the start when both Ferrari drivers appeared to be half asleep down to the first corner. Massa left a gap to the inside, which Alonso immediately squeezed into to take the lead, while Kimi Raikkonen did the same and allowed Hamilton to pass for third. But Lewis wasn't finished yet: the first right-hander is linked to a left-hander immediately afterwards, and going around the outside of Massa at the first turn allowed Lewis to be on the inside and ahead going into the left-hander. In the space of two corners Hamilton had vaulted from fourth to second and the F1 community got to see that the Melbourne start had been no fluke: he really could find passing places that were invisible to others.

With Alonso out front and charging, Hamilton played the team game perfectly, eased off a little and backed up the Ferraris, allowing Alonso to escape. It was the basis for a totally dominant victory from the world champion. Hamilton hadn't quite had Alonso's consistent pace – even though he did set the race's fastest lap – and quite early in the race decided to concentrate on defending his second place. Massa, frustrated at being held back to third while Alonso pulled out an ever-bigger lead, was desperate to pass Hamilton.

The opening lap had seen Hamilton in attack mode, now we were seeing him in defence – and he was flawless, always putting his car in exactly the right position to frustrate his opponent without ever resorting to unfair weaving. In fact it was Massa who began to get ragged, not Hamilton. On the fourth lap he thought he saw a gap to Hamilton's inside as they raced up to turn 4. He put the Ferrari down it. Hamilton saw him coming but judged that Massa had left it too late and so just stayed out wide on the left and braked as late as possible. Sure enough, Massa locked up and ran wide, being in front of the McLaren only for a second or so before Lewis was able to retake the place as he exited the corner. Within a couple of laps Massa was back on his tail and making a run at the same corner. This time Hamilton began to move across, to make it more difficult. Again he braked as late as possible – and again it tricked Massa into trying to brake even later, again causing the Ferrari to run out wide, this time across the grass and losing Massa two places. This was Massa's 72nd Grand Prix, Hamilton's second, but it looked for all the world the other way around.

Hamilton duly shored up his second position with a superb middle stint of the race, where he set fastest lap, cut a big chunk out of Alonso's lead and eased himself well clear of Raikkonen. But he was somewhat alarmed to find that he'd used up the full contents of his drinks bottle shortly after beginning his final stint. The hydration his trainer had insisted upon was now going to dry up. No matter, he thought. He'd done the hard work, kept the Ferraris behind. Fernando was up ahead and the team policy once the final stops have played out and the cars are running 1–2 is for the drivers not to race each other. He could do no more, so could now just relax, concentrate on keeping it on the road to the end and conserve his energy. Hence the concern when he received a radio warning that Kimi was just 6s behind and catching fast. 'I couldn't see him in my mirrors,' said Lewis afterwards, 'and it was difficult to read the gap on the pit board. I saw what the gap was to Fernando, saw it was quite big but I made the mistake of thinking that was the gap to Kimi.' This was a body blow, given his now dehydrated state. 'I just had to bite my tongue to bring me back to life and dig really deep, while still trying to preserve my energy.' Raikkonen was right with him by the last lap, but there was no way by. Hamilton took the flag in second. Two Grands Prix, two podiums.

As he went into cool-down mode on the in-lap he received the team's congratulations over the radio. What he said back was significant: 'I want to win. Doesn't matter if it's the next race. But sometime this year I'm going to have one,' he said. Given the power-play between the McLaren drivers and the strategic complications, it seemed more than an expression of ambition. More a warning that they couldn't expect him to continue to play the support role to Alonso the way he had here. As Alonso later acknowledged, it was Hamilton's delaying the Ferraris in the first stint that opened the window to Alonso's victory. By default, Hamilton had driven a perfect number two's race here, but he wasn't intending to do too many of them. 'It was maybe my toughest race,' he said. 'But next time I aim to come here better prepared, ready for the win.'

It was all coded. But listening between the lines, he wasn't satisfied to be Alonso's support. It had happened this time only because he was new to this place and the very trying conditions. 'Don't get used to it', Hamilton seemed to be saying to the team and Alonso.

Martin Whitmarsh seemed to acknowledge as much, saying: 'He will be winning races this year and there's no reason why he can't compete for the championship.' Had Alonso heard these words and not been celebrating a perfect victory, those thick, dark eyebrows might have formed into a frown.

Round 2 of 17:
Malaysian Grand Prix, Sepang, 8 April

1. Fernando Alonso (McLaren-Mercedes)
2. **Lewis Hamilton (McLaren-Mercedes)**
3. Kimi Raikkonen (Ferrari)
4. Nick Heidfeld (BMWSauber)
5. Felipe Massa (Ferrari)
6. Giancarlo Fisichella (Renault)
7. Jarno Trulli (Toyota)
8. Heikki Kovalainen (Renault)

Drivers' World Championship

1.	Alonso	18 points
2.	Raikkonen	16
3.	**Hamilton**	**14**
4.	Heidfeld	10
5.	Fisichella	7
	Massa	7
7.	Trulli	2
	Rosberg	2
9.	Kovalainen	1
	R. Schumacher	1

Just seven days after Malaysia, the F1 circus was performing in the much drier desert heat of Bahrain. Here was the first track on the F1 calendar of which Hamilton had prior experience – he'd won the 2005 F3 race here in spectacular fashion. Maybe coincidentally, maybe not, it was the first time he had a decisive and consistent edge in speed over team-mate Alonso. At no stage in the weekend did the champion threaten Hamilton's in-team supremacy. The only problem for Lewis was the Ferrari – or that of Felipe Massa, at least.

Bahrain's Sakhir circuit demands a lot of the brakes, with lots of high-speed entries into slow corners. Alonso was never happy with the feel of his McLaren's brakes. There was nothing mechanically wrong with them, it was simply that the hard compound material necessary to make them last on such a hard-braking track gave a pedal feel that Alonso found very difficult to have confidence in. He'd spent the previous five years with the very different braking system of Renault and was having a hard time adapting. Hamilton was having no such difficulties.

But for all that he seemed to have memorised the track from his previous visit, his recollection of how to get to it was initially a bit shaky. Former F1 drivers Martin Brundle and Mark Blundell were travelling from their hotel to the track on Thursday morning in their role as TV pundits. They stopped at a set of traffic lights and noticed a Mercedes M-class pull up alongside. The window came down and they were amused to see it was Hamilton behind the wheel, on his own, asking them directions to the circuit! 'It occurred to me that there he was, this megastar with no idea how big he had become back home because he hadn't been back here yet,' said Brundle, 'and he was just driving himself around with no minders. I wondered if that was one of the last little bits of normality he would ever experience.'

Amid his adaptation to the car and tyres, Alonso was also still feeling his way with the team, was still very conscious of how well Hamilton already knew everyone, of how he was the boss's protégé. He didn't feel entirely comfortable, and made no attempt at a charm offensive – he's not that sort of character. He felt it was up to the team to make him comfortable, to deliver the team leader status he felt he had been promised. Ron Dennis had noted his driver's apparent dissatisfaction, and particularly how irritated he seemed to be at the team's post-qualifying press conference in Australia when Hamilton was being asked all the questions. In the Bahrain paddock on the Thursday afternoon, Dennis took the opportunity to sit down with Alonso, trying to reassure him.

'We were just talking about a couple of things, life in general,' said Dennis afterwards, trying to downplay the situation, to keep a lid on the competitive cauldron that was developing within his team. 'It was a slightly paternal approach. We are trying to manage the drivers, keeping their feet on the ground and making sure everyone knows that we are privileged to have a double world champion in our car.'

Ron may have had only the best intentions, but Alonso later reported to Spanish journalists that he felt condescended to by Dennis. He felt his status as a double world champion justified a more equal relationship, a partnership rather than the very clear employer/employee dynamic that Dennis imposed.

Alonso's predecessor at the team, Juan Pablo Montoya, was not surprised by what was unfolding. In an interview with Associated Press later in the year he said: 'Fernando is a nice guy, but he was the No. 1 at Renault and he was used to winning and getting everything. Then he went to McLaren, and when [wife] Connie and I heard that Lewis was going to be his team-mate, we said "Oh my God". We immediately felt sorry for Fernando because Lewis is Ron's baby. Ron paid his whole career, so Ron wants him to win and not Fernando. He would rather see Lewis win, who is like his own child to Ron. Fernando is nothing to him.

'Ron, outside the work environment, is a great guy. But he's two different guys. The guy who I signed with and played golf with, he just didn't exist in the office. He was just a different person, you wouldn't even recognise him. He wants to control everything, and I think Fernando is [angry] about that because he is not used to someone controlling everything and did not like that Ron was like that. I think Ron is used to drivers who don't say anything back. They are very quiet and very nice and do what everyone says, and I came along and he didn't like that [I wasn't like that]. Now I guess Fernando is the same way. He thought he was going to come in and be No. 1, and he's just not. They try to make them be equal, but Lewis is genuinely a really fast driver. And apart from being really fast, he's Ron's favourite. It's just the truth, and it makes it bad for Fernando.'

Alonso never did properly dial himself into his car at Bahrain and this time it was Hamilton who qualified second – his first front-row start – and Alonso who was fourth, albeit with a heavier fuel load. Hamilton had been much the quicker in second qualifying – to the extent that it would have been pointless for Alonso to have wasted a set of his race tyres going for another lap, as he did in Australia. Lewis therefore had strategic preference, just compounding Alonso's disaffection.

Massa's Ferrari again had the edge on raw one-lap pace and started from pole, with the sister car of Kimi Raikkonen in third. After his errors in the previous race, Massa was determined to make amends here, and did so with a vengeance. He took the lead at the start and stayed there. Hamilton, after aggressively fending off Alonso down to the first corner, pressured Massa all the way to the first pit stops but could not find a way by. He then suffered an over-inflated set of tyres in the middle stint, allowing Massa to escape. For the short final stint, and back on correctly-pressured tyres, Hamilton was able to close up all the time he'd lost to the Ferrari, and crossed the line just 0.2s behind. But second is second. Raikkonen finished just behind, while Alonso had a very uninspired race, still struggling for confidence in his brakes, and was passed for fourth by the BMW of Nick Heidfeld. This result put Alonso, Raikkonen and Hamilton into a joint lead of the world championship. Hamilton's result also broke the record of consecutive podium finishes for an F1 rookie.

Given that he was sharing the lead of the championship, the previous McLaren position of not expecting Hamilton to be a title contender in his first year now looked unsustainable. Martin Whitmarsh admitted that he was transcending his rookie status. 'He clearly is going to be a championship contender this year. We are having to revise our expectations of him. Since I joined McLaren in 1989,' he said, 'I've worked with a lot of great drivers, including Prost, Senna, Mika Hakkinen and now Fernando Alonso. It's pretty clear that Lewis ticks all the necessary boxes. It's too early to analyse, but if the trend continues there is no reason why he could not become the greatest driver ever.'

Hamilton indeed was the talk of the paddock. Frank Williams spoke for most of McLaren's rivals when he said: 'I thought after we got rid of Michael [Schumacher], "Now we've got a chance again." But then another superhuman turns up. Michael was many things, but he was also a very,

very simple human. Hamilton is a different character I think, but purely in terms of calibre or quality of skill, what I'm seeing so early in this man's career is remarkable. Hamilton is still a baby, so to speak, but dishing out loads of trouble already. I mean that in the nicest possible way. I cry he's not in a Williams but I rejoice for F1. I really do.'

Alonso was by now heartily sick of hearing about how brilliant his team-mate was, and gave several ill-tempered responses to questions about him from the British media. Hamilton was getting under his skin. No team-mate had ever done that to Alonso before.

Asked about whether he expected to be able to fight for the title with his team-mate, Hamilton answered: 'Yeah, absolutely. I don't see why not. I have the same car and I seem to be as competitive as him. So as long as I can keep up this consistency, I know I can. I feel a lot more comfortable now that a win is going to be possible.'

Marc Hynes believes that beating Raikkonen in both Malaysia and Bahrain boosted Hamilton's confidence enormously. 'When he was in GP2 he'd be looking over that fence, like all of them, to the F1 paddock and trying to live up to what he thought an F1 driver should be. Kimi was always someone Lewis enjoyed watching and was impressed by – as was Alonso, but particularly Kimi. Suddenly, there he is among them – and beating them, slapping Kimi on the back on the podium saying "Well done, mate" after he's just whupped his ass. I think that demolished any inner questions he might have had about just where he stacked up. Here he was doing the same as he'd always done, except he's in F1 – and it's good enough to do this. It allowed him to settle into F1 properly, to relax into it – and when he's comfortable like that he's devastating.'

Round 3 of 17:
Bahrain Grand Prix, Sakhir, 15 April

1. Felipe Massa (Ferrari)
2. **Lewis Hamilton (McLaren-Mercedes)**
3. Kimi Raikkonen (Ferrari)
4. Nick Heidfeld (BMWSauber)
5. Fernando Alonso (McLaren-Mercedes)
6. Robert Kubica (BMWSauber)
7. Jarno Trulli (Toyota)
8. Giancarlo Fisichella (Renault)

Drivers' World Championship

1.	Alonso	22 points
2.	Raikkonen	22
3.	**Hamilton**	**22**
4.	Massa	17
5.	Heidfeld	15
6.	Fisichella	8
7.	Trulli	4
8.	Kubica	3
9.	Rosberg	2
10.	Kovalainen	1
	R. Schumacher	1

CHAPTER TWELVE

Team Tensions

Recognising the scale of challenge that team-mate Lewis Hamilton represented, Fernando Alonso responded with vigour. He had not enjoyed the Bahrain weekend, had felt humiliated to finish 12s behind a rookie. He needed to understand the car and the tyres better, in particular. He could feel his driving was not yet as instinctive as it had been during his title-winning years at Renault. The next Grand Prix was his home race, at Barcelona. The prospect of being humbled by a rookie British team-mate in front of hundreds of thousands of his fans did not appeal in the slightest. As such, he took charge of his destiny, began to throw around the weight that comes with two world titles. For the pre-race four-day Barcelona test, he campaigned aggressively to McLaren's Martin Whitmarsh to be allowed to share only with his friend, the test driver de la Rosa. He did not want to have to stand down for the final day to allow Hamilton time in the one car, as originally planned. Keen to demonstrate to Alonso that there was no Hamilton bias, Whitmarsh agreed.

Hamilton was not invited to the test. De la Rosa would do one-and-a-half days, Alonso two-and-a-half.

Running the car with new parts to enhance its aerodynamic performance that Hamilton wouldn't get to try until first practice, Alonso felt he had made much progress. 'After Malaysia I thought I had understood the car and the tyres,' he said, 'but I then realised I still had a lot to learn. In the test here I learned so many things about the tyres, the long runs and first lap performance. So there is no doubt that I can keep learning.' He sounded upbeat, confident. He was about to get a surprise.

With this backdrop, there was a very definite determination in Lewis Hamilton's first run in the car on Friday morning of the Grand Prix weekend. It may have been only a routine practice session, something normally devoted to doing tyre comparisons and set-up work. But for Lewis there was an added dimension this time: to compete with Alonso after having been denied the chance to test, to make a point to the team and the watching world. Alonso had already been pounding around for a few minutes as Hamilton took to the track. His first flying lap, in a car with upgrades he had not had the chance to try out beforehand, was 0.3s quicker than Alonso's best. Hamilton remained in front throughout the session, the pair heading the times but with Hamilton almost 0.4s ahead at the end. As Alonso climbed from his car in the garage, he had a face of thunder. It was easy to sense the bewilderment in his mind – how could this be? I'm the double world champion, I've tested the car for two-and-a-half days and he didn't, I was familiar with the new parts and he wasn't – and still he goes faster.

Into qualifying and Hamilton was 0.5s quicker in the first session, 0.1s faster in the second session. It wasn't looking

Hamilton at 12 performing at the 1997 Autosport International Show.

Twelve-year-old Hamilton with Ron Dennis, the man who would sponsor his rise all the way to F1. This is at the 1997 Belgian Grand Prix and is during the first year of Hamilton's McLaren backing.

A 14-year-old Hamilton meets Prince Charles at McLaren's Woking base. Hamilton was at the time racing in the JICA category of karting in Italy and Belgium under McLaren tutelage.

Lewis and MBM.com team-mate Nico Rosberg at the Formula Super A karting world championship meeting in September 2001. This was the only season of Hamilton's career in which he didn't win at least one race. He came into a team set up around Nico Rosberg in 2000 and in the following two seasons out-performed him. The two formed a close friendship regardless, though that couldn't be said of the respective fathers.

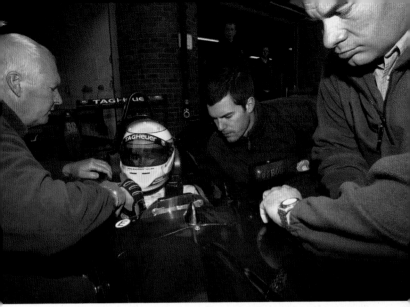

Manor Motorsport's John Booth (on left) oversees Hamilton's first run in a Formula Renault, Mallory Park 2001. A few laps later Hamilton crashed the car, but later lapped very quickly in the repaired machine.

Hamilton locks an inside wheel on his Manor Motorsport Formula Renault as he turns into Druids at Brands Hatch, on his way to victory during his 2002 campaign, his first season of car racing.

July 2003, and Hamilton shares the podium with James Rossiter and Mike Spencer after a stunning victory in the Croft Formula Renault race. Despite a disconnected rear damper, he fended off Spencer for lap after lap.

Lewis with Nelson Piquet Jr in the 2004 Marlboro Masters F3 meeting at Zandvoort. Two years later the pair would be locked in battle over the outcome of the GP2 championship, a battle that Hamilton would win, thereby paving his graduation to F1.

Hamilton flat-out through the Monaco tunnel in his ART GP2 car during qualifying in 2006. In the opening minutes of the session, with everyone else playing themselves gently into the tricky circuit, he was fastest by seconds.

Hamilton moments after securing pole position by the margin of 8s for the Monte Carlo round of the 2006 GP2 championship. He went on to dominate the race. A year later he would be fighting for victory here in the Grand Prix itself.

Hamilton sprays the champagne with Adam Carroll after a sensational performance in the GP-support GP2 race at Silverstone in 2006. His thrilling performance in this race had the crowd on its feet but also gave his career the final push of momentum to get him into F1.

Stirling Moss and Lewis Hamilton separated by five decades but united as two Grand Prix greats. Here th chat during Hamilton's GP season of 2006.

hortly after clinching the 2006 GP2 title, Lewis touches base with stepbrother Nicholas, ere with Linda Hamilton (on right), mother of Nicholas, stepmother of Lewis.

ewis and father Anthony Hamilton together celebrate the GP2 title. They came into he weekend not knowing if they were continuing with McLaren and left it feeling ncreasingly sure that Lewis would be driving for McLaren in F1 in 2007.

The newly crowned 2006 GP2 champion walks off the podium with an F1 future apparently secured. But he still wasn't sure exactly what Ron Dennis meant by 'giving him a chance'. He would find out very soon.

Spraying the champagne in Melbourne after taking third place on his F1 debut. He ran for two-thirds of the race's distance in second place, ahead of team-mate Fernando Alonso.

A new sort of life: making an appearance for a team sponsor in downtown Kuala Lumpur. The level of attention now he was in F1 made his life very different in a short space of time.

Hamilton and Ferrari's Felipe Massa in the midst of their early battle for second in the 2007 Malaysian Grand Prix. It was a battle that Hamilton won after Massa ran onto the grass attempting to pass.

Relieving Alonso of second place in the opening seconds of the 2007 Spanish Grand Prix
Alonso has just banged wheels with the Ferrari of Felipe Massa, sending himself across the
gravel and allowing Hamilton and Kimi Raikkonen (on the left of the picture) to pass.

Joy uncorked as Hamilton
alights from the cockpit as
a Grand Prix winner for
the first time. His winning
drive came in his sixth
Grand Prix start.

10 June 2007, Montreal, the scene of Lewis Hamilton's first Grand Prix victory. Although he led from start to finish, a series of safety cars meant he had to go through four nerve-wracking restarts.

Anthony in characteristic pose, sheltering his boy from the sun and the attention on the eve of a race, in this case the 2007 American Grand Prix at Indianapolis. It's a scene they've played from the British karting tracks of the 1990s all the way to F1.

Fending off team-mate Fernando Alonso for the lead of the 2007 American Grand Prix at Indianapolis. Twice Hamilton had to get defensive to keep the reigning world champion behind him, and at one stage Alonso was on the radio telling the team to move Hamilton aside. It was to no avail, as Hamilton took his second Grand Prix victory in seven days.

Natasha Bedingfield, Hamilton and rap star Pharrell Williams leaving a party hosted by another rapper, P Diddy, in July 2007.

A professional greeting of respect between Alonso and Hamilton at the beginning of the 2007 British Grand Prix weekend. The McLaren team-mates remained on reasonable terms for most of the season, despite extreme strains in their relationship.

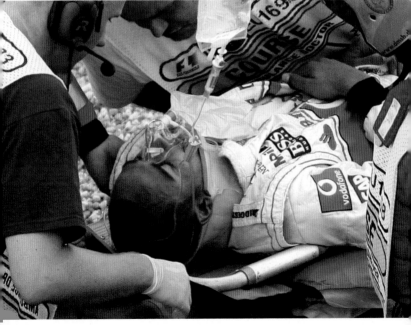

Loaded onto a stretcher and carried into an ambulance after his qualifying crash during the European Grand Prix weekend. The accident was caused by a loose right-front wheel.

Hamilton faces the cameras and microphones on his return to the track after his dramatic crash during qualifying for the 2007 European Grand Prix at the Nürburgring. McLaren team boss Ron Dennis looks on.

Sportsman of the Year at the GQ Men of the Year awards, September 2007. Here he receives his prize from Naomi Campbell.

Tense moments: Hamilton sits with test driver Pedro de la Rosa and McLaren MD Jonathan Neale during the second FIA World Council hearing of the McLaren espionage case in Paris.

Hamilton and Alonso as the safety car finally pits and allows the 2007 Japanese Grand Prix to get under way. Hamilton won in commanding fashion and Alonso crashed out, putting Hamilton 12 points clear at the top of the championship with just two rounds remaining.

Ferrari's superior getaway system ensured that Kimi Raikkonen accelerated ahead of Hamilton in the opening seconds of the Brazilian Grand Prix, with Raikkonen and Felipe Massa forming an impenetrable Ferrari barrier down to the first corner.

Hamilton attempted to re-pass team-mate Fernando Alonso into turn 4 on the opening lap of the Brazilian Grand Prix, locked up and ran wide. He rejoined in eighth place, but a later gearbox malfunction and a failed strategy gamble finally put paid to his world championship hopes.

like Alonso could win this on pace, but he had a plan to combat that. In line with Alonso's requests, McLaren had changed how they decided their fuelling strategy between the two drivers, with a less rigid system that gave more scope for each driver and his engineer to deviate further from the standard theoretical optimum, in order to distance themselves further from what the team-mate might be doing. As such, Alonso opted to run light, reckoning on using a low fuel load to take pole position in the final session. Hamilton accepted a heavier fuel load worth an extra three laps but which would penalise him in final qualifying. Alonso was hoping this would put at least one Ferrari between them, enabling him to sprint clear and build up more of a lead than could be clawed back by Lewis's three extra laps up to the stops. Everything about Alonso's choices in this weekend appeared to be geared to beating Hamilton and the Ferrari rivals seemed almost incidental to him.

So it was quite a blow for Alonso when he was beaten to pole position by a scant few hundredths of a second by Massa's Ferrari. It made it less likely he could lead and sprint away, it brought Hamilton – who on his heavier fuel load had qualified fourth – closer. Now all Hamilton needed to do was stay close to Alonso, then bang in the three fast low-fuel laps and he would leapfrog ahead at the first stops – or alternatively take on more fuel than Alonso at the first stops and thereby be primed to leapfrog ahead at the final stops. Either way, he was looking good.

Given this, Alonso *had* to beat Massa into the first corner to stand any chance of beating Hamilton. If he could put the Ferrari between him and his team-mate, he might be able to build up enough of a gap that Hamilton would be too far behind at the first stops to be able to leapfrog him.

He was not prepared even to think of an alternative: it was going to happen, zero-compromise. So as the lights went out and the Ferrari and McLaren headed down to the first turn, with Massa defending the inside line, Alonso going for the outside, there was an inevitability about what happened. Alonso tried to bully his way ahead, Massa was not up for being bullied and held his line. The two cars touched, flicking Alonso's car off the track and across the gravel. Massa continued, still leading, and as Alonso took his wild ride and rejoined the circuit he was passed by two flashes of colour – Hamilton and Kimi Raikkonen. Lewis had outfumbled Kimi down to the first corner and was now ahead of his team-mate too. It was difficult not to think that Hamilton's pressure and Alonso's pride had triggered Fernando into adopting his ill-considered plan. It was arguably the first pressure crack of the four title contenders. And Hamilton was the guy who appeared to have induced it.

Massa was able to parlay his pole into a second consecutive victory – with Hamilton again second, a result that moved him into a clear lead of the world championship. Alonso took third only because of the retirement of Raikkonen ahead of him when the Ferrari's engine failed. Hamilton and Massa joked with each other as they prepared to walk onto the podium. 'I'm going to beat you soon,' warned Hamilton. He felt confident in saying this – as coming up next was Monaco, a track on which he had never lost and where his performances in the junior formulae were invariably devastating.

Round 4 of 17:
Spanish Grand Prix, Barcelona, 13 May

1. Felipe Massa (Ferrari)
2. **Lewis Hamilton (McLaren-Mercedes)**
3. Fernando Alonso (McLaren-Mercedes)
4. Robert Kubica (BMWSauber)
5. David Coulthard (Red Bull-Renault)
6. Nico Rosberg (Williams-Toyota)
7. Heikki Kovalainen (Renault)
8. Takuma Sato (Super Aguri-Honda)

Drivers' World Championship

1.	**Hamilton**	**30 points**
2.	Alonso	28
3.	Massa	27
4.	Raikkonen	22
5.	Heidfeld	15
6.	Kubica	8
	Fisichella	8
8.	Rosberg	5
9.	Coulthard	4
	Trulli	4
11.	Kovalainen	3
12.	Sato	2
	R. Schumacher	2

CHAPTER THIRTEEN

It All Gets Dirty

If the Spanish Grand Prix was the first to reveal the intensity of the fight between Hamilton and Alonso, the first time that Alonso was so rattled by Hamilton's pace that it affected his on-track actions, then Monaco two weeks later was where it all spilled over into animosity. For Lewis it was a winnable race, but he felt his challenge was suppressed by the team in favour of Alonso – in the interests of a safe 1–2 for McLaren. With characteristic frankness, Hamilton angrily said afterwards to the world's press: 'It says number two on my car so I guess I'm the number two driver.' When Lewis gets angry, a slight Jamaican twang comes out in his words – and you could hear it quite distinctly here. 'It's says numba two on ma ca, so I guess I'm the numba two drivurr.' He was angry. The guy sitting a metre to his right – Alonso – now began to get angry too, at what he saw as the belittling of his victory. The team boss sitting in his office in the McLaren Communications Centre listening to the audio of the conference now became furious. It was all about to kick off.

Monte Carlo's street circuit is regarded as the ultimate test of a Grand Prix driver. It's the slowest on the calendar but inside the car, the proximity of the walls and barriers makes it feel the fastest. It's like guiding an Excocet through a letter box. The course through streets more usually populated by billionaires in traffic queues was devised as a circuit in the late 1920s, a tourist attraction with a glamorous Riviera backdrop. Unlike conventional tracks, you don't so much master this track as get into its rhythm. All sorts of seemingly impossible deeds can be conjured when a master driver becomes at one with it. The difference here between fast and inspired is enormous – far greater than at conventional tracks.

It is the circuit that made Hamilton's hero Ayrton Senna come over all mystical when describing a qualifying lap here. 'Ayrton was my favourite driver,' said Lewis that weekend, 'and when I first started watching Formula One it was the red and white car at the front, and as a little boy I was always dreaming of driving that car and I am driving it now and, so, you know, when you come to Monaco … I have lots of memories of watching him win here and when he lost a race, when he crashed, and I was definitely emotional when he passed away, but still … it is great to be racing here and to be doing as well as he always did when he was racing.'

The essential circumstance that made Monaco 2007 such an explosive race was that the McLaren-Mercedes were by some margin the fastest cars around the Monte Carlo streets. It was only ever going to be a fight between their drivers. McLaren thus wanted to ensure they maximised this opportunity, and their focus all weekend was to achieve a 1–2. In terms of risk management, the best way of converting their performance superiority into the perfect result was always going to conflict with the wishes of one of the drivers.

Circumstances decided that driver was Hamilton. But, denied his maiden victory at a track where he felt he had a real performance advantage over Alonso, Lewis was certainly not taking such a philosophical view.

Lewis had raced three times at this track – twice in F3, once in GP2 – and won on all three occasions. At times his superiority here had been outrageous, such as during the early stages of GP2 qualifying when he had been lapping four seconds faster than anyone else. 'He came into this race with only victory on his mind,' revealed Ron Dennis. 'In the lead up to it he was constantly saying "This is my race". He was convinced this was going to be his first Grand Prix win.'

This was Hamilton's state of mind as he took to the track. The conventional wisdom is that around the initially dusty streets of Monte Carlo you play yourself in gently, build up your rhythm, don't take risks. Hamilton was in no way interested in the conventional wisdom – that was for other people. Totally confident in his own huge ability, he attacked the place from the off. Even on his installation lap on Thursday morning, he approached the fast left-hand sweep of the swimming pool section with the car sliding outrageously sideways, yet fully under control. At that moment it was easy to imagine how this was a driver who would come to excite and inspire in the years ahead.

Hamilton's driving style is based around a total ease with oversteer, where the rear of the car slides before the front. At most circuits this style is not inherently superior to an understeer or neutral handling characteristic, but at Monaco it is. The track's short-duration corners demand instant direction change rather than stability. Anyone able to live with an oversteery set-up gets paid back here, each corner accumulating the advantage of generating the direction change from the rear of the car, getting the turning moment completed earlier and allowing the driver to be harder and earlier on the power. It brings with it attendant risks – it's easier to hit the wall.

Hamilton was immediately setting the pace around the track, quicker than team-mate Alonso by between 0.3 and 0.4s whenever they were running together during the practices. Hamilton's opening session was curtailed by a starter motor problem, allowing Alonso time to catch up as the track got quicker. In the afternoon, Hamilton was trying the fast super-soft tyres for the first time when he got out of shape at Ste Devote corner and hit the barriers, putting him out for the rest of the day. The old sages shook their heads, said it had only been a matter of time, that you couldn't attack Monaco like that and not get bitten. They said also that the track time lost to the accident would set him back for the rest of the weekend, that he would be playing catch-up now. They went quiet on Saturday as he took up where he'd left off, his audacious, swashbuckling style very apparent as he went quicker than his only rival Alonso in morning practice and first qualifying – maintaining his consistent 0.3s advantage over him. 'I just love this place,' he said. '180mph between the barriers; it's just such a buzz.' In second qualifying Alonso ended up marginally quicker – but only because he'd had a second run, his first having been 0.6s adrift of Hamilton's, who didn't try to respond.

For the final session, Hamilton felt confident enough in his superiority over Alonso to be fuelled significantly heavier. This tied in well with the team covering themselves for the complications that might arise in the race if a safety car was triggered – always a strong possibility at this track. For his part, Hamilton felt he could beat Alonso to pole *and* have enough fuel to run longer to the first stops. He was fast enough, he believed, to have his cake and eat it. Hamilton's car was duly fuelled to run five laps longer than Alonso's – a very significant difference, worth around 0.3s in Alonso's favour in qualifying.

The final session began with a dark cloud threatening. McLaren reckoned it might be about to rain and so had both their cars fitted with new tyres, ready for Alonso and Hamilton to do flat-out flyers right from the start, despite being at their heaviest. As it turned out, the rain never did come and so they had each wasted a new set for nothing. But the lap times were interesting: Alonso 1m 16.1s, Hamilton 1m 15.9s. Despite a weight penalty worth three-tenths of a second, Hamilton was two-tenths faster. Weight-corrected, in other words, he was now 0.5s faster than the world champion in the same car around F1's most demanding race track.

Unfortunately for Lewis, these times wouldn't count; for with the rain holding off, the track getting quicker as it rubbered in and the cars becoming faster as they burned more fuel off, the critical new tyre laps would come at the end of the session. And Hamilton encountered a problem on each of his two runs then. The first time he glanced the wall exiting Casino Square. It did no damage, but it slowed him. Alonso's run at this time got close to Hamilton's earlier effort, but still Lewis was provisionally quickest. It all hung now on their final runs. Alonso went out first, Hamilton a few seconds later as the session built to a crescendo, the two McLarens in a class of their own well clear of the rest.

Alonso finally went faster than Hamilton's earlier effort and put himself onto provisional pole. But Hamilton was already smashing Alonso's time in the first sector of the lap, being 0.35s ahead by the time he reached Casino Square.

But ahead of him was another car – Mark Webber's Red Bull – on an out-lap. Hamilton was baulked all the way from Casino down to the corner before the tunnel about half-a-mile further on. The lap was ruined. Even then, he was still just 0.2s off Alonso – and therefore faster, weight-corrected, despite the delay. But weight-corrected didn't count for pole – that belonged to Alonso.

Hamilton was deeply frustrated by Webber's actions. 'He's always the guy in the drivers' meetings saying "Watch your mirrors" and he goes and does that! I was already 0.35s up. It would have been pole by 0.5s.' This, remember, despite carrying 0.3s-worth of extra fuel. It had been an astonishing display, albeit a frustrated one.

With hindsight, that errant Red Bull cost Hamilton a likely start-to-finish victory at Monaco. Without it, he would have started from pole and, being fuelled heavier to the first stops, would only have increased his advantage. Overtaking is virtually impossible here and track position is therefore everything. Now Hamilton had to hope that he could use his extra five laps to put himself in the position he would have been virtually guaranteed had he not been baulked during that critical lap.

There was much speculation before the race about whether the two McLarens might try to fight it out down to the first corner. But that was something that had been discussed within the team and discounted. The run down to Ste Devote was too short to make passing feasible, the risk of collision too high. Lewis had agreed not to fight the corner out with Fernando. Instead he aimed his car directly onto the back of Alonso's as the lights changed – but was surprised at how slowly Alonso had got away. It looked very much like Alonso had been trying to make Hamilton vulnerable to being passed at the start by Massa's Ferrari, but Felipe had backed out of trying a marginal move, thereby frustrating Alonso's plan. The two McLarens quickly began distancing themselves from the rest of the field, Hamilton following Alonso's every move.

For Alonso this part of the race was critical. Knowing that Hamilton was fuelled much longer, he needed to build some distance on his team-mate to have any chance of not being leapfrogged by him at the first pit stops. Accordingly, he pressed on, hoping to set such a pace that Hamilton might over-stress his tyres on his heavier fuel load. It didn't look like Alonso's plan was going to work until, on lap 10, the gap suddenly began to build: Hamilton was indeed suffering problems with his front tyres. They had begun to grain, a process whereby the tread blocks tear and are unable to provide their normal grip. The aerodynamic turbulence of this generation of F1 cars made the loads on a closely following car very inconsistent – enough to damage the tyres, particularly if they were of a soft compound like the ones used at Monaco. It was a phenomenon that Alonso would suffer later in the year at Indianapolis when following Hamilton – something that cost him a likely victory there. For seven laps Hamilton was losing up to 1s per lap compared to his earlier pace, while Alonso was able to maintain his initial speed. Soon the gap had built up to 7s, which was going to be comfortably enough for Alonso to retain position over Hamilton after they had both stopped, despite Hamilton's scheduled five low-fuel laps.

For Lewis, this was not looking good. But then: hope on the horizon. Just as his tyres completed their graining phase and he began lapping at his earlier speed, and even faster, so Alonso was coming up to lap backmarkers. They proved particularly uncooperative and Hamilton sniffed his opportunity, quickly closing the gap down. By the time both had scythed their way through them, that 7s gap was back down to 4.2s, and Alonso was called in for his first fuel stop. Theoretically, Lewis should now have had five laps on his low fuel load with Alonso refuelled for 29 laps and therefore heavier to the tune of 1.2s per lap. That should have given Hamilton around 6s advantage in those five laps – comfortably enough to overcome the 4.2s lead Alonso had.

He was therefore dismayed when he was called in just three laps after Alonso, and before he'd had time to build the gap that would have leapfrogged him ahead after stopping. Furthermore, he was held in the pits for around 1.5s longer than Alonso had been, as they fuelled him heavier. It all meant that instead of leapfrogging past, he rejoined 4s behind.

From the team's perspective, there was a good reason for bringing in Hamilton prematurely. It was to do with the likelihood of a safety car. In four of the previous five Monaco Grands Prix, a safety car had been triggered. The risk was that it might be deployed here before Lewis had stopped. If this had happened, it would have dropped Hamilton behind those cars on a one-stop strategy and denied McLaren their 1–2. Bringing him in early was the no-risk option. Anything else was just allowing an unnecessary race between their two cars. With hindsight, Lewis never had any chance of winning this race once Alonso had got to the first corner in the lead. To have prevented that, Lewis needed to have been on the pole position denied him by Webber the day before.

Not knowing or caring about any of this, Hamilton knew only that the team had apparently prevented him fighting for a victory he felt was very achievable. He was furious and began to cut whole chunks out of that deficit. Alonso, seeing the gap close, responded and upped his pace too. The two were racing each other absolutely flat-out, the rest of the field nowhere in sight.

In the McLaren pits, things were getting tense. This was jeopardising the team's chances of a 1–2. Not only did it increase the chance of one or both of them crashing, there was also the matter of a very marginal brake material to consider. The chosen brake gave great stopping power, but at the expense of durability if it was used too hard for too long, especially on a heavy fuel load. From the team's perspective, a perfect result was at risk of going up in a cloud of brake dust and possibly a crashed car.

Ron Dennis instructed each driver's race engineer to tell them to stop racing each other, to back off. Neither complied. Hamilton, in fact, did not even answer. Alonso replied to the effect of 'Tell him to back off. Then I will.' Still they lapped flat out, and still the gap was closing. Eventually Dennis himself came onto Hamilton's radio, and told him in no uncertain terms he was to back off. Hamilton complied, immediately dropping his pace by 0.6s. Alonso, wracked by much the same paranoia of team favouritism as Hamilton now was, continued to push hard for another four laps. Only then did he comply – and even then it was only for another four laps before upping his pace again. Hamilton, noting this, upped his in response. Like a trick birthday candle that relights, a race had broken out again! Alonso set the race's fastest lap on lap 44 and Hamilton responded with a lap just 0.2s slower, despite being fuelled for ten laps more (around 0.5s-worth).

Again in a bid to foil any safety car interference, Alonso was brought in three laps early for his final stop, with his lead out to over 10s. Hamilton had enough fuel for another ten laps and, just like last time, could theoretically have used those extra laps to wipe out the deficit and leapfrog ahead. But again the team played safe and got his stop out of the way early – just two laps after Alonso's. Again he had been contained, and again he was furious. He ignored team instructions to back off in the final stint to save the engine and brakes, and instead put himself right on Alonso's gearbox in the closing laps – just to show the world that he could have won had he been allowed.

In truth, there was no conspiracy to favour either driver. The team just wanted to ensure a 1–2. That's what the governing body, the FIA, accepted after launching an investigation into a possible breach by the team of the regulation that outlaws team orders. But that wasn't Hamilton's concern. All he knew was that he'd been denied by his own team the chance of his first F1 victory on a day when he was certain he had the performance to do it. It was an anger no doubt intensified by the psyched-up state in which he'd approached this very special event, absolutely determined and confident this was his weekend.

On climbing out of the car and taking part in the podium ceremony, Lewis took time out, despite his anger, to find brother Nicholas and hand him the runner-up trophy. 'He's a very important person to me,' said Lewis afterwards, 'and I just wanted to show him that.'

The outside world had known nothing of the drama within the team as it had happened, but one or two of us who were there were suspicious of the timing of Hamilton's stops, particularly the second one, given that the time he was stationary at the first stop suggested he could have run for much longer than two extra laps over Alonso. In the press conference I asked him about it – and he wasn't shy with an answer. He confirmed he had been brought in early and, when pressed, made his bitter comment about 'It says number two on my car so I guess I'm the number two driver'. Only at this point did most of the media correspondents realise that Hamilton hadn't simply been beaten in a straight fight – and the British newspaper journalists duly got enraged on behalf of their partisan readers, beating a path down to Ron Dennis at the team's motor home. He explained as best he could, but the subtleties of race strategy and non-existent safety car periods are difficult to convey to a general audience.

'We are scrupulously fair at all times in how we run this Grand Prix team,' he said. 'We will never favour one driver, no matter who it is. We don't have team orders, we had a strategy to win this race. There will be places where they will be absolutely free to race, but this isn't one of them. This race is nothing about the drivers other than the necessity for them to drive really quickly and give us the opportunity to determine the outcome of the race. And that's my job.

'Team strategy is what you bring to bear to win a Grand Prix; team orders are what you bring to bear to manipulate a Grand Prix. We do not, and have not, manipulated Grands Prix unless there are some exceptional circumstances.

'This is a place where one driver pushing another driver – if it's from a rival team – is a way to induce a mistake. Everybody in the pitlane and media would be saying "What an idiot the team principal of McLaren is for allowing his cars to compete [against each other], and one of them is in the barriers." I have a clear conscience about this race.'

Although the Hamiltons were deeply disappointed, Anthony had just about managed to get it all into perspective by the evening. 'We're over-achieving even our wildest dreams,' he conceded. 'It would have been great to have won but we've got another ten years in this business. It'll come to us eventually.'

Hamilton was not the only unhappy McLaren driver. Alonso felt his victory had been devalued. He was irritated when McLaren did not point out that he too had been brought in early for his second stop (even though it was only three laps, compared to Hamilton's ten, and the first stops were more crucial). He claimed that Hamilton had been unprofessional in revealing to the media what had happened. And he felt that his victory had been hard-won – he'd not made a single error and had led throughout. There was, he felt, no inevitability about it being Hamilton's race if it had played out naturally, that we didn't see if he had performance in hand if needed. These were valid points to some extent, but if he had performance in hand over Hamilton there was no evidence of it at any stage of the Monaco weekend. From the beginning of Thursday practice through to the weight-corrected lap times in the race, the best evidence suggests that Hamilton was the quicker guy all weekend – sometimes by a devastating margin.

In light of the controversy caused by the differing strategies of each driver at Monaco, the team decided on yet another change in how it would decide on their respective refuelling stops in future. From now on, McLaren decided, each driver would be fuelled identically for their new tyre runs in final qualifying. It was McLaren's way of trying to provide transparency and equality to two hyper-competitive drivers each convinced he could give nothing away to the other. Unfortunately, it was to lead to another debacle later in the year – one with more serious consequences than this one.

Round 5 of 17:
Monaco Grand Prix, Monte Carlo, 27 May

1. Fernando Alonso (McLaren-Mercedes)
2. **Lewis Hamilton (McLaren-Mercedes)**
3. Felipe Massa (Ferrari)
4. Giancarlo Fisichella (Renault)
5. Robert Kubica (BMWSauber)
6. Nick Heidfeld (BMWSauber)
7. Alexander Wurz (Williams-Toyota)
8. Kimi Raikkonen (Ferrari)

Drivers' World Championship

1.	Alonso	38 points
	Hamilton	**38**
3.	Massa	33
4.	Raikkonen	23
5.	Heidfeld	18
6.	Fisichella	13
7.	Kubica	12
8.	Rosberg	5
9.	Coulthard	4
	Trulli	4
11.	Kovalainen	3
12.	Wurz	2
13.	Sato	1
	R. Schumacher	1

CHAPTER FOURTEEN

Victory – At the Double!

When Lewis Hamilton was trying to downplay his disappointment at not winning the Monaco Grand Prix, he said, 'Oh
well, next time.' Remarkably, that's exactly what happened.
Two weeks after his Monte Carlo disappointment, he
registered his first Grand Prix victory with a commanding
performance in Montreal. Seven days after the Canadian
race he repeated the feat with victory in the USA Grand Prix
at Indianapolis. The double victories not only boosted him
into a significant lead in the world championship, thereby
putting more pressure on his team-mate Fernando Alonso,
as well as the Ferrari drivers – it also had an enormous
impact on his negotiating position and income potential.
Something that father Anthony Hamilton was not slow to
capitalise on.

'We can no longer say "Maybe we'll fight for the world
championship",' said Anthony. 'We've nailed our colours to
the mast ... there are no holds barred – it's a fair fight as far
as we're concerned.'

Lewis accepted that position but counselled caution. 'The next dream is obviously to win the world championship. But at the moment we have to be realistic again. I'm still a rookie and there are going to be some hard times – it's bound to happen.'

Montreal's Circuit Gilles Villeneuve was another track new to Hamilton, a place where no prior testing is permitted and where none of his junior categories ever raced. The man-made island on which it is situated sits in the middle of the St Lawrence River and was created for a trade exposition in 1967 and was used also for the 1976 Olympic Games. The circuit was created in time for the 1978 Canadian Grand Prix, an event that had a fairy-tale ending when Canadian Gilles Villeneuve took his maiden Grand Prix victory, for Ferrari. The circuit was named in his honour after he was killed during qualifying for the 1982 Belgian Grand Prix, three years before Lewis was born. Gilles Villeneuve was a driver a lot like Lewis Hamilton: spectacular, brave in the extreme, incredibly fast, from a humble background, very down-to-earth and natural. The track named after him is an unusual one, a combination of long straights and slow chicanes and as such very tough on brakes. It's also very bumpy, thanks to the harsh Canadian winters that allow ice into the crevices, which expands and causes damage, and is visibly 'old-school' in that it's lined by barriers and walls rather than open run-off areas. It's unforgiving of mistakes – and induces them easily, thanks to a track surface that tends to break up as the race weekend progresses and the dust and rubber 'marbles' that build up and make the track spectacularly slippery off-line.

Hamilton was very respectful of the place after his first experience of it in the Friday practices. 'The layout looks simple enough but it's a real challenge – physical, mental and technical,' he reported before going back to his hotel to give it all some more thought. He definitely needed to find a little more lap time, as he was consistently a couple of tenths adrift of Alonso. The good news was that the McLaren-Mercedes again seemed to be the class of the field, albeit by a narrower margin than in Monaco. It rode the kerbs beautifully, a very important quality on this track, in that it largely determined how fast you could attack the many chicanes and therefore how quickly you went down the following straights. A night's sleep seemed to have brought the answers Hamilton sought, as his deficit to Alonso was wiped out. On Saturday morning he went fastest of all, just as he did in first and second qualifying. His advantage over Alonso was small, but definitely there. Into the final qualifying run-off and each equally fuelled after the strategy-induced contretemps at Monaco, it was nip-and-tuck between them. Hamilton began his final run first and duly beat his own time to remain on provisional pole, but Alonso – a few seconds behind – was even faster in both the first and second sectors of the lap. It looked like Fernando was going to snatch it at the last moment – until he got on the power fractionally too early at the hairpin and ran out a little wide, getting marbles onto his tyres, preventing him from attacking the final corner as hard as he might have. Lewis was on pole – the first of his F1 career. He now had a pole, a fastest lap, lots of podium finishes, and was sharing the lead of the world championship. All that was missing was a win.

He put that right the following day. He took off in the lead at the start and stayed there, keeping his nerve through five safety car periods. Each time he would build up a lead, it would be taken away from him by the safety car and he'd have to do it all over again. But each time he was faultless. This was not a word you could have ascribed to Alonso's performance. Over-ambitious at the first turn, he ran straight on over the grass trying to prevent Nick Heidfeld's BMW from passing. He would later make four similar errors during the course of the race, and was also unlucky in the timing of the first safety car. These various difficulties limited him to a seventh place finish. In combination with Hamilton's victory, it put Lewis eight points clear at the top of the championship. One of the safety cars was to extricate Hamilton's friend and karting rival Robert Kubica from the remains of his BMW after suffering a huge, barrel-rolling accident on the flat-out approach to the hairpin. A misunderstanding with Jarno Trulli saw the Pole leave the circuit at around 175mph. Remarkably, he sustained only a sprained ankle but it was without doubt the biggest non-injury accident in the sport's history and a fantastic testament to the safety of current F1 cars. Hamilton, who'd seen the wreckage and the extrication crew as he passed each lap under the safety car, was kept informed over the radio, though it was some time before there was any news.

It was an emotional moment as Hamilton took the chequered flag, and there were few in the paddock not genuinely delighted for him. A lot of very big names were suitably impressed. Double world champion Emerson Fittipaldi spent the weekend with McLaren, the team with which he won the second of his titles in 1974. He told Adam Cooper in *Autosport* magazine: 'Every lap he turned the steering wheel in exactly the same place. He made the initial turn in then just drove with the throttle, drifting the car. He was better than anybody else out there … incredible control, amazing. He's in a zone of calm and comfort like a veteran of ten years; his personality, the way he approaches the sport. I'm very impressed.'

Britain's last world champion, Damon Hill, was asked for his views. He replied: 'People should not underestimate what he has achieved in an incredibly short space of time. Yes, he's with a good team, and yes, he's got a good car – but, to be winning Grands Prix and be putting in performances like that race after race, takes something special. He may be young and in his first season, but this guy is the real deal. If you're good enough in this sport, you're old enough – and, boy, is Lewis good enough. He's leading the world championship and winning races, so his confidence will be sky-high. And he's shown he can handle the pressure. We shouldn't get too carried away but we could be looking at the next British world champion.'

Other greats followed. Mario Andretti: 'He's a rare, rare talent. A rookie like this comes around once in a generation. You just try to step back and appreciate it.'

Jackie Stewart: 'I think Lewis is going to rewrite the book. We'll see a new generation of what I call properly prepared, professional racing drivers. I'm talking about fully rounded; [Michael] Schumacher became that, but even Schumacher wasn't as good as he should have been, not in terms of the driving but the total package. I believe Lewis will create the benchmark for a whole generation of drivers. Niki Lauda and James Hunt changed the culture of racing drivers, but they weren't role models. They said nothing, didn't give a damn. Lewis Hamilton can become a role model.'

Ron Dennis was spotted with a tear in his eye, and later said: 'Lewis's race was faultless. He looked after his tyres, pushed when he had to push, all the restarts were perfect, he really didn't put a foot wrong. The preparation for Lewis to enter F1 has been ongoing for ten years. I don't think anyone's entered F1 better prepared. That's not just through my efforts, but also the efforts of his family and his own commitment, passion and dedication. And also sacrifice. He's never hesitated. He's focused on being a great F1 driver, and what we've all experienced today is just the beginning.'

'I'd like to dedicate this to my Dad,' said Lewis in the press conference. 'Without him this wouldn't have been possible. You wouldn't believe the amount of work he's put into my career. He had nothing when he was younger. He lost his mum at a young age and just to see his family be successful is a real pleasure to him.'

Anthony wasn't there to hear that. He was outside, in the paddock, walking on air and taking in the congratulations of people, only some of whom he recognised. 'Good things come to those who wait,' he said. 'My son's just won the Canadian Grand Prix! How silly does that sound? Today was hard work. With the restarts it felt like five Grands Prix, not one. We always tried to do the best at whatever it was we were doing. Getting to F1 was just the next step that came along. We just do it as a job. To be honest this could be GP2, F3 or karting. We apply ourselves in the same way. You should never look ahead and set an outlandish target – you just get egg on your face if you don't achieve it. I haven't noticed any change in him since Australia. Not a bloody thing. He's loving it. A lot of young guys racing karts dream of F1, and he is really enjoying it. He has just been laughing in his helmet and enjoying it – that's what he does. Nothing scares him.'

Round 6 of 17:
Canadian Grand Prix, Circuit Gilles Villeneuve, 17 June

1. **Lewis Hamilton (McLaren-Mercedes)**
2. Nick Heidfeld (BMWSauber)
3. Alexander Wurz (Williams-Toyota)
4. Heikki Kovalainen (Renault)
5. Kimi Raikkonen (Ferrari)
6. Takuma Sato (Super Aguri-Honda)
7. Fernando Alonso (McLaren-Mercedes)
8. Ralf Schumacher (Toyota)

Drivers' World Championship

1.	**Hamilton**	**48 points**
2.	Alonso	40
3.	Massa	33
4.	Raikkonen	27
5.	Heidfeld	26
6.	Fisichella	13
7.	Kubica	12
8.	Wurz	8
	Kovalainen	8
10.	Rosberg	5
11.	Coulthard	4
	Sato	4
	Trulli	4
14.	R. Schumacher	2

Hamilton barely had time to take in the enormity of his achievement in Montreal, or even begin to reply to the 200 texts of congratulations from friends. Four days after the race he had to be in Indianapolis for the beginning of the American Grand Prix weekend. In between times he was in New York for two days for a Mercedes-Benz appearance, then it was off to Washington for Exxon Mobil. His Wednesday evening flight from Washington to Indy was cancelled due to bad weather and he didn't arrive at the track until Thursday morning. His fame arrived ahead of him and local TV stations were mad keen to get a few words. In one interview he pulled out a crucifix from around his neck and spoke of the power of God. Most of the Americans lapped it up.

Then he was straight into the FIA press conference and fielding questions about what Fernando Alonso had recently said to Spanish radio journalists – that he felt Hamilton as a British driver in a British team was being favoured.

'I find it strange he said that,' said Lewis, 'because I feel that ever since he joined, the team have been extremely motivated to push us both toward winning. Ron and the other guys on the team have been working very hard to make sure we have equal opportunity. It's probably always going to be difficult in a business, but obviously I've got a great relationship with all the guys in the team because I've been with them since I was 13. At the end of the day when Fernando came into the team, they were extremely excited and I feel built a very good relationship with him. So I don't see why he would say that. But I guess because he is Spanish and I am English, he might feel that way, but I don't agree with it personally.

'I doubt very much that he was expecting me to do as well as I have. But I don't know whether that's why he would be saying what he's saying. But definitely coming into the team, he's the two-time world champion and he's not really been challenged before. Well, I think he had some challenges in the past but not really had probably someone as close as me and as good a friend off the track probably. So it's a very difficult situation.'

The words were delivered with his characteristic wide-eyed openness, the body language relaxed. What he was saying was hardly dynamite, but by F1 driver standards at an FIA press conference, it was frank. Watching and listening to him, you do not doubt for one moment that he is genuine.

As for the track, it was new to him and just as at Montreal he found unlocking the last couple of tenths from it impossible on Friday, and Alonso had a small but consistent advantage. But come Saturday and he was much more attuned to it, though still lagging slightly behind his teammate. The McLarens were again comfortably faster than the competition. The Ferraris were again struggling, and in addition the team were fielding questions about why their former chief mechanic Nigel Stepney had been suspended from his job at the factory, and whether the rumours of his giving away technical secrets were true.

With the McLarens fuelled equally for the top-ten run-off session at the end of qualifying, Hamilton opted to burn off more of his load than Alonso, shortening the length of his first race stint but ensuring he was lighter when the time came to fit the new tyres and try for pole position. Against the run of play, Hamilton took the pole by a small margin from Alonso, who made a small but crucial error on his best lap.

This pretty much defined the race. Hamilton shot off into the lead, Alonso tried sitting it out with him into the first turn, but Lewis calmly moved left to take up his approach to the right-hander, obliging Alonso to back off to avoid an accident. It was firm but fair. Just as Hamilton had suffered with tyre graining while running in the turbulent slipstream of Alonso at Monaco, so the roles were reversed here and Alonso lost too much ground in the first stint to be able to take advantage of his extra lap up to the stops. Afterwards, Alonso appeared to be slightly faster, and at one stage they ran side-by-side down the pit straight at over 200mph inches apart, but again Hamilton used the advantage of his line to move across and force Alonso to cede on the approach to the corner. A lap later and Alonso swerved sharply over to the McLaren pits and angrily waved his fist. According to team insiders, he was at this stage of the race screaming on the radio that he was faster and that the team should tell Hamilton to move aside. When they declined to do so, he made the gesture.

Hamilton reeled off the remaining laps and duly took his second Grand Prix victory in a week, extending his lead in the championship to ten points. It was a great Father's Day present to Anthony, an even greater present to himself. In the space of a week he'd arrived at two circuits completely unknown to him, set pole at them both, and won the race at them both, beating a double world champion with prior experience of them in the same car. By any standards this was a stunning achievement.

Alonso was asked afterwards if he thought Hamilton's moves were fair, and was giving a non-committal answer when Hamilton interrupted and made his position very clear: 'May I just say in the rules you're only allowed to make one move down the straight, and going into the corner you're allowed to move back to your position or at least move back again to try and get yourself around the corner.' He knew what he'd just achieved and, polite as always, made it clear he was in no mood to hear even the slightest detraction.

Round 7 of 17:
USA Grand Prix, Indianapolis, 17 June

1. **Lewis Hamilton (McLaren-Mercedes)**
2. Fernando Alonso (McLaren-Mercedes)
3. Felipe Massa (Ferrari)
4. Kimi Raikkonen (Ferrari)
5. Heikki Kovalainen (Renault)
6. Jarno Trulli (Toyota)
7. Mark Webber (Red Bull-Renault)
8. Sebastian Vettel (BMWSauber)

Drivers' World Championship

1.	**Hamilton**	**58**
2.	Alonso	48
3.	Massa	39
4.	Raikkonen	32
5.	Heidfeld	26
6.	Fisichella	13
7.	Kubica	12
	Kovalainen	12
9.	Wurz	8
10.	Trulli	7
11.	Rosberg	5
12.	Coulthard	4
	Sato	4
14.	Webber	2
	R. Schumacher	2

CHAPTER FIFTEEN

Espionage and Rap Stars

By the terms of his contract, Lewis Hamilton's double victories in North America and the points they netted were believed to have taken him over £1 million in earnings from the team. It may sound a lot, but in the league of F1 driver earnings it was relatively modest. His team-mate Alonso, as a double world champion, was on roughly ten times that amount. Now that Hamilton had shown he was capable of Alonso-matching performances, it was time to renegotiate. Anthony Hamilton and Ron Dennis were now in that process – though on the eve of the French Grand Prix were a long way from any agreement.

While Dad looked after business off-track, Lewis was attending to it around the sweeps of Magny Cours for the French Grand Prix meeting. After their disappointing North American form, Ferrari had hit back with a raft of aerodynamic upgrades here, and definitely seemed to have the edge in speed over the McLaren-Mercedes. Lewis and Fernando Alonso looked fairly evenly matched through the first two qualifying sessions, but starting the third session Alonso suffered a gearbox failure, one that couldn't be repaired in time to get him back onto the track. This left him down in tenth on the grid, effectively scuppering any chances he had of fighting for the win. Hamilton meanwhile fought Felipe Massa's Ferrari for pole, but lost out by a few hundredths of a second and would line up second. However, he had been able to compete with the Ferrari only by dint of a much lighter fuel load, and during the race it was all he could do to keep the two red cars vaguely in sight. He was a distant third, keeping intact his record of finishing every Grand Prix so far on the podium, but after the consecutive victories it was something of a comedown. Kimi Raikkonen won from Massa, while Alonso could get only as far as seventh from his compromised grid slot. The result increased Hamilton's championship lead to 14 points.

Round 8 of 17:
French Grand Prix, Magny Cours, 1 July

1. Kimi Raikkonen (Ferrari)
2. Felipe Massa (Ferrari)
3. **Lewis Hamilton (McLaren-Mercedes)**
4. Robert Kubica (BMWSauber)
5. Nick Heidfeld (BMWSauber)
6. Giancarlo Fisichella (Renault)
7. Fernando Alonso (McLaren-Mercedes)
8. Jenson Button (Honda)

Drivers' World Championship

1.	**Hamilton**	**64**
2.	Alonso	50
3.	Massa	47
4.	Raikkonen	42
5.	Heidfeld	30
6.	Kubica	17
7.	Fisichella	16
8.	Kovalainen	12
9.	Wurz	8
10.	Trulli	7
11.	Rosberg	5
12.	Coulthard	4
	Sato	4
14.	Webber	2
	R. Schumacher	2
16.	Button	1
	Vettel	1

It was between the French and British Grands Prix that McLaren's season took a serious turn for the worse. Investigators hired by Ferrari raided the home of McLaren's chief designer Mike Coughlan and found CDs containing what was essentially an operating manual for the Ferrari F2007. Coughlan claimed he'd got the original paper document from Ferrari's Nigel Stepney in a continuation of the communication they had been having since the beginning of the year. On Coughlan's behalf, his wife had the documents transferred to disk at a local copying shop. The shop's owner was suspicious of Ferrari-headed documents being copied and got in touch with Ferrari, who then initiated the investigation. As the news broke, Stepney and Coughlan were each suspended from their teams.

Coughlan and Stepney were in deep trouble – but so too was McLaren. Ferrari naturally wanted to know to what extent the information in the documents had leaked into McLaren. Ron Dennis was adamant that none of it had reached the team, that it was a case of two disaffected employees colluding for their own ends. Ferrari were naturally dubious about that, and as well as initiating their civil action, also advised the sport's governing body, the FIA, of their concerns. The FIA felt there was a serious case to be answered by the team in terms of Article 151C of the sporting code (which concerns acting in a fraudulent way and bringing the sport into disrepute), and convened an extraordinary meeting of the World Motor Sport Council to be held on 26 July, the week after the European Grand Prix in Germany. Among the penalties available to the governing body if it judged McLaren to be in breach of the sporting code was disqualification from the championship and a ban from competing in future. The entire company was potentially at stake, not to mention the championship prospects of its drivers, Hamilton and Alonso.

Although easier said than done, Lewis tried simply to ignore the furore surrounding the team as he made his first appearance as an F1 driver at his home race.

On the same Thursday that the espionage story broke, he was helicoptered to Milton Keynes for a promotional event for McLaren sponsor Vodafone. This involved a demonstration drive of a kart and meeting and watching in action some of the young kartists trying to follow in his footsteps in the British Racing Drivers' Club 'Star of Tomorrow' series.

Although a little rusty on his karting technique, he was soon getting himself back in the groove. His impression on some of the kids present was akin to Jesus walking among his disciples. He chatted extensively with them and gave a few words of advice to the group afterwards.

'I was always gaining places in the races,' he said, 'especially at the beginning. No matter what position you start in, you have to attack and try to take as many places as you can. But it's not all about winning it at the first corner. It's about taking your time, and pacing yourself throughout the race, knowing you have 10 or 15 laps, knowing that you have got to take two people on that lap, two people again on another lap, or maybe three or whatever on the last lap. Going into a race and having a strategy is the key to winning. You have to keep on enjoying it, but there's a lot to it. You have to make sure, with your opportunity, to extract the most out of it. Even when you have a bad kart and you can't win, get the points or finish as high up as you can, and don't be disappointed with it. Come away from it, and try to come back stronger.' The kids hung onto his every word before then scrambling for autographs.

And with that he was away, helicoptered back to his rarefied existence, in this case the F1 paddock at Silverstone, back to the fantasy they all dream of but hardly any achieve. A fantasy that includes having your music heroes as friends you can dine with. A big rap fan, Hamilton had already met Pharrell Williams – who showed up to support him at the Canadian Grand Prix – and P Diddy. He'd also met singer Natasha Bedingfield and had been photographed with her – 'I hardly know her,' he said. 'All I did was give her a hand to help her out of the car. I was just being a gentleman. Honest!'

It didn't stop the newspapers running stories about a possible romance, especially now that he was no longer together with girlfriend of four years, Jodia Ma, the two having agreed to be merely friends. Lewis was reported as having bombarded Bedingfield with calls, asking for a date – to no avail. 'Unfortunately, she has a boyfriend,' said Lewis. 'Otherwise ...'

He'd been invited to attend the Prince's Trust Concert at which Bedingfield was performing, but had declined on account of it being on the evening of the French Grand Prix. 'The next day I was playing golf at Woking,' he recalled, 'and I got a call saying P Diddy had invited me to a special meal that night. I wanted to finish the last nine holes so I seriously considered not going. But I'm so glad I did. They waited for me to arrive and then sat me down next to P Diddy himself! Then he, Pharrell, Natasha and me went on to a house party afterwards.

'The weird thing was, when we got there, there were all these celebrities – and yet I seemed to be the main attraction. I expected to be the big nobody, the guy they didn't know all that much about and, perhaps, hadn't even seen race. But people were coming up and asking me for my number – and asking if I wanted theirs. How cool was that! It was a very new and very strange experience. But I have to admit I quite enjoyed it.'

'Next day I was driving down the road and had P Diddy on my iPod. And I was thinking, "I've got his telephone number. He's my friend – ridiculous."'

Maybe he'd had his head turned. He won't have been the first. He was a fit, good-looking 22-year-old leading the world championship. Why wouldn't he be enjoying some of the lifestyle that can come with that? He needed to be careful, though. As he was doubtless aware, the music industry is far more indulgent of wild lifestyles than sport, and then there was his wholesome image to consider. Both Anthony and Lewis are keen for him to be a role model, for their own reasons as well as commercial ones. But this was no longer 1999, he no longer needed a chaperone, and Anthony was no longer waiting to see he got back before curfew.

Throughout the British Grand Prix weekend, Hamilton was clearly very aware of the support he had from the crowd and was evidently keen to reciprocate. He spent way longer than is normal for any driver signing autographs and waving to the fans in the grandstand. He seemed to genuinely enjoy it. 'I don't know about other drivers,' he said. 'I don't know if it's part of my personality – but I like to make people happy and when I'm out there and I sign extra autographs, to see the amount of support you have, to see the flags waving, and when I drive round, I do see the Hamilton flags and all that. So I get a big buzz from that and a lot of energy, so I'm finding this weekend quite a positive.

'There has not been that many negative comments made, so I have been able to keep all this positive energy and it's definitely comforting to hear such nice things. But having my world turned upside-down is … I'm very lucky I have very good balance and a sense of awareness so even though it's turned upside-down I can still get on with my life. But it's been really tough, obviously, walking on the streets and people coming up to you. It is strange. Taken from my past experience when I used to go up to Formula One drivers, I wanted to be slightly different. I wanted for people to be able to approach me and to try and give them as much time as possible. That's what some Formula One drivers didn't do when I was younger.'

Although he was happy to devote as much time as possible to the fans, he did admit that trying to dovetail all the demands of his off-track time was tough. 'That's definitely been one of the toughest challenges – trying to manage your time and maximise the time you have off. I haven't had much time off. Obviously the marketing department work extremely hard to make sure we don't have too many days, but especially here, coming after a race in Magny-Cours, we didn't get many days off and we were straight back into appearances and everything. So to be able to divide out your energy, and it's mostly mental energy that you are losing, to try not to empty that bottle that you need the whole weekend and to keep everyone happy, keep a smile on and make sure you say the right things is really, really tough. It is probably one of the trickiest parts of the job.'

Out on the track the following day, it was a special moment as he drove down the pitlane and saw the huge response of the fans, the waved banners, the union jacks. Another first, another very special moment to try to imprint on his memory. But there were becoming so many of them, it was hard to keep up.

The McLaren was not in its element around the high-speed bends of the track. This was Ferrari territory. Only around the tight infield at the end of the lap was the McLaren better than its rival. Overall, the red car seemed just that little bit faster throughout the weekend. Furthermore, Lewis didn't seem to be getting the best out of his car. Alonso, with a slightly different rear suspension set-up, had a consistent edge throughout the weekend and seemed the McLaren driver most likely to take the challenge to the Ferraris. This was Hamilton's least competitive performance of the season to date, a particular disappointment given that it was his home event.

Coming into qualifying, however, McLaren had a plan. Realising he was unlikely to be able to fight with Alonso and the two Ferraris for the victory, they were planning to try for the consolation of pole position by fuelling him light. It would at least give the crowd something to cheer. Alonso was not at all happy with this. He was close to the pace of the Ferraris and felt that if they acted as a team strategically – like a team that was configured around him, as he felt he had been promised prior to joining – they could beat them. To do this, it would be better to fuel them both light, in which case Alonso would likely take pole, with Hamilton alongside him. Alonso could then sprint away and Hamilton could be used to slow the Ferraris down, giving Alonso the chance of building up a big enough gap to overcome his early fuel stop compared to the Ferraris. But McLaren overruled him. He would be put onto an optimum fuel strategy – meaning he was unlikely to get pole – and Lewis would be fuelled light. It was just one more Alonso gripe against the team in a long list of them.

It was all very well running a lighter and therefore theoretically faster car, but Hamilton still had to deliver the lap when it counted. On his first new-tyre run, he was only fourth fastest despite his weight advantage. He was in trouble. 'I just struggled to get the car balanced all week-end,' he would later say. 'I think I made a wrong decision on set-up coming into qualifying. The car just never felt quite beneath me.' In particular he was struggling through Copse corner, the near-flat-in-seventh first turn taken at over 185mph. Some drivers were claiming to be able to take it without a lift of the throttle. But Lewis never did.

As the last of the top four runners to go out on his final

set of new tyres, he had it all to do in front of an expectant crowd. It was time to dig deep. Just as he was beginning his lap, Kimi Raikkonen was finishing his, and now the Ferrari was on a provisional pole position, with Alonso second and Felipe Massa's Ferrari third. All except Lewis had now completed their runs. This time he was determined to try Copse flat. It was all-or-nothing. So he screamed down the pit straight to begin his lap with only that thought in his mind. The corner entry rushed up to him, he turned the wheel, kept his right foot mashed to the bulkhead. The split-second messages he got from the car were of red alert – it wasn't going to go through flat. He momentarily lifted, but not for as long as previously: he'd got through there almost flat. He checked the speed display on his steering wheel – it was showing a higher exit speed than previously. Good, pole might still be possible. He attacked through the rest of the lap and in the middle sector, where the deceleration and acceleration zones of Stowe, Club and Abbey corners pay back a lighter weight, he was fastest of all. Checking the sector time as he exited the flat-out Bridge corner, he could see he was on course for pole. All he had to do now was not mess up through the tight twists and turns of the complex.

Outside, the commentator was keeping the 100,000-plus crowd informed of their hero's progress. They had no way of knowing he was on a light fuel strategy and therefore compromised for the race. All they knew was that he seemed set to take pole away in a dramatic last-moment turn-around. He crossed the line 0.102s faster than Raikkonen – and the whole place erupted. Pole position at his home Grand Prix in front of the adoring crowd! Yet another piece of folklore that in years to come will become part of the sport's fabric.

It was a very special sporting moment, even if in reality it meant little. Weight-corrected, he was still the slowest of the four McLaren/Ferrari drivers, still struggling for outright pace, something that would be revealed in the race the following day. But for now it was a moment to savour: 'I was screaming in the car,' he said. 'I could hear the crowd even above the engine. I don't know if they could hear me or not, but I've just about lost my voice.'

He converted his pole into the lead of the race as the lights went out, but Raikkonen was shadowing his every move, despite the Ferrari being fuelled heavier. 'I kept trying to open up a gap,' Lewis explained, 'but Kimi was extremely fast and was able to stay right with me.' On one occasion the Ferrari driver thought he saw a gap on the inside of the McLaren going into Brooklands corner, and tried putting his car into it, but Hamilton was having none of it and boldly cut across the Ferrari's bows. The crowd loved it, but the reality – as both drivers suspected – was that the lead was going to change at the pit stops. Hamilton made his stop at the end of the 16th lap, four earlier than Alonso, two earlier than Raikkonen. Both rivals were therefore able to continue running light after Hamilton had rejoined refuelled and heavy – and both therefore were able to build up the necessary gap to enable them to come out of their stops ahead of him. Raikkonen duly went on to win, with Alonso doing well to keep him under pressure. A difficult middle stint with tyre graining saw Hamilton fall well off their pace – and although he finished third, he was over half a minute behind them at the end. Had not Felipe Massa's Ferrari been forced to start from the pitlane after stalling on the grid, then he too would likely have beaten Hamilton and thereby spoilt his record of finishing on the podium for every race.

It was by far the least competitive Hamilton performance of the year. Alonso was putting him under pressure, and afterwards made a barely disguised criticism of the team for not configuring the combined strategy of both cars around him. 'We need a bit more consistency,' he said, 'and a better approach to the races from the team. Then it will be better.' Had they been prepared to use Hamilton as his foil against the Ferraris, in other words, this would have been a winnable race despite the Ferrari's slight pace advantage.

For Hamilton, this was a concerning time. His form was tailing off at a crucial time, amid a blur of rap stars, espionage trials, salary negotiations and life decisions.

Round 9 of 17:
British Grand Prix, Silverstone, 8 July

1. Kimi Raikkonen (Ferrari)
2. Fernando Alonso (McLaren-Mercedes)
3. **Lewis Hamilton (McLaren-Mercedes)**
4. Robert Kubica (BMWSauber)
5. Felipe Massa (Ferrari)
6. Nick Heidfeld (BMWSauber)
7. Heikki Kovalainen (Renault)
8. Giancarlo Fisichella (Renault)

Drivers' World Championship

1.	**Hamilton**	**70 points**
2.	Alonso	58
3.	Raikkonen	52

4.	Massa	51
5.	Heidfeld	33
6.	Kubica	22
7.	Fisichella	17
8.	Kovalainen	14
9.	Wurz	8
10.	Trulli	7
11.	Rosberg	5
12.	Coulthard	4
	Sato	4
14.	Webber	2
	R. Schumacher	2
16.	Button	1
	Vettel	1

CHAPTER SIXTEEN

In the Blink of an Eye

A second-rate movie script about a rookie F1 driver fighting for the world championship would not be complete without a scene of him on a stretcher, oxygen mask strapped to his face, being carried from the wreckage of his car. This scene duly played out during qualifying for the European Grand Prix at the German Nürburgring track. A worried loved one rushes to his bedside, in this case former girlfriend Jodia Ma. The hero then checks out and bravely races the following day.

With the FIA's World Council hearing regarding the espionage case coming up the following Thursday, it was difficult for McLaren to focus on the race weekend. Hamilton, Alonso and the team arrived fresh from a test at Spa the previous week, in preparation for the Belgian Grand Prix there later in the year. In the meantime, McLaren's lawyers were preparing their submission for Thursday, the team desperate to prove their innocence, knowing the frightening potential prospects if they didn't. Hamilton issued a statement outlining his full support for the team – as did Mika Hakkinen, who won his two world titles with McLaren. Hamilton said: 'Although I've only been with the team for a year I have known Ron for nine years now and this [fraudulent conduct] is something that Ron would never do. That's why I have such great belief in the team. I do feel that McLaren is one of the most honest teams out there. There are always teams trying to bend the rules in some way but I truly believe we are the most honest.' From Fernando Alonso there was no such statement of support.

The practice sessions went well enough, with Hamilton fastest on Friday morning, second to Raikkonen in the afternoon and also on Saturday morning. Alonso appeared to have a small edge in the first two qualifying sessions, but all was to play for as they prepared to do their first grid-deciding new-tyre runs in the final session. An out-lap to warm the tyres, then full on it. He'd just gone fastest of all in the first sector and was approaching the flat-out left-right flick of the Schumacher Esses at 160mph. As he eased the steering wheel left there was no response from the car. Lewis later said it didn't register that there was a problem, and his initial reaction was to treat it as if it were just understeer and apply a little more lock. But already there was tyre smoke from the right-front wheel. The wheel had been incorrectly torqued due to a faulty wheel gun. As the wheel shifted on its stub axle, the tyre came into contact with a carbon-fibre body part that cut the tyre, collapsing the carcass, and the suspension then failed. The car flew over the kerb, barely touching the gravel trap before embedding itself hard in the tyre barriers. He didn't lose consciousness, but was heavily winded and in some pain from his legs. The session was red-flagged as the rescue crew attended to him. He climbed out of the car unaided, but fell as he tried to stand. Great care was taken with his removal in case of spinal injuries. He was eventually laid out on a stretcher and gave the crowd a wave of reassurance as he was being loaded into the waiting ambulance. He was taken to the circuit medical centre.

Alonso had been on an out-lap and now returned to the pits. His wheel had been torqued with the same gun as Lewis's. It was checked – and found also to be insufficiently tightened.

After a check-up at the medical centre, Hamilton was flown to the Koblenz Bundeswehr Hospital for a precautionary CT scan. Former girlfriend Jodia turned up at his bedside, having made a flight from London. He was given the all-clear later that night and would race the following day. But he would be starting back in tenth, with Raikkonen's Ferrari on pole from Alonso and Massa.

The formation lap began with a huge black cloud about to drop its load at the southern tip of the circuit, and only the lowly Spyker team had the foresight to bring one of their cars in for a change to wet weather tyres as the race got under way. Hamilton took off like a rocket from his compromised grid position, passing four cars before the first corner. Ahead of him through the first two turns were the scrapping BMWs of Robert Kubica and Nick Heidfeld. The team-mates touched, sending Kubica spinning into Hamilton's path. Lewis tried to go around the back, but his left-rear tyre caught the errant car and punctured, leaving him to limp back to the pits for a replacement. Before the lap was out, the heavens opened and almost everyone came in for wet weather tyres. Hamilton rejoined well down on account of how slowly he'd had to drive back. Incredibly, the Spyker of F1 debutant Marcus Winkelhock was now leading the race, thanks to his team having put him on wet weather tyres before the race had started.

Between the end of the first and second laps, a lake formed in the braking zone to turn 1 – and car after car aquaplaned on it and into the gravel trap, including Hamilton's. The race was then suspended to await more favourable conditions. Although all the other cars that had ended in the gravel were now out of the race, Hamilton had kept his engine running throughout, and upon being craned out and put back on the track, he was able to simply select a gear and drive to the reformed grid! With the worst of the storm over, the race restarted, with Lewis a lap down in 17th place. A premature gamble to change to dry weather tyres delayed him even further, and it was all he could do, after an incident-packed afternoon, to finish ninth. Remarkably, it was the first time in his ten-race F1 career that he had not finished on the podium. Even worse news, as far as his championship aspirations were concerned, was that Alonso won after an inspired battle with Massa and thus brought himself within two points of Hamilton's championship lead.

Behind the podium, Dennis congratulated his driver and Alonso did not even acknowledge his presence. Alonso was also involved in an angry exchange with Massa about the wheel-rubbing that occurred as Fernando passed the Ferrari. There was some levity when the dignitary chosen to present the constructor's trophy to Dennis turned out to be Ferrari's Michael Schumacher, a task that Michael appeared to find rather awkward.

McLaren's focus then switched fully to Thursday's FIA hearing over the espionage allegations. McLaren's personnel and its lawyers faced a six-hour trial in which they tried to convince the council that Coughlan had acted in his own interests in receiving Ferrari information from Stepney and that none of the knowledge he gained was used by the team. The council found that the team had contravened the relevant article of the sporting code in bringing the sport into disrepute, but as there was no proof that the Ferrari information had leaked into the organisation, there would be no punishment.

Ferrari were incensed at the decision, saying that it 'legitimises dishonest behaviour in Formula 1 and sets a very serious precedent,' and that it was 'highly prejudicial to the credibility of the sport'. Ferrari President Luca di Montezemelo promised that the matter was far from over. Within a few days came confirmation that Ferrari were appealing the judgement, and a court of appeal hearing was duly set for 13 September. Hamilton's title chances could have yet gone up in a cloud of courtroom acrimony and his wondrous on-track performances could count for nothing.

Round 10 of 17:
European Grand Prix, Nürburgring, 22 July

1. Fernando Alonso (McLaren-Mercedes)
2. Felipe Massa (Ferrari)
3. Mark Webber (Red Bull-Renault)
4. Alexander Wurz (Williams-Toyota)
5. David Coulthard (Red Bull-Renault)
6. Nick Heidfeld (BMWSauber)
7. Robert Kubica (BMWSauber)
8. Heikki Kovalainen (Renault)

Drivers' World Championship

1.	**Hamilton**	**70 points**
2.	Alonso	68
3.	Massa	59
4.	Raikkonen	52
5.	Heidfeld	36
6.	Kubica	24
7.	Fisichella	17
8.	Kovalainen	15
9.	Wurz	13
10.	Webber	8
	Coulthard	8
12.	Trulli	7
13.	Rosberg	5
14.	Sato	4
15.	R. Schumacher	2
16.	Button	1
	Vettel	1

CHAPTER SEVENTEEN

'Pitlanegate' –
The Making of a Man

Fernando Alonso's grievances with McLaren had made the team a hostile place. Lewis Hamilton's relentless pace had triggered these grievances. In a team that was doing its utmost to provide equality for its drivers, the competitive paranoia of any driver with a very fast team-mate meant that both at different times felt the other had been favoured. In the midst of all this was the spectre of the ongoing espionage case, and as if that were not enough for the McLaren management to deal with, both drivers were trying to negotiate new terms for their future contracts. These factors came to a head in spectacular fashion in the final qualifying session at the Hungaroring.

Lewis flew into Budapest on Wednesday, having spent the time since the last race in Finland with his trainer. 'I feel 100 per cent better than I did,' he reported at a Thursday appearance for Vodafone in the centre of the city. He'd felt poorly post-Germany, possibly as an after-effect of the accident, but was now raring to go on a track at which he'd driven such a sensational GP2 race the year before. Just like in the previous two races, he was trying to ignore the ongoing espionage case against the team and was concentrating on the car and track.

The practices suggested that tyre usage was going to be absolutely key to the weekend. Bridgestone had brought the two softest tyres in their range – designated super-soft and soft. On Friday no one could get the super-softs to work. They would grain spectacularly even before a single lap was completed. But with the more rubbered-in surface of Saturday, some drivers were finding they could make them last long enough to do a very fast lap. Hamilton could do this. Alonso could not. The champion's very different driving style and the extra load he put on the front of the car made the difference. Going into qualifying, Alonso was resigned to the fact that he was going to have to do his time on the harder tyre, while Hamilton was confident he could make the faster, softer tyre work. As such, Hamilton was much the favourite for pole position, as the Ferraris lacked the one-lap pace of the McLarens, even though they were comparably fast over a multi-lap run.

Hamilton duly went faster than his team-mate in Q1 and Q2. Now for the critical grid-deciding Q3. To understand what unfolded next requires an explanation of the fuel-burn phase of the complex qualifying procedure. Before the session starts, the cars are fuelled with as much as is needed not only for qualifying but also the first stint of the race. In the early laps of Q3 the cars burn fuel off to make them as light as possible when they fit their new tyres and attempt their fast laps. Between qualifying and race, each car is then allowed to replenish according to how many laps they have run in the session – at a predetermined weight per lap.

Complex enough in theory, it becomes more so in operation. Because when you are running your fuel-burn laps and not going for a fast time, you can use less fuel than you will be credited for – giving you a longer, more advantageous, first stint of the race. So you don't need to fuel quite as heavily to get your required stint as would be suggested by the fuel credit figure. This of course means you can be lighter for qualifying.

McLaren, in its quest to give absolute equality to both drivers, would calculate the likely fuel consumption in advance, and because it habitually got its cars out onto the track ahead of all the others – on account of having the ability to idle at the end of the pitlane for a long time without overheating – would allocate which driver would run at the front and set a fast pace in the fuel-burn laps and which would run behind at a slower pace and use less fuel. The difference in pace was to ensure there was a gap of around 12s between the cars when they came in to have their new tyres fitted, so the second car could be serviced without queuing or rushing the crew.

On this occasion, Alonso was scheduled to be the one running at the front and Hamilton was supposed to run 2–3s per lap slower behind for six laps. Their respective fuel loads accounted for the big difference in fuel consumption between them that would result. As the driver instructed to set a faster pace, Alonso had extra fuel to compensate, so that when they came to fit their new tyres and go for a time, they would have their nominal correct loads. The plan was to run Hamilton slightly longer to the first stops, and as such he was supposed to be slightly heavier than Alonso by the time they had each done their fuel-burn laps. But taking into account that he would be running the fuel-burn laps more economically, he would begin the session with less of a weight disadvantage than he would have when they each came to put on their new tyres. Confusing, but essential knowledge in understanding what unfolded next.

Against the plan, it was Hamilton who got down to the end of the pitlane first. What's more, he then refused to move aside and swap positions when out on the track. Now fuelled lighter and running in front, he had effectively tricked himself an advantage. He could run a hard pace in the fuel burn *and* have a lighter fuel load, thereby guaranteeing that he would be significantly lighter than planned when the time came to qualify. It would compromise his race strategy, but the pole position it was likely to get him would probably be more advantageous than an extra lap up to the pit stops – especially given that he was still running longer to them than Alonso. This way, he could get pole *and* have a better race strategy, aided by the fact that he could make the faster soft tyres work in qualifying and Alonso could not.

Several times the team asked him to move aside for Alonso, but he declined to do so. Alonso, realising immediately he'd been tricked and was not going to be able to get pole, went into fuel-saving mode, trying to minimise his fuel burn to give him a chance of retaliation by giving himself more laps to the first stop.

Alonso was brought in a lap short of his original fuel-burn allocation and fitted with his new tyres, this putting him ahead of Hamilton in the pits. There was a delay as Alonso discussed his tyre pressures with his engineer, thus bringing Hamilton quite close behind. They each completed their first runs, with Hamilton setting a provisional pole. They then returned for the final set of new tyres. Alonso was still in the pits as Hamilton arrived there. Alonso was held by the team for 20 seconds as they calculated where the gap in the traffic would be, to ensure that no other cars could be coming out of the pits as he was on his flying lap. The lollipop man holding the car then lifted his stick and Alonso was free to go. But he did not go. Realising a perfect opportunity for revenge on Hamilton had fallen into his lap, he stayed where he was for a further 10 seconds, despite the team repeatedly telling him to go. He left with just enough time to get to the start/finish line to begin his lap before the session ended. But it was too late for Hamilton. Alonso duly set pole position on his lap and Hamilton was denied the opportunity to respond.

Hamilton assumed at this moment that the team had deliberately denied him his new-tyre run by instructing Alonso to remain stationary – as punishment for his earlier refusal to move aside during the fuel-burn laps. He thought it was the team, and not Alonso, who had thwarted him. So as he crossed the start/finish line out of time, he relayed his displeasure to them over the radio. Ron Dennis returned with an equally angry response. The exchange was reported in the media as:

HAMILTON: 'Don't you ever **cking do that to me again.'
DENNIS: 'Don't you **cking speak to me like that.'
HAMILTON: 'Swivel.'

The Hamiltons were adamant that Lewis had not sworn during the exchange and insisted afterwards that McLaren issue a statement to that effect. This came the following week. The Hamiltons insisted that Lewis had actually begun the exchange with a sarcastic comment of 'Very funny', and that he had not uttered the word 'swivel'. Without access to the tapes of the radio exchange it's impossible to know the reality. What is certain is that both parties were furious.

Dennis threw down his headphones and marched off towards the collecting area where the drivers would arrive. On the way he grabbed Alonso's personal trainer, Fabrizio Borra, and took him with him. There was speculation that the trainer had been counting Alonso down as he sat in the pits, though this is unlikely. It is more feasible that Alonso simply used the scroll menu on his steering wheel to see a countdown of the end of the session. 'I took him with me,' explained Dennis later, 'because I thought there was a likelihood the drivers would both be in an emotional state and I wanted him, as a Spanish-speaker, to keep Fernando cool while I did the same with Lewis.'

Dennis could be seen talking animatedly with both drivers as they went into the weigh-in garage. Hamilton appeared to respond angrily while Alonso simply blanked his team boss as if he wasn't there – just as on the Nürburgring podium.

In the press conference afterwards, the two drivers sat next to each other and proceeded to give completely different accounts of why Alonso delayed Hamilton in the pits. At this time, Hamilton's triggering of the situation by his refusal to allow Alonso into his agreed position during the fuel burn was not known. They each tried not to lie while at the same time not divulging what had happened. At this time, Hamilton was still under the impression that his delay had been engineered by the team, not Alonso, and said he was looking forward to speaking with them. 'As Fernando said, he was told to stop and wait. His wheels were on, his blankets were off and he was told to wait. I imagine that I probably lost half-a-minute, I would say, from my in-lap coming in to waiting behind Fernando. At least 30 seconds, so it definite-

ly needs a good explanation.' He would later get that explanation – that only 20 seconds were from the team. The other
10 seconds – the critical delay that lost Hamilton the chance
of the lap – were purely of Alonso's making.

At one point, someone asked Alonso why he had sat so
long in the pits. Before he could answer, Hamilton said:
'Your guess is as good as mine', then apologised for answering the other guy's question. Alonso simply advised the
questioner he should ask the team. He would do so – along
with pretty much every other journalist – an hour later at the
team's own press conference.

In between times, Anthony Hamilton visited the race
stewards. Livid at Alonso's obstruction, he enquired what the
regulations were concerning protesting at being impeded
by another competitor when that other competitor was on
the same team. He was told that an enquiry into the matter
was ongoing.

Meanwhile, the chief steward, Tony Scott-Andrews, was
surprised on returning to his room in race control to hear a
shuffling behind the sofa. He asked who was there and was
first amazed then amused to find that it was none other than
Lewis Hamilton, hiding in order to avoid his team boss!
Despite him saying he was looking forward to getting an
explanation from his team of what had happened, he was
also – in the cold light of day, away from the adrenaline zone
of the cockpit – somewhat nervous of facing Dennis about
having triggered the whole thing!

The two had spoken by the time of the team's press
conference. Hamilton had been apprised of Alonso's part in
the delay and Dennis had registered his 'disappointment'
with Hamilton's behaviour in the fuel burn. Hamilton later
explained: 'I came back, everything was quiet, we didn't

really speak too much. I went back to my engineers, we did the same job as always, a debrief. Then we had a sit-down with Martin Whitmarsh, Fernando and his mechanic and me and my mechanic, and we went through what the programme was and they asked me why I didn't do the part that they wanted me to. And so I explained to them. I said: "I made a mistake, I apologise, it won't happen again. But it has happened, let's forget about it and move on. We are both on the front row so we can still smile." And I thought that because of the argument I had with Ron over the radio, he was obviously angry, I thought that perhaps he was just teaching me a lesson, so I just took it on the chin. That is why when I went to the press conference I said I wouldn't have thought Fernando would do something like that, but I have reasons to believe otherwise now.

'I think it is always difficult. I have had it with every team I have been in. When you have the two most competitive people in the team, possibly the two most competitive people around, both wanting to win, it puts the team under immense pressure. It is just extremely hard for everyone to play fair and to make it easy. That's why sometimes it appears that one driver is favoured over the other. That's why sometimes I feel he is favoured and vice versa.'

In an attempt to smooth over the incidents and prevent the discontent within the team from spreading, Dennis came up with a cover-story for the press gathering that was part-true but not the whole truth. He first of all apologised for Hamilton's absence, saying that Lewis was too 'hot' (in the angry sense of the word) to take part. Alonso sat to his side while Dennis tried to explain what had happened. It was only at this point that the world outside the team discovered Hamilton's fuel-burn stunt. Dennis used Hamilton's actions to explain that it brought the whole choreography out of sequence and resulted in Hamilton's own disadvantage. When questioned about the delay in the pitlane at the second tyre stop, Alonso claimed he was being counted down by the team and that he had no knowledge that Hamilton was queued behind him. Dennis did not contradict this. It later emerged that in fact Alonso was being told to go as soon as the lollipop was lifted, but chose to remain stationary for the critical extra 10s. Dennis was publicly trying to protect Alonso, apparently even to the extent of muddying the waters a little. It was a dangerous line to tread, given that his reputation for honesty was central to his defence in the forthcoming appeal court hearing about the espionage case.

Part-way through the conference, Dennis had to leave on account of having been called to race control by the stewards investigating the incident. This created an extraordinary situation whereby Alonso was left to be interrogated by the press without the 'protection' of Dennis. It was made even more extraordinary a few minutes later when Hamilton suddenly appeared and sat in front of his allocated microphone! He apologised for his lateness, claiming he'd been watching the start of the GP2 race and had lost track of time. Now, as questions were fired at both drivers, they gave at times absolutely opposing explanations. They couldn't both be true! Hamilton explained that in all his time in the team he had never been told to use a radio countdown as the cue to leave the pits, that always it was the lollipop man. He also said he regretted his own actions in going against team instructions during the burn-off phase. The questions were coming thick and fast, Alonso getting visibly irritated, when Dennis's deputy Martin Whitmarsh stepped in and called a halt to the conference.

There had been a clear conflict between the team's interests and Hamilton's. Lewis's actions in refusing to move aside in the fuel burn had triggered the problem in the first place. Informally protesting at Alonso's retaliation had certainly not helped the team, in that they were now under investigation for the incident. There have since been conspiracy theories that the fuel-burn non-compliance was engineered by the Hamiltons beforehand, as a mechanism to show that Lewis was not prepared simply to be an instrument of the team, that he was going to fight his corner, that the team could forget any ideas about acceding to Alonso's continued demands for team leadership.

Regardless of the truth or otherwise of this theory, there was always going to be an awkward crossover point for Hamilton driving for Ron Dennis, the man who had largely made his career. He could not forever remain the grateful protégé; he did at some point need to show he was prepared to fight his own corner. He'd done as much in the aftermath of Monaco. Now he'd initiated a situation where he was underlining that willingness to put aside any question of gratitude in order to fight his biggest rival for the world championship. Whether it was with his father's help or not, Lewis Hamilton had followed through on his sensational performances and showed he was prepared to use the power they brought into how he conducted his relationship with the team – even if he was a little nervous of the fallout! The balance of power had definitely swung some way towards him. And that will doubtless have had a bearing on their negotiating position. As any of those karting rivals will tell you, don't ever under-estimate the intensity of ambition of the Hamiltons.

The stewards heard evidence from the team, listened to

radio transcripts, asked for explanations from Dennis and others. During the course of this, Alonso's explanation of having been counted down by the team was dismissed, unsupported by the evidence. The stewards then deliberated long into the night about what action to take. Eventually they found that Alonso had been guilty of impeding a competitor, with the assistance of the team. He was to be demoted five grid positions – dropping him from pole to sixth, with Hamilton now on pole. Furthermore, the team would be ineligible for constructors' points.

While Lewis may have been happy with the first part of the judgement, he felt guilty about the lost constructors' points – especially as the mechanics' bonus money was paid on this basis. Some were not slow in letting Hamilton know this, and he made a point of going round to each team member on Sunday morning and apologising. 'With Ron, obviously yesterday he wasn't very happy. I told him my views, he respected those. He said: "OK, I respect that because it is part of your personality and perhaps in your situation maybe that was better for you or whatever." And so we came to a mutual understanding and started on a clean slate today. Still it is not great because of all the problems we are having already with the FIA and with Ferrari. It is just more pressure on the team.'

The grid penalty was just the final straw for Alonso. He portrayed it as yet more vindication of his belief that the team should be centred around him, with a clear number one status and Hamilton in support. This was never going to happen, but on Sunday morning Alonso tried once more to press his case with Dennis, who once again outlined why the team would continue to operate on a basis of equality for both drivers. By now in quite an emotional state, Alonso suggested that if Dennis was not prepared to slow Hamilton down for the rest of this season, or maybe engineer him not finishing the odd race, Alonso would show the contents of his company lap-top to the FIA, suggesting there were e-mails on it that would be very interesting to anyone examining the espionage case. Dennis could barely believe what he was hearing. On the one hand, his driver seemed to be threatening blackmail. But shocking even beyond that was that there might be evidence that the Coughlan/Ferrari information had indeed leaked into the team itself – the refutation of which was central to McLaren not having been punished by the FIA at the previous hearing.

'At this point I called Martin Whitmarsh into the room,' said Dennis. 'Martin and I agreed that Fernando should inform the FIA. When Fernando left, I phoned [FIA President] Max Mosley myself to tell him what had happened. Half an hour later, Fernando's manager came back and said he was sorry, that Fernando had been angry and wanted to retract everything he'd said and that it was a load of old rubbish. So I picked up the phone again and called the FIA to keep them up to date.'

But it was too late. In the event, it didn't matter that Dennis had turned the information in; Mosley already had it, sourced from elsewhere. It concerned the e-mails between test driver Pedro de la Rosa and Alonso from the beginning of the season, in which de la Rosa had asked Mike Coughlan for the Ferrari's weight distribution, then relayed the answer to Alonso, assuring him it was good information as it came from Nigel Stepney.

There were those at McLaren in Hungary who wanted Alonso to be thrown out of his drive there and then. But Dennis counselled caution, pointed out that they were in the midst of a world championship battle with Ferrari and could not afford to discard a driver of Alonso's ability.

The pressure on Hamilton as he went into the race was enormous. He was in pole position, but had got himself into enormous trouble with the team. 'Going into the race there was a big cloud over my mind,' he admitted. 'It was difficult to stay focused because obviously you had this feeling in the team. The team weren't getting any points. So you didn't know whether the team hated you, whether they just hated the situation or who they blamed. So it was difficult but I just tried to come here with a smile on my face and tried to remain positive for everyone and do the same procedure as always.'

He took off into the lead and stayed there throughout, soaking up big pressure from Kimi Raikkonen's Ferrari virtually all the way and coping with a worrying steering problem in the last third of the race. Around a track where passing is virtually impossible, Alonso was restricted to a fourth-place finish. McLaren duly appealed against the decision to be stripped of constructors' points – and a hearing was scheduled for 18 September, five days after the espionage appeal hearing. McLaren's lawyers were certainly being kept busy.

In taking his third Grand Prix victory, Hamilton had been absolutely faultless, the eye of calm within an incredibly stormy environment. One thing was certain, though: he left the weekend with no one in any doubt that he was more than able to fight his own corner. He was even willing to *start* the fight. He was no longer anyone's protégé, and even Ron Dennis may have come to realise this during this extraordinary weekend. This isn't a sport where gratitude has much currency, not if it means compromising on performance.

The balance of power had changed subtly. Earlier in the season, Ron's wife Lisa had said: 'You feel more protective of [Lewis] than any other driver Ron has employed. It's a little hard for me to judge how Ron feels, but when I watch him giving him a lecture it's the same as when it's our son, Christian. He's very paternal towards him.' Well, that was probably gone now. And from Lewis's viewpoint it needed to be so. He was always going to need to shrug off Dennis's paternal interest; there was room only for one father, and his name was Anthony. Lewis was not relaxed with the idea of a paternal relationship with his boss; he had moved into a phase in his life and career where it needed to be more one of partnership in success, each critically valuable to the other professionally. 'I have been working with Ron for nearly ten years now,' he said, 'so OK, it is quite a big event, but I think the relationship we have is very, very strong and something like this is not going to come between us. We will move on to bigger and better things.'

Hamilton's actions during the Hungarian Grand Prix weekend may not have endeared Lewis to everyone, but as an indication of the qualities required of a great Grand Prix driver, he'd just ticked yet another box.

Round 11 of 17:
Hungarian Grand Prix, Hungaroring, 5 August

1. **Lewis Hamilton (McLaren-Mercedes)**
2. Kimi Raikkonen (Ferrari)
3. Nick Heidfeld (BMWSauber)
4. Fernando Alonso (McLaren-Mercedes)
5. Robert Kubica (BMWSauber)
6. Ralf Schumacher (Toyota)

7. Nico Rosberg (Williams-Toyota)
8. Heikki Kovalainen (Renault)

Drivers' World Championship

1.	**Hamilton**	**80 points**
2.	Alonso	73
3.	Raikkonen	60
4.	Massa	59
5.	Heidfeld	42
6.	Kubica	28
7.	Fisichella	17
8.	Kovalainen	16
9.	Wurz	13
10.	Webber	8
	Coulthard	8
12.	Trulli	7
	Rosberg	7
14.	R.Schumacher	5
15.	Sato	4
16.	Button	1
	Vettel	1

CHAPTER EIGHTEEN

Paparazzi and Pounds Sterling

Ron Dennis was keen to get his team back on an even keel after the storm of Hungary, and as such extended invitations to both Hamilton and Alonso to spend a few days on the boat of Mansour Ojjeh, Dennis's equity partner in McLaren. Hamilton accepted, Alonso declined.

Hamilton evidently enjoyed his time there – as the rest of the world could see. Pictures of him spending time with Ojjeh's 18-year-old daughter Sara were splashed all over the front pages of the world's newspapers. Pictures of them swimming together, diving off the boat, walking on the beach, sitting in a restaurant. It was a similar story when he then returned to Britain and spent a night out with friends in London. Pictures duly appeared of him with yet another girl.

He was keen to set the record straight when he eventually turned up in the paddock at Istanbul on Friday. But first he had some talking to do with his team-mate. The drivers usually appear at the track for the first time on Thursday, but this time Dennis had arranged for Hamilton and Alonso to meet at a venue in the city, and he insisted they talked through any issues they may have had with each other following the events of Hungary.

'After the last race I called Fernando and said, "Look, we can't go for the next three weeks without talking,"' he explained on Friday, '"or just relying on the media reporting on the fact that we're at war, when we're not. We need to discuss the last race and move forwards. At the end of the day we're team-mates and need to get on." He agreed, but he was busy and I was on holiday, so we didn't meet up until yesterday. First of all we discussed our holidays. It was relaxed. I put my hand up and apologised for everything that happened at the last race and he said, "Yeah, me too."'

'I told him I had a huge amount of respect for his achievements, that I'm easy to get on with and find him to be the same. We agreed that we didn't have a problem with each other and needed to push on and fight for the world championship on the team's behalf.

'We've had a lot of time to think about what happened in Budapest and don't want to go back there again, because we need harmony in the team. We've settled our differences and know where we want to go, and I feel very comfortable that we can both go out there and battle for the title, which is what the sport is all about.'

As for the holiday pictures that had so captured the imagination of newspaper editors, he was dismissive, saying: 'It's all a bit disappointing. All those stories were wrong. I was supposed to go away with the lads, but I thought that was a bad idea in the middle of a season when I'm leading the world championship. I thought I'd give myself a chance to recover, and do some training, and I was invited onto the

Ojjehs' boat. There were 13 of us, including three Ojjeh daughters, all of whom had their boyfriends there, and we all got on so well. We had a fantastic time partying and then in the second week I got back into my training. I wasn't expecting to find photographers there, but what you don't see in "that" picture are 12 people at the back of the boat throwing each other in the water. It wouldn't be so bad if I was getting off with all these women, but I'm not.

'My ex-girlfriend and I made a decision: we were both 22 and at the start of the year I told her the next few months would be hard for her because I'd be away a lot in the coming months. At that point she was only in the UK because of me and had a few problems with her family. So she went back and we decided to see how things were after my first three races. She has her career to consider and we came to a decision to part, but we're still great friends and talk all the time, but the papers keep bringing the subject up, which is pretty devastating for both of us. Now I'm supposedly dating one of the Ojjehs, which is completely untrue.

'She has a boyfriend and we're just great friends. Then, the other day, I went out with my best friend, his fiancée and another friend. The papers claimed she was a new girlfriend and one of the others was my bodyguard, so now I was supposedly cheating on someone I'm not even going out with … I also hear I'm supposed to have slept with [singer] Dido, but I certainly don't remember that. It's just not me. I'm not a playboy. I haven't been out and bought loads of fast cars and I'm not dating lots of different women. If I was, fair play, write about it, but I'm not. I'm trying to lead a normal life.'

The question then came up about how all this might impact on his choice of home. Rumours were already circulating that he was searching for a suitable property in the tax haven of Monte Carlo. Asked if he might consider leaving the UK, he allowed: 'It is possible, but it's down to the media, really. I don't so much mind a few people coming up to me at home – I get quite a buzz from that. I wasn't surrounded when I came out of the cinema last week, but I was bullied by two particular photographers who wanted snaps. If that's what my life has to be … There are some people who just want to push you into a corner. I just want to live a normal life – and if I can't do that, I want it to be as normal as possible so I can enjoy it without it being spread across the tabloids.'

There were many things going on here behind the scenes, probably not all under Lewis's control. On the one hand there was a serious financial imperative to reside in a tax haven. On the other there was a real desire within his camp for him to be seen as a positive role model. The two impera-tives conflicted. Maybe a bit of intrusive paparazzi activity was a convenient way of resolving this conflict. Just a year earlier he'd have given anything to be in this position, even if it was unpaid. That's how fast success had caught up with him. It was a nice problem to have.

Around the fast sweeps of the Istanbul Park track, the Ferraris were in their element and definitely faster than the McLarens. Their superiority was less evident in qualifying because of their usual difficulty in warming up their front tyres – and so Hamilton was able to make a fight of it for pole position. He ended up losing out to Felipe Massa by 0.04s, but would start from the front row ahead of Raikkonen and Alonso. Again, Hamilton seemed to have the edge in speed over his team-mate, with Fernando deciding to qualify on the harder tyre, looking to find a technical advantage that might allow him to compete.

Raikkonen's Ferrari was much quicker off the grid than Hamilton and slotted immediately into second, this the foundation of a dominant Ferrari 1–2 led by Massa. Hamilton was looking set for a solid third place when he suffered a sudden delamination of his front right tyre just after exiting the fast turn 8. 'As I exited [turn 8] I saw some bits fly off the tyre and as soon as I braked for turn 9 it just exploded. I went off and almost hit the barrier.'

He managed to wrestle the car back to the pits, where the tyres were changed. The tyre decompression had damaged some of the aerodynamic appendages on the car, and it was all he could do to hold off Heikki Kovalainen's Renault to finish fifth. The incident also allowed Alonso, who had been running a long way behind, to grab third place, bringing him to within five points of Hamilton at the head of the championship table.

After the race he was asked if he had any recollections of the last time a British world championship contender was wrestling to control a car with tyre failure – Nigel Mansell in Australia in 1986. 'No,' Lewis smiled in reply. 'I was one at the time.'

Round 12 of 17:
Turkish Grand Prix, Istanbul Park, 26 August

1. Felipe Massa (Ferrari)
2. Kimi Raikkonen (Ferrari)
3. Fernando Alonso (McLaren-Mercedes)
4. Nick Heidfeld (BMWSauber)
5. **Lewis Hamilton (McLaren-Mercedes)**
6. Heikki Kovalainen (Renault)

7. Nico Rosberg (Williams-Toyota)
8. Robert Kubica (BMWSauber)

Drivers' World Championship

1.	**Hamilton**	**84 points**
2.	Alonso	79
3.	Massa	69
4.	Raikkonen	68
5.	Heidfeld	47
6.	Kubica	29
7.	Kovalainen	19
8.	Fisichella	17
9.	Wurz	13
10.	Rosberg	9
11.	Webber	8
	Coulthard	8
13.	Trulli	7
14.	R.Schumacher	5
15.	Sato	4
16.	Button	1
	Vettel	1

CHAPTER NINETEEN

Alonso Hits Back

In the Wednesday before the Italian Grand Prix, the McLaren/Ferrari espionage case took a new turn. The FIA announced that the originally convened court of appeal hearing had been cancelled and replaced by a reconvening of the World Council 'in light of new evidence' on the matter. For McLaren – and Lewis Hamilton – this was a disturbing development. The new evidence was the uncovering of the e-mails between test driver Pedro de la Rosa, McLaren designer Mike Coughlan and Fernando Alonso – as well as records of the frequency of phone texts between Coughlan and Ferrari's Nigel Stepney. McLaren were going to be re-tried on the original case, but with more evidence against them this time. The case would be heard on the Thursday before the Belgian Grand Prix, which followed one week after the Italian race at Monza. The spectre of McLaren's banishment from the world championship came back onto the horizon.

Following Dennis's phone call to Mosley in Hungary outlining Alonso's threat to reveal his e-mails, Mosley sent out a letter to Alonso, Hamilton and de la Rosa telling them that if they had any information pertaining to the case they should share it with the governing body. In exchange the governing body would show the drivers 'leniency'. Hamilton had no information to give, but the two Spanish drivers did – and duly released their e-mail correspondence. This showed that the Ferrari information had indeed spread further into the McLaren organisation than was claimed by McLaren in the original hearing. Into the bargain, it was announced at Monza that McLaren had been fined $50,000 for having raced a modified gearbox in the Hungarian Grand Prix without having subjected the car to the required crash re-test when a new design is used. The team had argued that the gearbox had been merely a modification, not a re-design, but the FIA did not accept this. There was a widespread feeling that the team was being targeted.

As ever, it was Hamilton's lot to try to put any thoughts about the espionage case to the back of his mind and concentrate on his on-track performance. Although the McLarens were much the fastest cars around the Monza track, Hamilton had a real challenge on his hands trying to match the pace of team-mate Alonso. The world champion had forgone his frequent attempts at using different components or tyres to try to out-perform Hamilton and instead just concentrated on finding a better set-up and then driving faster. On the evidence of Monza, it was a strategy that worked brilliantly. Hamilton was chasing Alonso's pace throughout the weekend and never did quite manage to match it. Alonso took a commanding victory from pole position, with Hamilton having to put a stunning late-race out-braking move on Kimi Raikkonen's Ferrari just to finish second. Alonso now lay just three points behind Hamilton in the championship with four races to go.

That Alonso should suddenly step up a gear in the midst of his very poor relationship with the team was quite characteristic. A solitary figure within the team, he is at his best when he perceives an injustice against him, when he uses his fiery character to fuel some magnificent performances. Hamilton may have been quicker more often in the season to date, but Alonso – with the prospect of a third consecutive world title in the offing – was now digging deep.

Hamilton remained positive, however, still outwardly confident he could remain in front. His relaxed demeanour and sharp humour was present in the press conference when a journalist asked Raikkonen what he had been talking about with Hamilton on the grid. Both Kimi and Lewis denied that any such conversation had taken place. Then, off-mike, Hamilton said to Raikkonen: 'Must've been some other black dude.'

Round 13 of 17:
Italian Grand Prix, Monza, 9 September

1. Fernando Alonso (McLaren-Mercedes)
2. **Lewis Hamilton (McLaren-Mercedes)**
3. Kimi Raikkonen (Ferari)
4. Nick Heidfeld (BMWSauber)
5. Robert Kubica (BMWSauber)
6. Nico Rosberg (Williams-Toyota)
7. Heikki Kovalainen (Renault)
8. Jenson Button (Honda)

Drivers' World Championship

1.	**Hamilton**	**92 points**
2.	Alonso	89
3.	Raikkonen	74
4.	Massa	69
5.	Heidfeld	52
6.	Kubica	33
7.	Kovalainen	21
8.	Fisichella	17
9.	Wurz	13
10.	Rosberg	12
11.	Webber	8
	Coulthard	8
13.	Trulli	7
14.	R.Schumacher	5
15.	Sato	4
16.	Button	2
17.	Vettel	1

While the rest of the F1 travelling circus gathered at Spa on Thursday in preparation for the Belgian Grand Prix, senior McLaren personnel were in Paris for the FIA World Council hearing. The prognosis for the team seemed to be grave. There was a widespread belief that they were about to be banished from the championship – which would likely have left Hamilton and Alonso powerless to prevent one of the Ferrari drivers overcoming their points lead in the remaining races. There was also the possibility that the drivers, as well as the team, would be penalised on account of having benefited from McLaren's access to Ferrari information.

In the event, neither of those things happened. The hearing found McLaren guilty of the charges, imposed a fine of $100 million and stripped the team of all 2007 constructors' points – meaning that Ferrari automatically became world champion constructors. But the drivers' championship was left unaffected, doubtless to the huge relief of Hamilton and Alonso. Mosley had reportedly been keen for the drivers to have been penalised too, but is believed to have acceded to commercial rights representative Bernie Ecclestone's desire that the drivers' championship was not interfered with. From a commercial perspective, the possibility of the remarkable black rookie winning the world championship at his first attempt was a very powerful story, and it would have been very anti-climactic if the fight was declared null and void in a courtroom.

So the fight continued onto the Spa circuit, set in the dramatic Ardennes valley. The long high-speed corners suited the Ferrari's characteristics better than the McLaren's, and throughout the weekend the Italian team looked the stronger force. Kimi Raikkonen duly reeled off a dominant win over team-mate Felipe Massa. At McLaren there was acrimony between the two drivers as a result of a territorial dispute between them at the first corner. Just as at Monza, Alonso appeared to have a slight edge in speed over Hamilton throughout the weekend and had qualified third, one place ahead of him. The Ferraris arrived at the hairpin corner of La Source first, with Alonso tucked up behind them on the inside and Hamilton trying to go around the outside. As the two McLarens went side-by-side through the corner, Alonso deliberately used up all the track on the exit, forcing Hamilton to drive off the circuit onto the tarmac run-off area to avoid a collision. He rejoined without losing much momentum, once again side-by-side with his team-mate as they raced down the hill towards the spectacular and dangerous Eau Rouge corner, taken flat out in top gear at around 185mph. Hamilton was on the outside, so Alonso therefore had the advantage as they entered the corner with their wheels just inches apart. Had they interlocked, there would have been an accident of monumental proportions. For a split-second Hamilton considered staying flat-out and committed to his line. He had pulled off such a move here in F3 on his then team-mate Adrian Sutil, and wondered whether it might work in an F1 car.

But then common sense prevailed. He lifted briefly and conceded the corner. He never got as close again and Alonso took a solid third, 9s ahead of Hamilton. Afterwards, Lewis had harsh words about Alonso's behaviour on that first lap. 'At the first corner all of a sudden Fernando came sweeping across me, and he knew I was there, so ... I did the best job I could to get by him down the straight, but it wasn't enough. I wouldn't say it was fair, but it was hard.

'There was enough room for us all to get round fair and square. I just feel that for someone that's always complaining about people doing unfair manoeuvres, he has gone and swiped me and pushed me as wide as he could. I was just really lucky there was a run-off area so I could take that. At Eau Rouge it's impossible to take two Formula One cars through there without taking each other out, so I just lifted.'

Talking of the worry of the World Council meeting in the lead-up to the race, he used the opportunity of ratcheting up the psychological pressure on his team-mate: 'It's been a tough week, and for sure a lot tougher week for me than for Fernando.' When asked why, he replied: 'I feel more attached to the team, I guess, and I care a bit more, I think.'

This was a clear reference to Alonso's original threat of exposing his lap-top contents to the FIA in his negotiations with Dennis.

Asked of his feelings about Max Mosley's assertions that the championship would be tainted, he was having none of it. 'I don't really have anything to say to or about Max Mosley. We've all worked hard this year. The way I feel is that the team has done nothing wrong, and neither have I. I have just taken the opportunities I've been given and done the best job I could with it. I don't see why people should say, if I win it's a tainted championship.'

Tainted or not, if he wanted to win it, he needed to respond to Alonso's new-found vein of form.

Round 14 of 17:
Belgian Grand Prix, Spa, 16 September

1. Kimi Raikkonen (Ferrari)
2. Felipe Massa (Ferrari)
3. Fernando Alonso (McLaren-Mercedes)
4. **Lewis Hamilton (McLaren-Mercedes)**
5. Nick Heidfeld (BMWSauber)
6. Nico Rosberg (Williams-Toyota)
7. Mark Webber (Red Bull-Renault)
8. Heikki Kovalainen (Renault)

Drivers' World Championship

1.	**Hamilton**	**97 points**
2.	Alonso	95
3.	Raikkonen	84
4.	Massa	77

5.	Heidfeld	56
6.	Kubica	33
7.	Kovalainen	22
8.	Fisichella	17
9.	Rosberg	15
10.	Wurz	13
11.	Webber	10
12.	Coulthard	8
13.	Trulli	7
14.	R.Schumacher	5
15.	Sato	4
16.	Button	2
17.	Vettel	1

CHAPTER TWENTY

Water Margins

With a masterful victory in the wettest Grand Prix in living memory, on a day when title rival Fernando Alonso crashed out, Lewis Hamilton seemed to lay one hand on the world championship trophy in Japan, with two races still remaining. Seven days later, he had to relinquish that hold after crashing out of a wet Chinese Grand Prix as his two title rivals Kimi Raikkonen and Alonso finished first and second. Which set up a three-way title fight down to the wire.

Although the Fuji circuit, nestling at the bottom of the mountain of the same name, was another circuit of which Hamilton had no previous experience, this time he wasn't alone: virtually none of the others had either. Fuji Speedway had not been used by F1 since 1977, long before most of the competing drivers here had even been born.

Hamilton arrived with a fresh perspective. He'd been troubled by his inability to match Alonso in the previous two races and sought to understand why. The morning after the Belgian race he had visited the factory and met up with his engineers to look through the data of the previous two races. 'I spent a couple of days there,' he revealed, 'trying to understand where I'd gone wrong. I had followed a different path to Fernando, thinking it was the right way to go, but we were wrong – so we ended up miles apart. These cars are so complex that when you get the set-up just a little bit wrong, you're not able to get that extra out of it – even if you try driving a bit harder. I found it difficult getting the maximum from it and that's been down to my experience. But after spending time at the factory, I really feel I know what went wrong and am much more comfortable about it now.'

It was probably significant that for the three-day Spa test earlier in the year, Hamilton had driven only on the first day and thereafter the car was shared by de la Rosa and Alonso. Hamilton was happy with the set-up he'd found by the time he'd left, but the two Spaniards then developed the car more to Alonso's taste. As had already been shown by the e-mails between them that were uncovered during the espionage trial, Alonso and de la Rosa worked very closely together. There may even have been a feeling of the two of them against Hamilton – as a later e-mail from de la Rosa to Alonso suggested. Talking about a possible flexible rear wing development prior to the Italian Grand Prix, the safety of which he was not very comfortable about, Pedro had joked: 'Maybe we can get Lewis to try it at the Monza test!'

Several times during the year, Hamilton had tested on the first day, with Alonso and de la Rosa then following on. It is perfectly feasible that Alonso took Hamilton's set-up as a baseline, then fine-tuned it to be more in line with his own driving style, with de la Rosa's help, thereby giving himself an advantage. In F1 terms, there would be nothing at all unethical in that – especially when you are fighting your team-mate for the world championship. From Hamilton's perspective, he was maybe a little slow to realise the disadvantage of testing on the first day and allowing Alonso to follow. Just another little bit of information to be stored away in the experience bank.

For the three remaining races there was no prior testing, so giving Hamilton one less thing to worry about. Significantly, McLaren played their part in relaxing him too, while leaving Alonso – barely on speaking terms with the team – to his own devices. 'We cleared all Lewis's corporate duties coming into this weekend,' said Martin Whitmarsh. 'We told him to just relax, do some training with his trainer Aki Hintsa and clear his mind. We told him to stop worrying about all his off-track stuff, where he is going to live etc., and just come here fresh and prepared.' Lewis followed the instructions to the letter and arrived in Japan a week ahead of the race, getting his body clock attuned and relaxing into the weekend, as he explained: 'I came out here a few days early to be a bit of a tourist. I quite like the Asian culture. I don't really get hassled on the street here and can enjoy just walking around.' A little reminder of how life used to be just 12 months and an eternity earlier, before F1 and its audience of billions rocketed him to a different life. 'I came out to take my mind off things and prepare for a new attack, a fresh approach.'

For all that he was relaxed, he was feisty about his prospects – and seemed to have decided upon a bit of psychological warfare with his team-mate, happy to take up the bait offered by journalists' questions about Spa.

'I will be a lot more aware of him around me,' he said, sounding more than ever like a boxer shadow-boxing his opponent in the build-up to the fight. 'You wait and see. I will be driving to keep the car on the track and be fair to everyone but if that's how aggressive he wants to be then I can be just as aggressive. But I am not going to take silly risks and take myself off, or anyone else. I just have to make sure I am ahead of him so it won't be an issue.

'I feel I have nothing to lose. He is the one defending the world championship, so really there is more pressure on him. In the last two races he has done very well. I don't know if he has unloaded a load of baggage, not feeling any weight from the team. He seems to be quite happy with himself all of a sudden.'

Here was Lewis playing the media, using it to try to unsettle his opponent. He was now straying into sensitive territory – about team loyalty – and happily painting himself as the good guy and Fernando the villain. All part of the game.

'The funny thing is when you are in a relationship with a certain amount of people you do the best job you can and want to show to everyone that you are the one for the team. In this situation I was a rookie and he is the two-time world champion coming into the team. He is the one that was looked at to bring it home, but eventually I have earned more respect from them, and since what's gone on in the last few weeks they've realised who the real people are in the team and who they really should back. I feel my bond with the team is even stronger.'

This was strong stuff at a time when the team were desperately trying to demonstrate equality of opportunity – to not give Alonso any grounds for claiming that Hamilton was favoured. Lewis ploughed on, as fearless as on the track.

'It has been a little bit strange for me as during the season you walk into the communication centre and Fernando is with his group and there is my family and they are very separate. We tried our best to bring them together and at one point it looked like they didn't want to know. Then we spoke to each other at Turkey and it seemed to go a lot better from there. Then when we arrived at Spa [where the team were facing the prospect of disqualification from the championship and ended up being fined $100 million and losing all their constructors' points] just for some reason he was sitting there laughing and joking as if nothing had happened. I don't understand it.'

So there was the reason the team should support him. But almost certainly it was a message aimed not at the team, but at unsettling Alonso – just as Alonso had clearly unsettled him by his apparently blasé attitude at Spa while in the midst of out-performing him.

'I want to win this title fair and square. Not once have I approached the team members and asked to be favoured. It is just not something I have done at any team – asking for better equipment. It is better when you both have equal opportunity. It means you both have got to do the best job you can. After Monaco they didn't know what to do with the strategy so they made us equal and gave us equal fuel loads, and whoever out-qualifies the other has done the better job. If it is equal I have to work harder or he has to work harder to stay ahead of me. I want to win it the right way. The best feeling ever is when you know you have won and you have beaten someone as talented as he is with the exact same equipment and exactly the same opportunity.'

This was all a clear reference to Alonso's demands earlier in the season, before his relationship with the team had broken down, for preferential treatment. Now fully into the subject, Lewis continued: 'I don't understand why he would ask for that. It shows how much of a threat I am and that he is worried – which is great; it is always good to have your opponent worried. But then it is strange; you try to understand these people but then the whole idea of what sort of person they are is completely miles out of the ball park. He is not the person I imagined him to be, but that's the way it is.'

Still he wasn't finished with the Alonso-baiting. He then fired off an early warning about any ideas Alonso might have of settling the championship by driving him off the track – the way that Ayrton Senna had done to Alain Prost in 1990 or Michael Schumacher had tried on Jacques Villeneuve in '97. 'I think it will be interesting to see during the last three races whether he'll have the thing Michael Schumacher had, where he'll do anything – *anything* – i.e. he doesn't care whether he runs himself or anyone else on the grid off the road. Will he do absolutely anything? I guess that's one of the questions, will he break under pressure? We'll just have to wait and see. It will ruin his reputation more than mine, because I'd never do that.'

The newspaper journalists were loving this: fantastic copy straight from his lips. But he was as happy to use them as they were to use him, just inviting the provocative question and reeling off another from-the-hip answer. 'Do you think you and Fernando can still be team-mates next year?' a journalist asks, just waiting for the quotes to roll into his recorder.

Lewis obliges with: 'No I don't. I mean, if the team wants to keep him they keep him, but I'm here to stay as long as they want me. Any dreams that I have had about what I would like to be doing ten years in the future have slightly changed …' In what sense? 'About where you would want to be. This season has helped reconfirm in my mind where I want to be, where I want to live out my career, and that is here. I'm really happy and comfortable here. So long as they want me, there's no reason to move anywhere else. It's up to the team. They've got to be smart and think about it: I know they've got politics and sponsors and all that sort of stuff, but they've got to do what's right and I'm sure they will. I don't know who else would slip in here, but I'd much rather it were Fernando in a Ferrari and me in a McLaren.'

Colours nailed to the wall, then. And this may have been the one piece of information that was targeted at the team: I'm happy to commit to you indefinitely and have no wish to decamp to your biggest rivals. And as such I'd prefer it if the other guy wasn't here in future. Would make it easier for all concerned. Easier for me to deliver for you.

After such a blockbusting performance in front of the dictaphones it would have been a little embarrassing if he'd failed to produce the goods on the track. But Hamilton is remarkable in how he invariably produces his best stuff when under the most pressure. Saturday practice was rained off, and into qualifying on a damp track it looked for a moment as though he was going to get caught in traffic on his crucial Q1 run. This would have been disastrous for his race and title chances, would have left him 17th on the grid, at best. With the seconds of the session counting down and Alonso already comfortably through, Hamilton had time for just one more lap. He couldn't afford to blow it. He didn't – and got himself through to Q2, where he proceeded to go quickest, 0.1s ahead of Alonso. For the final session, Hamilton and Alonso were fuelled equally but had differing plans in how they were going to attack: in still wet conditions, Alonso decided he was going to make only one stop for fresh intermediate tyres, reckoning on finding more time from keying himself in to the tricky conditions than there was by making a second stop for another set of tyres. Hamilton opted for the conventional two new-tyre runs, making his session more interrupted. It would also mean Alonso burned off more fuel – making him a lap lighter and therefore potentially faster.

For much of the session it looked like Alonso's plan was a sound one, as he consistently led the times. Lewis made his first stop for new tyres and on the subsequent lap didn't even beat Alonso's best fuel-burn time. Alonso then made his one and only stop for new tyres and improved upon his own provisional pole. Coming in for his final set of new tyres, Hamilton was truly up against it now. Time left for just one flying lap – with Alonso's 1m 25.438s as the target. In the first sector he went faster, in the second he was slower by about the same amount. It all hung on the twisty uphill section at the end. He emerged from the gloom of the final corner, a vision in silver and red, yellow helmet atop the cockpit, and sprinted for the line, jinking left past a slower car with a terrifying speed differential. He crossed the line to trip the electronic beam: 1m 25.368s. As he lifted off and passed the on-track TV screen, he saw his time and position and began a celebratory dance – as much as one can within the tight confines of the cockpit. Hamilton 1st, Alonso 2nd, the Ferraris on the second row. A perfect preparation for the fight – and a perfect backing up of the strong words.

Conditions on race day were appalling, with the track awash and walls of fog rolling in. Those with long F1 memories were taken back to this place in 1976 when, under similar conditions, Niki Lauda had pulled out of the race for his own safety and thereby handed the world championship to James Hunt. There was speculation that the race may be cancelled this time, but in the end it was decided to start it under the safety car. The cars would line up in grid order behind it and racing would begin when it was deemed safe enough. Bernd Maylander led the field around in the silver Mercedes coupé, the two McLarens somewhere in his wake. Visibility was virtually zero, and even at safety car speeds this was lethally dangerous. Drivers were reporting over their radios that the race could not start under these conditions. The cars were aquaplaning from puddle to puddle, but worse than that was that at 190mph on the long main straight, visibility was no more than a few metres. Ferrari had sent Kimi Raikkonen and Felipe Massa to the grid on intermediate tyres rather than the extreme weather wets of everyone else. This was contrary to specific instructions from the race director that had been e-mailed to all teams around an hour earlier. Ferrari claimed they didn't receive the e-mail. Regardless, they were instructed to bring their cars in and have the correct tyres fitted, dropping them down to the back but allowing them to refuel.

Conditions did not get any better. As drivers braked and accelerated, trying to keep temperature in their brakes and water out of their engines, they were passing other cars without even being aware they'd done so, before then falling back again. For 18 laps they circulated like this before the race director decided it was time for the show to begin. As Maylander switched off his flashing lights and made for the pits, the race would be on as the cars passed the start/finish line. Hamilton began playing cat and mouse with Alonso, alternately accelerating and braking, trying to ensure he wouldn't be close enough to him to try a pass into the first corner. Just before the final corner he accelerated hard, as if making the break. Alonso reacted and went with him – just as Hamilton was again standing hard on the brakes. Alonso had to (illegally) pass him to avoid running into the back of him, and only then did Hamilton accelerate for real and sprint for the line. He was thus comfortably ahead into the first turn and, as the only driver able to see where he was going, built up a lead of around 3s over his team-mate.

This gap was to prove crucial because it allowed him to make his refuelling stop and rejoin in clear space. Alonso, having to stop a lap earlier and being 3s behind, just failed to clear a gaggle of cars that had yet to stop – and so Hamilton's lead over him increased substantially. In between the two McLarens were a group of cars that had yet to stop and with tyres that were fully warmed. Lighter and grippier, they began to close down on Hamilton – and the first of them was Robert Kubica's BMW. Hamilton knew he was there only from his pit signs, because the spray and his misted-up mirrors meant non-existent visibility behind him. On the 36th lap, Kubica tried a move down the inside of turn 13. Hamilton didn't see him and turned in, the two cars collided and spun. Both were able to restart, but it had given the McLaren team palpitations. Hamilton radioed that he had a vibration in the car; the team checked the telemetry and told him not to worry, all was OK. Just a couple of laps later, in a near-repeat incident, Sebastian Vettel's Toro Rosso tried to pass Alonso and made hard contact. The McLaren restarted after a spin, but Fernando now had to cope with a damaged floor and bodywork, giving him less downforce just as the rain began to fall harder. A river was streaming across the track on the exit of turn 5, and on the 41st lap Alonso lost control over it and aquaplaned hard into the banking, destroying his car. Hamilton's title chances had just received a massive boost.

The safety car came back out while the Alonso debris was

cleared, with Hamilton leading the race. Hamilton was becoming a little concerned at how closely the second-placed Red Bull of Mark Webber was following him, and was radioing to the team to tell them to get him to hold off. Webber in turn was being hassled by the Toro Rosso of Vettel. All three were trying to keep their brakes up to temperature and to clear their engines by braking and accelerating. It all came to a point of impact on lap 45 as Hamilton veered to the right of the safety car, trying to create a gap into which he could accelerate and clear his misfire. Vettel became distracted, thinking Hamilton was retiring – and when he looked up, found he was about to crash into the back of Webber. Both the Toro Rosso and Red Bull were out of the race. Upon the resumption of racing, Hamilton took off into an uncontested lead and 19 laps later crossed the line as the winner, 9s ahead of the battling Heikki Kovalainen and Raikkonen. It was his fourth victory of the year, the third on a track that was new to him. He now had a 12-point lead with just two races remaining. It was hard to envisage how he could not win the title.

He received a clue as he arrived in Shanghai a few days later. There, the paddock was awash with rumours that Hamilton was under investigation for the manner of his driving while behind the Fuji safety car. A Japanese fan had recorded the Vettel/Webber incident on video camera and posted it on the YouTube website, and it offered a clearer view than the official coverage of Hamilton pulling sharply to one side just before. There was talk of a Hamilton grid penalty for the Chinese race. Webber stoked the fire, saying that Hamilton had done 'a shit job' in keeping a consistent pace behind the safety car.

Cynics viewed this threat as a handy way of keeping the

world championship battle open until the final round, with Hamilton the victim of his own success. There was talk of manipulation by the powers-that-be. Asked about the prospect of a penalty, Hamilton played his cards carefully, but beautifully, saying: 'I don't think I put a foot wrong and I didn't do anything to harm anyone else or put anyone else in danger. But I've come to China and no doubt I'm going to be punished for something. I just think it's a real shame for the sport. Formula One is supposed to be about hard competition – fair – and that's what I've tried to do this year, just be fair. If I've been in the wrong, I've been the first to put my hand up, or apologise at least … but there's been some really strange situations this year where I'm made to look the bad person, or by the looks of it this weekend could be given a penalty. It's just a shame for the sport and if this is the way it's going to keep going then it's probably not somewhere I really want to be.'

Those last few words had a real sting to them. Lewis Hamilton was fast on his way to becoming the biggest star the sport had ever seen, with a level of fame that could soon transcend the sport itself. On account of both his rookie success and his race, he had the power to do enormous good for F1's interests throughout the world. He also had the potential to seriously damage it if he were to walk from it and explain why he had done so. There was a very clear threat in those last few words – and he was the only driver, actually the only participant of any sort, with the power to make it. He wasn't explicitly saying he would leave the sport if he felt he was unfairly treated. But he'd floated the idea out there and may well have made the likes of Bernie Ecclestone and the FIA step back from the brink. The idea of the most famous racing driver in the world going on to chat shows to explain why he had walked out on F1 just didn't bear thinking about.

On Friday evening Hamilton, Vettel and Webber sat in with the stewards, who listened to their testimony. Hamilton was eventually cleared and no penalty was imposed, and Vettel's original penalty of ten places on the grid for causing an avoidable accident was rescinded. The following day, F1's commercial chief Bernie Ecclestone was ringing in his endorsement of Hamilton, saying: 'He has been a real breath of fresh air and has resurrected F1. I have been in motor racing longer than I care to remember but I have never seen anyone like him. He has been nothing short of a miracle worker. We lost a big hero in Michael Schumacher but in Lewis we have another. But for him I'm not sure where the sport would be heading.

'It is painfully obvious to me that the right guy to be world champion is Lewis. In fact my main fear would be if he didn't win it. Kimi Raikkonen barely talks to anyone and as such has done little for the sport, and as for Fernando Alonso, in his two years as world champion he has done nothing. He hasn't really been an F1 campaigner at all, but if Lewis wins the drivers' championship he will act like a real world champion. He will know exactly what is expected of him and what he has to do.'

He knew what was expected of him on Saturday afternoon too, as he recorded a brilliant final lap to secure pole position ahead of Raikkonen's Ferrari. Team-mate Alonso was back in fourth – and convinced he had been nobbled. Just 0.1s slower than the lighter Hamilton on his first Q3 new-tyre run, he suddenly found himself 0.5s slower on the final run, despite a lap that he felt was quick and error-free. Seeing conspiracies everywhere, he later claimed that the pressures of his tyres had been set too high.

The race began in wet conditions, with everyone on intermediate tyres. Hamilton took off into an ever-increasing lead
over Raikkonen, with Alonso back in fourth. This was the
first time that Hamilton had used F1 intermediates for any
length of time, and with hindsight he should maybe have
given them an easier time in these early laps, when his
fuel load was high. Although he was impressively extending
his lead by around 0.5s each lap, he was taking a lot out
of the tyres, which tend to wear out very quickly once the
track begins to dry, which it was soon doing. The first of the
leading quartet to stop, the team left him on the existing set
of tyres, as they were expected to last for the next stint and
are faster in this part-worn state than a new set. By stopping
later, Raikkonen was able to cut Hamilton's lead down from
8.5s to 4s, but still it looked like Lewis was in good shape,
especially given that Alonso was still fourth, around 17s
behind. All Hamilton needed to do on this day to secure the
world crown was finish ahead of Alonso.

It began going wrong on the 26th lap, just as the rain
began falling again. Hamilton got to experience the sudden
catastrophic reduction in grip of a worn intermediate tyre in
wet conditions. 'It was like driving on ice,' he recalled.
Raikkonen was now right with him and within a couple of
laps had passed to take the lead. Now the white stripe of
canvas could be seen on the right-rear tyre of Hamilton's
car. At this point the team could have brought him in and
fitted new tyres – and surely should have. But they froze in
a dilemma. Which tyres to put him on? New inters or dries?
Their weather man was saying the shower was going to last
only for a couple of minutes and thereafter it would be dry.
In which case, dry weather tyres were the answer. But what if
the shower continued? Then he'd be on the wrong tyres and

Alonso, fuelled to run three laps longer, would get to choose with the benefit of those extra laps. So they kept him out there, the white ribbon of canvas getting wider every lap. Eventually they called him in. He came down the pitlane to the sharp left corner, braked, and that right-rear lost grip, twitching the car suddenly sideways. Hamilton corrected the slide but in doing so had run out of space in the tight confines – and he clattered across the gravel trap, doing no more than 20mph. For a brief moment it looked like he might keep enough momentum up to get it out the other side, but no – it stopped, beached up to its floor, rear wheels spinning uselessly. This couldn't be happening – on the cusp of the world title – but it was. Lewis desperately asked the marshals to push him, to no avail; it was stuck fast. He climbed out and walked disconsolately the short distance to the McLaren garages, shook the hands of his crew, apologised to the bosses on the pit wall, then walked back out to face the cameras.

'You can't go through life not making mistakes,' he said, 'and I can still win it in Brazil, and fully intend to.' With that he was off before the race had finished. A victory for Raikkonen brought him right back into the title hunt, and Alonso's second put him just four points behind Lewis.

Afterwards, McLaren held their hands up to their misjudgement. Had they just brought Hamilton in as soon as his tyre problem became apparent, and fitted a set of dries, he would have finished second and clinched the title – because the rain did hold off, just as forecast. Had the rain continued and Alonso changed to inters and Hamilton been forced to come back in to change again, then Alonso would have been second, Hamilton fourth. Which would still have left Hamilton seven points clear going into Brazil.

In desperately trying to beat their own man – Alonso – they ironically ended up costing Hamilton. Ron Dennis even admitted 'We weren't really racing Kimi, we were racing Alonso,' saying everything about how that particular relationship was at an end. Hamilton may now have been de facto number one at McLaren, but could he still become number one in the world?

Round 15 of 17:
Japanese Grand Prix, Fuji, 30 September

1. **Lewis Hamilton (McLaren-Mercedes)**
2. Heikki Kovalainen (Renault)
3. Kimi Raikkonen (Ferrari)
4. David Coulthard (Red Bull-Renault)
5. Giancarlo Fisichella (Renault)
6. Felipe Massa (Ferrari)
7. Robert Kubica (BMWSauber)
8. Adrian Sutil (Spyker-Ferrari)

Drivers' World Championship

1.	**Hamilton**	**107 points**
2.	Alonso	95
3.	Raikkonen	90
4.	Massa	80
5.	Heidfeld	56
6.	Kubica	35
7.	Kovalainen	30
8.	Fisichella	21
9.	Rosberg	15

10.	Wurz	13
	Coulthard	13
12.	Webber	10
13.	Trulli	7
14.	R.Schumacher	5
15.	Sato	4
16.	Button	2
17.	Vettel	1

Round 16 of 17:
Chinese Grand Prix, Shanghai, 6 October

1. Kimi Raikkonen (Ferrari)
2. Fernando Alonso (McLaren-Mercedes)
3. Felipe Massa (Ferrari)
4. Sebastian Vettel (Toro Rosso-Ferrari)
5. Jenson Button (Honda)
6. Tonio Liuzzi (Toro Rosso-Ferrari)
7. Nick Heidfeld (BMWSauber)
8. David Coulthard (Red Bull-Renault)

Drivers' World Championship

1.	**Hamilton**	**107 points**
2.	Alonso	103
3.	Raikkonen	100
4.	Massa	86
5.	Heidfeld	58
6.	Kubica	35
7.	Kovalainen	30
8.	Fisichella	21

CHAPTER TWENTY-ONE

Heartbreak on Hold

There's always a neurosis about F1, and it invariably surfaces in situations of high pressure. Coming to Brazil, the sport had its first three-way title showdown in 21 years and that was more than pressure enough to trigger the paranoia and conspiracy theories that were already underlying this remarkable season.

Noting Alonso's comments about his tyre pressures during qualifying in China, the Spanish motor sport authority had requested to the sport's world governing body, the FIA, that there should be a neutral representative in the McLaren garage during the Brazilian Grand Prix weekend in order to ensure fair play between Alonso and Hamilton. The FIA agreed and duly nominated a Brazilian official to station himself in there. It seemed just another act of humiliation for McLaren, but it didn't make a fuss, simply worked around him.

In reality, it was little more than window-dressing. There is no way any outside observer could follow every little piece of preparation and know for certain exactly what was going on around him. The technical procedures are so complex, the cars themselves so intricate, that any number of ways of ensuring that one car was better than another would be impossible to pick up. But the man was there – and more importantly, was seen to be there by the outside world. Even Alonso was dismissive of the situation: 'I don't agree with that decision,' he said, perhaps a touch disingenuously, 'but it's not up to us. If they decide to do that it's OK, but we don't need anything like that in the garage.'

He was sitting next to Hamilton as he was saying this, and given the war of words between them in the previous weeks they seemed remarkably relaxed with each other, chatting amiably between questions, poking occasional fun at the other in their answers. Cynics wondered if Alonso was now on a charm offensive to remain at McLaren, given that in the week leading up to the race, Ferrari announced that they had extended Felipe Massa's contract to the end of 2010. With Kimi Raikkonen contracted to them until the end of '09, there appeared to be no space for Alonso at Ferrari.

But although much of the attention was focused on the battle for the title between the two McLaren drivers, Ferrari's Raikkonen was still a very dangerous opponent. Although he was seven points behind Hamilton, a victory would ensure that Lewis had to finish at least fifth in order to take the crown. If Alonso were to win, Hamilton would need to finish second. There were all sorts of computations, but although the numerical odds much favoured Hamilton, the practicalities were potentially complex. Ferrari – with their other driver Massa out of championship contention – could run their campaign with a two-pronged strategy. Massa could be used to control the McLaren drivers, leaving

Raikkonen to escape. McLaren, with both their drivers in contention, could not use one to help the other. Raikkonen had the simplest task, in that all he could do was win the race – nothing less would be good enough – and then see how the others did. But for Hamilton, the man with everything to lose, striking the balance between attack and circumspection was going to be difficult.

'I don't plan to take a strategic approach,' he said. 'I don't think you can because so much is out of your control. The best way is just to attack and try to win, as always. Obviously with a win – that's the best way, to go out with style, but any way I do it would be with style because it has been a phenomenal year. Who'd have thought I'd still be leading the championship with the bits of bad luck I've had – all to do with tyres, funnily enough – but it has been phenomenal and I'm going into this weekend to try to win.'

He'd chilled out between China and here at his family's home – 'my real home,' as he put it – in Tewin, the plain and unpretentious place he'd lived in full-time until his F1 career exploded and ended his ordinary existence; before he needed to be thinking about tax havens, or good luck messages from his music idols.

Interlagos was another track he'd not seen before. He was asked if he'd tried it on the McLaren simulator. Questions about the simulator never fail to irritate him. He was stung by his portrayal as a 'robo-driver', as though his speed and success were down to programming rather than natural gift. 'No,' he replied. Did he not find it useful? 'If I did I would use it', came the immediate short shrift response.

The best way of learning the place, as ever, was to get out there and drive it. The track was wet as practice began on Friday morning, and would remain so throughout the session. He quickly got to terms with it, though he was surprised by how smooth it was after being led to expect bumps. Sitting between two lakes, the ground beneath the circuit is constantly shifting, creating the bumps that have always characterised the place. Each year they would re-surface it, and all that seemed to achieve was to replace one set of bumps with a different set. But this time, the circuit had commissioned a more thorough reworking – and for the first time ever, Interlagos was a smooth track. Which was potentially quite a significant point in the battle for the championship. McLaren came here expecting to have a faster car than rivals Ferrari, as it always handled bumps better. Now there were no bumps ... Furthermore, the new surface was jet-black. When the sun came, the track would retain more heat than the previous greyer surface – and the McLaren tended to overheat its tyres more than the Ferrari. So tailored to Ferrari did the circuit changes seem to be that some speculated they had been guided by local hero, Ferrari's Felipe Massa.

Although Hamilton found no problems with the car or circuit, he did find himself in trouble with officialdom again. This time, McLaren had transgressed a tyre usage regulation. During that first practice it had used two sets of wet weather tyres on Hamilton's car – which was not allowed. A new regulation had been introduced earlier in the year in an effort at containing costs, stipulating that only one set per session could be used. McLaren – and two other teams – had overlooked it, and there was a real concern that the stewards of the meeting might penalise Hamilton with a grid penalty. In the end, they simply fined the team 15,000 euros.

The afternoon session was held on a damp but drying track and in these conditions Hamilton indulged himself with his phenomenal car control, flinging the McLaren through the damp patches and catching the spectacular slides as if it were child's play. He looked in a different league to everyone else, and the timing beams reflected that. He was quickest by a substantial margin. But it didn't count for much. Qualifying, on the other hand, did. Held under a brilliant blue Saturday sky, the track temperatures were scorching and the place was filled close to capacity. In the dry, the Ferraris seemed to have a definite edge in performance. As the sessions progressed, it all came down to the final new-tyre runs of each of the four McLaren/Ferrari drivers. Alonso was struggling. At no stage in the weekend did he get the McLaren working to his satisfaction, complaining that it was difficult over the kerbs, normally its strong suit. Hamilton found no such problems, but had adopted a different set-up. Pole position was going to be fought out by Hamilton and the Ferrari drivers.

Ferrari's Felipe Massa was the first to complete his new-tyre runs and put himself on a provisional pole. Raikkonen was next to make his run but as he stormed down the back straight that leads to turn 4, he was aware of Hamilton's car leaving the pitlane exit road to begin its out-lap. Raikkonen needed Hamilton to stay over to the left so as not to impede him, but instead the McLaren began moving towards the right, as if about to take up the racing line into the corner. He didn't complete the move and instead moved back across out of the way on the left. But it did compromise Raikkonen's speed through the corner. It disturbed the airflow over the Ferrari's wing, and as Kimi turned in he found himself light on grip and had to rescue a big oversteering slide. He completed the lap but it was 0.24s slower than Massa's.

Hamilton proceeded to do his lap and was actually slightly ahead of Massa's time as he completed the second of the lap's three sectors. But into Juncao, a tight left-hander leading onto a long drag up the hill that merges with the start/finish straight, something made Lewis be conservative, just as he'd insisted he wasn't going to be. 'I didn't want to lose what I'd gained,' he said afterwards in reference to how quick the early part of his lap was. Slower than before through the corner, this penalised him all the way up the hill – and he crossed the line to take second-fastest time, 0.15s slower than Massa. With hindsight, that decision not to attack the final corner was a crucial moment.

Upon climbing from the car, he spoke to Raikkonen and apologised if he had got in the way. Raikkonen simply shrugged and patted him on the shoulder. But in the press conference that followed, the matter came up, introduced in quite an aggressive manner by *L'Equipe* journalist Anne Giuntini. Hamilton explained that he'd initially believed he could get around the corner without impeding Raikkonen, then realised he'd misjudged the closing speed and at that point moved back out of the way. It was a difficult one to call. It definitely had the effect of spoiling Raikkonen's lap, but if it was deliberate it had been done in a masterfully subtle way. Giuntini was not to be deterred and questioned Hamilton's sportsmanship. At which point Hamilton got visibly annoyed. When Giuntini persisted, he concluded by saying he didn't want to talk to her. Afterwards, the journalist had to be led away from verbal attacks on both Anthony Hamilton and Ron Dennis.

Ferrari agreed with Giuntini's analysis of the incident and their sporting director visited the stewards of the meeting to complain. Again, the prospect of a possible Hamilton penalty became very real. But in the end the stewards viewed it as a simple racing incident and informed Ferrari they would not be taking action.

It was clear by now that there was something of a backlash against Hamilton, among both the non-British media and certain other F1 drivers. In a sport that had believed it had rid itself of the dominance of one man with the retirement of Michael Schumacher the year before, perhaps Hamilton's performances were making them concerned about history repeating itself. Maybe the idea of a rookie world champion was plain embarrassing to more established drivers. Maybe some believed it would somehow demean the sport if someone could just walk in and claim its biggest prize at his first attempt.

But the Brazilians were definitely not part of any backlash. The crowd here clearly loved him. Hamilton merchandise – including T-shirts with twinned flags of Brazil and the UK – sold out, reportedly outsold even that of home boy Massa. Hamilton's mixed-race credentials made him irresistible to a city where every race under the sun is represented. They are hugely passionate F1 fans but no one has ever quite lit them up like their beloved fallen warrior Ayrton Senna, Hamilton's boyhood hero. But Hamilton's swashbuckling, passionate, exciting style is exactly the sort of thing that used to stir them up about their own great countryman.

As the drivers took to the back of the flat-bed truck for the drivers' parade on the eve of the race, the crowd packing the Carlos Pace Stadium to its rafters went crazy. Massa and Hamilton were the only ones they cared about, and thousands of people began to make derogatory chants to Alonso – presumably for no other reason than he was seen in simplistic terms as Hamilton's enemy. Just to add to the pressure on Hamilton, England had lost the rugby world cup final to South Africa on Saturday, so all British sporting attention was now focused on him.

To all outward appearances, Hamilton was not unduly affected by the enormity of the moment as he prepared for what might be the biggest day of his life, as the favourite to achieve something that no one in the long history of the sport had ever before achieved. But you wondered if that could really be the case as he sat there on the front of the grid waiting for the lights to change, a savage sun shining down, the fans cheering and whistling. As the lights went out and the field surged forwards, Raikkonen's Ferrari was much quicker off the line and overtook Hamilton even before they arrived at the corner. Raikkonen was side-by-side with team-mate Massa, forming an apparently impenetrable Ferrari barrier to Hamilton. As they dived into the Senna Esses together, Raikkonen corrected a rear-end slide that cost him some time and, with the instincts of thousands of racing miles, Hamilton prepared to take advantage, getting as close as he could to the Ferrari's rear. But Raikkonen was wise to him, knew he needed to stop himself being vulnerable onto the back straight, and simply lifted his accelerator momentarily at just the moment Hamilton was expecting him to accelerate. It's one of the oldest tricks in the motor racing book, and Lewis was forced to lift in avoidance. It may have been a bit of tit-for-tat from Kimi after Lewis had spoilt his lap the day before. More likely it was just the competitive drive of the moment. Just as Hamilton was forced to lift, so Raikkonen was accelerating away, leaving Lewis fumbling. Worse, it had allowed Alonso to get a run on him too, the other McLaren forcing its way through on the left. From second down to fourth in the first two corners, this wasn't a great start for Hamilton. But it wasn't disastrous either. All he needed to do was keep his car on the road. He didn't need to win this race. But with the adrenaline flowing, irritated at being mugged by Raikkonen, he was determined to re-pass Alonso into turn 4. Alonso played it perfectly, placing his car in the middle of the track, forcing Lewis to try the outside. He did so, braked – and immediately locked a wheel, sliding off the circuit onto the run-off tarmac. He was still going but was now down to eighth. For the first time all year, Hamilton had looked like a rookie, like someone caught up in the intensity of the moment and allowing it to cloud his judgement. It was an incredibly un-Lewis-like error of judgement.

He quickly began to put things right, slipstreaming past Jarno Trulli for seventh as they began the second lap. Next on his radar: the BMW of Nick Heidfeld, who appeared rather more determined to defend than Trulli. For four laps Hamilton pressured him, once clattering his car hard across the turn 5 kerbs as he tried to line up the BMW. A few corners later he finally got ahead, at the same place as he'd passed Trulli. Now he was up to sixth, just one away from the place that would guarantee him the title assuming Raikkonen won – as looked likely. The Ferraris were drawing away from Alonso at an incredible rate and so long as they kept going were clearly going to finish 1–2, well ahead of Alonso.

Hamilton's title campaign still looked well on course as he now began to close on the fifth-place Red Bull of Mark Webber. But then disaster. As Hamilton pulled on the down-shift paddle approaching turn 4 on the seventh lap, the McLaren's gearbox found only neutral. Repeated downshift attempts brought no response and Hamilton coasted along as car after car overtook. The McLaren engineers looking at their monitors in the garage could see the problem. It was not insurmountable; the electronics controlling the hydraulic mechanism that changes the gears had suffered a glitch and simply needed to be rebooted. This involved a complex sequence of the clutch lever and the down-change paddle – and the team relayed these instructions to Hamilton as his car coasted pitifully slowly. He did as requested, and after around 20 seconds the gearbox came back to life and he once more had a fully healthy car. But he was now back in 18th place, almost half a minute from the required fifth place. Once again, he set about making the lost places back up.

As he made his first refuelling stop at the end of the 22nd lap, his target still looked achievable. At this point the team took a calculated gamble to try to boost his recovery. They decided to fuel him for a short second stint of just 14 laps and fit the slower super-soft compound tyres (the regulations demand that you use each of the two specifications of supplied tyre). These tyres were expected to be unsuited to the scorching track temperatures, so it seemed to make sense to have them on for the minimum time. He would then make a second stop and be refuelled to the end. It was a good plan – but it foundered on Hamilton's unexpectedly high tyre-wear. As he left the pits from his first stop the team looked at the tyres they had just removed – and realised they were almost completely worn out. This was after a stint of just 22 laps. The second stop that his light fuel load now committed him to was 35 laps from the end. There was no way tyres that had only just made 22 laps were going to complete 35 – and McLaren realised with dismay that they would need to make a third stop. The extra 28–30 seconds that this would cost finally dashed Hamilton's hopes. Had they just stayed with a standard two-stop strategy with a long middle stint and a short final one on the super-soft tyres, there's every indication he would have garnered that vital fifth place. As it was, he could finish only seventh. Raikkonen won the race, with Alonso third. The result gave the Ferrari driver the title with 110 points. Hamilton and Alonso were tied on 109. One point between the three of them after 18 races. The rookie dream was over.

As Raikkonen told his story in the winner's press conference, Hamilton took time to thank his crew and sheltered in the McLaren garage, away from the clamour that awaited him outside. When he did eventually appear, he put on a very convincing brave face. 'I went into the race thinking, "Whatever happens today it has been a phenomenal year." Who'd have thought I'd be leading the world championship going into the final race? With a little luck I might have done it, but it's a great feeling to have been in that position. The team has done a phenomenal job all year, absolutely amazing. We all wanted to win the rugby world cup and the F1 world championship, but it obviously wasn't to be England's turn. But it's my first year of F1 and next year we'll bounce back stronger, for sure.'

They were the words, and he probably was trying to believe them himself. But there will have been a moment, whether in the car, in the garage, at the team end-of-season party that night – a party planned in the expectation of a celebration – or maybe in his hotel room later, when he will have felt the pain. He would not have been human if he didn't think, however fleetingly: 'Why did I stay out on that worn tyre in China?'; 'Why did they put me on that short second stint today?'; 'How did I lose a 12-point lead in two races?' He alluded to this on the Monday morning, saying: 'Sure, later on in the evening I felt it more. It's tough on everybody.'

He also gave his reaction to the news – which emerged from the track on Sunday evening some hours after the race ended – that he may yet get his title because three of the cars that finished ahead of him, the BMWs of Nick Heidfeld and Robert Kubica and the Williams of Nico Rosberg, were under investigation for having their fuel cooled below the permitted temperature. By making the fuel denser, this would confer an advantage by giving faster refuelling and a temporary power boost afterwards. The stewards decided not to take action as there was too much doubt about the accuracy of the ambient temperature. McLaren served notice of appeal to the stewards' decision. Were Rosberg, Kubica and Heidfeld disqualified and Hamilton moved up to an official fourth place, it would give him 112 points, enough to take the championship. But it would be a hollow victory – and Lewis himself felt as much: 'If they [BMW and Williams] are wrong, they are wrong, but I want to win on the track. You want to win the race and do it in style. Being promoted after some people have been thrown out is not the way I want to win it. It would feel weird after Kimi did such a fantastic job in the last two races and won on Sunday. Having it taken away would be a bit cruel and probably not good for the sport.'

But what had been really good for the sport, regardless of who won the title, was Hamilton's impact upon it. This whirlwind of speed, attack and panache had excited the purists, but not half as much as the onlooking outside world. The rookie world champion dream was over, but no other record of achievement looked safe from this phenomenon.

For the black kid from a Stevenage council estate, this was, to borrow one of his expressions, 'sweet'.

Round 17 of 17:
Brazilian Grand Prix, Interlagos, 18 October

1. Kimi Raikkonen (Ferrari)
2. Felipe Massa (Ferrari)
3. Fernando Alonso (McLaren-Mercedes)
4. Nico Rosberg (Williams-Toyota)
5. Robert Kubica (BMWSauber)
6. Nick Heidfeld (BMWSauber)
7. **Lewis Hamilton (McLaren-Mercedes)**
8. Jarno Trulli (Toyota)

Drivers' World Championship

1.	Raikkonen	110 points
2.	**Hamilton**	**109**
	Alonso	109
4.	Massa	94
5.	Heidfeld	61
6.	Kubica	39
7.	Kovalainen	30
8.	Fisichella	21
9.	Rosberg	20
10.	Coulthard	14
11.	Wurz	13
12.	Webber	10
13.	Trulli	8
14.	Vettel	6
	Button	6

CHAPTER TWENTY-TWO

Shipping Out
and Getting On

Lewis Hamilton had flown into Brazil as leader of the world championship, on the verge of a unique achievement. He left it as the defeated finalist, with that unique achievement forever out of his grasp. Unless, of course, the Paris appeal court found in McLaren's favour in a few weeks. The likelihood of that seemed remote in the extreme. Even if Rosberg, Kubica and Heidfeld were disqualified from their respective fourth, fifth and sixth places, there was no compunction to promote Hamilton from his seventh place, merely an option. For the FIA to deliberately choose to change the outcome of the world championship – and in favour of someone driving for a team that it had recently disqualified from the constructors' championship – would be against all logic, and Hamilton put it to the back of his mind.

He flew home to Tewin, and later enjoyed a Sunday lunch there with his extended family. A few days later he paid a visit to Great Ormond Street children's hospital and met with some of his young fans. It was when leaving the hospital and answering reporters' questions that he revealed he had decided to leave Britain and was planning on setting up home in Switzerland. It would be fair to say that British press reaction to the news was largely negative. The taxation benefits of such a move for a well-paid sportsman were obvious, and on those terms it was entirely understandable, but when he chose to couch it purely in terms of the invasion of his privacy in Britain, it was hard not to be cynical.

'It was a tough decision,' he said. 'My dream for years was to move to London – I stayed at a friend's house this weekend in London and I woke up in the morning and just knew it was where I wanted to be. But I'll meet new people, new faces, and I do have a few friends there and my family and friends from home will be able to come and visit me. [Here] you lose your ability to go places – you don't understand what that means until you get there and you really struggle to lead a normal life. When you come home and everybody knows you, it makes it so much harder to do normal things. I can't go to the cinema. I go to the bathroom in a petrol station and people come in there for autographs.'

A measure of how much his success had transcended the world of F1 came with his appearance on British TV chat show *Parkinson*. The show's host, veteran interviewer Michael Parkinson, pursued the Switzerland question and made the point about lower taxation. Only then did Hamilton allow that it had been 'one of' the factors in his decision. He then went on to relate another tale of invasion of privacy. 'I am just a normal person and this is quite an unreal experience. I've gone literally from nowhere, and I have been leapfrogged into being this superstar. It's a really weird experience. Just the other night I went to a book-signing event with my dad and we drove home, got out of the car, and got ambushed by some people that followed us all the way home. You sort of worry for a second, and wonder what they want. And that's becoming more and more usual.'

Another little indication of how Hamilton's performance had moved F1 further into public consciousness came when Parkinson remarked to Conservative party leader David Cameron – who was sharing the interviewees' couch with Hamilton – that former Labour leader and Prime Minister Tony Blair 'was your Alonso'. By this time, it had been announced that Alonso and McLaren had indeed split two years short of their allocated contract time. The press release phrased it in neutral terms, saying that the partnership 'had just not worked out for whatever reason', but no one was in any doubt that the animosity between Alonso and team boss Ron Dennis – and critically Alonso's conduct in trying to use the espionage case as a lever in his negotiations with Dennis – had brought about a complete collapse of the relationship. A collapse in which Hamilton's exceptional performances had played a key part. A few weeks later, Alonso confirmed that he would be returning to Renault, the team with which he had won the 2005 and '06 world championships.

Hamilton continued to insist that his relationship with Alonso remained OK. 'We're not close friends,' he said, 'but it's not as strained as has been widely reported. We get on as well as any other two people working together. He doesn't call me up to come to my house, but we say "hi" – sometimes we play PlayStation, sometimes we have dinner together. At the end of the year we had a big hug and we said what a phenomenal year it had been, and I said it had been a pleasure working with him.' The question of who would replace Alonso as Hamilton's team-mate at McLaren-Mercedes remained open.

On 21 November 2007, four weeks after the final race, the FIA International Court of Appeal convened in Paris to hear McLaren's appeal of the Brazilian Grand Prix results. The decision of the Brazil GP stewards not to disqualify the BMWs of Robert Kubica and Nick Heidfeld and the Williams of Nico Rosberg, for allegedly using fuel chilled to below the permitted temperature, remained intact. Doubts about the accuracy of the ambient temperature, upon which the permitted fuel temperature is based, were the basis of allowing the results to stand. This doubt was successfully picked up by the BMW and Williams defence lawyers. Everyone concerned breathed a sigh of relief, for the credibility of the sport would have taken a further serious knock on top of 'Spygate' had the outcome of the world drivers' championship been changed weeks after the final race.

A couple of weeks later, Hamilton was the star guest at British motor racing's most prestigious get-together, the annual Autosport Awards in London, the event at which Hamilton had first introduced himself to Ron Dennis 13 years earlier. To no one's great surprise, the magazine's readers had voted him International Driver of the Year, British Competition Driver of the Year, and Rookie of the Year, the first time anyone had achieved all three accolades in the same season. But there *was* a surprise in store for Lewis. Viviane Senna, sister of Hamilton's childhood hero Ayrton, walked on stage to present him with his awards, and Lewis was visibly moved – even more so as she started to speak. 'Hamilton,' she said, lightly touching his cheek, 'is more than just a special pilot. He reminds me so much of my brother – both as a driver and a man. He has the same kindness in his eyes. God bless you for your whole life.' It was a poignant moment as they hugged. Lewis then had the unenviable task of following the moment up with some words.

'Ayrton played such a big part in my life,' he said. 'Through karting and single-seaters, I was always watching his videos. I never imagined I would get to meet someone close to him. I'm honoured you could come here – it's such a great pleasure for me, and I'm just speechless.' He then went on to talk about his season, and was particularly illuminating about the opening races. 'At the beginning of the year I wanted to take the other drivers by surprise,' he said. 'That was probably why I did so well in the first corner [at Australia and Malaysia], but I think they caught on after that. I was given a lot of respect, but they quickly realised I wasn't here to mess around.' He signed off by dedicating it all to his family.

The comparison with Senna had appeared *again*, this time from the late man's sister. Such comparison with the sport's icons upset many of the traditionalists. But when Senna himself made such an impact upon F1 in 1984 or Michael Schumacher did the same in 1991, there were similar outcries about early claims of the supremely high level they were operating at. Hamilton had out-done even those two in his rookie achievements, largely because he entered the category with a more competitive car. Eleven years earlier, Jacques Villeneuve had enjoyed similar success in his rookie season, but Hamilton's performances carried so much more resonance simply because of how tough a time he gave his double world champion team-mate Alonso. The

Spaniard was assumed to be the man who would inherit Schumacher's role as F1's standard bearer and it was difficult not to feel for him when, just as he'd helped ease Schumacher into retirement by defeating him for two consecutive years, he immediately encountered a rookie team-mate who threatened that stature. Alonso might reasonably have expected a longer reign than that.

Hamilton's attacking style and spectacular oversteering car control invite obvious comparisons with Senna. He had yet to regularly show the mesmerising one-lap qualifying pace of the late Brazilian, although his incredible Shanghai pole lap was certainly worthy of direct comparison. In the heat of the ultimate title pressure, Hamilton had faltered, just as Michael Schumacher had several times in his career. Only time will tell whether his fumbles in Brazil – and to a lesser extent in China – come to be seen as typical or as exceptions. Schumacher carried the trait throughout his career. Both Schumacher and Senna also resorted to outrageous professional fouls in their time, territory that Hamilton has not – as yet – definitively entered, although there are those who insist that his interruption of Raikkonen's qualifying lap in Brazil was an example of just that. Let's just say the verdict's still out on that. The bravery of his overtaking moves has drawn comparison with Nigel Mansell, one of the most excitingly combative performers the sport has seen. There is no doubt whatsoever that Hamilton is already one of the greats, regardless of the brevity of his time in the sport – no matter how offensive the traditionalists find that. What emerges in the coming seasons will simply be down to the competitive circumstances in which he finds himself – i.e., how competitive his machinery is in what is a totally machinery-dependent sport.

Jacques Villeneuve went on to win the world title in his second year – and Hamilton is now aiming to emulate that feat. But Jacques' father Gilles, the Ferrari ace, was widely recognised as the fastest driver of his time – and was almost certainly more gifted than his son – but never won a world title before his death in a qualifying accident for the 1982 Belgian Grand Prix. Jenson Button, for one, gave warning of how it didn't necessarily follow that, just because Hamilton had come so close to a title in his rookie year, he was bound to win it next time. 'It just doesn't work like that,' warned Jenson. 'He may never get such a chance again.'

But Hamilton was his usual irrepressible self when talking of his chances. 'I will be chasing it until it happens,' he said. 'That's part of my personality. There's not been one person I've met who goes as far as me. Some people just bail out right at the end and I still manage to do that little bit further. I will keep on going until I reach my goal.'

Earlier in the year, bookmakers had stopped taking bets on the outcome of British Sports Personality of the Year, so much was Hamilton the overwhelming favourite. As it happened, that lost them a lot of potential revenue, for Hamilton's failure to clinch the world crown shifted the public's votes towards boxing's Joe Calzaghe, the world super-middleweight champion, undefeated in 44 fights. Hamilton was runner-up in the voting, ahead of another boxer, defeated world heavyweight contender Ricky Hatton. Calzaghe garnered 28 per cent of the British public's votes, Hamilton 19 per cent. Hamilton – fresh from losing his road licence in France for speeding at 120mph on the autoroute – was just as publicly magnanimous towards Calzaghe as he had been a few weeks earlier towards Kimi Raikkonen, saying: 'He's a worthy winner. I can't say I have totally followed his career – what Joe Calzaghe does is very different to my job – but he's been phenomenal.'

This was mid-December, and even as Hamilton was leaving the latest ceremony and dodging the paparazzi yet again, behind the scenes events were unfolding that could yet ensure that the '07 McLaren espionage affair compromised Hamilton's 2008 season. As part of their investigation into the affair, the FIA had examined McLaren's 2008 car to determine whether it carried any of Ferrari's intellectual property. If they found that it did, there was a possibility they could refuse to sanction it to race. The consequences of that on the already beleaguered team would be devastating and would place a question mark over its entire future. The FIA report stated that several of McLaren's 2007 developments could have been influenced by information gleaned from the Ferrari documents. But no details of their findings on the '08 car were released – leaving McLaren to sweat.

To minimise the risk of their new car not being granted the all-clear, McLaren issued a letter to the FIA expressing their regret that the Ferrari information had indeed spread further into the McLaren organisation than they had originally believed, and accepting that the FIA's investigation had brought this to light. Two weeks later, McLaren and the FIA jointly released this letter, the FIA labelling it a statement of 'apology' – and at the same time the FIA announced that the matter was now finally closed. Few observers were in any doubt that McLaren had issued the grovelling letter in order to safeguard their continued participation in the sport.

With that in place, negotiations over Hamilton's contract with the team – ongoing since the middle of the season –

at last reached a conclusion. On 3 January 2008 it was announced that Hamilton and the team had extended their commitment to each other to the end of 2012. The deal was reported to be worth £50 million over the five years. 'While last year was my first year with the team in Formula 1, I have been connected to McLaren and Mercedes-Benz since 1998 and feel that I could easily drive for this team for the whole of my Formula 1 career,' said Lewis.

Two days later, McLaren launched the 2008 car at Mercedes' Stuttgart museum. Revealed also was the identity of Hamilton's 2008 team-mate: Heikki Kovalainen, the young Finnish driver who had entered F1 at the same time as Hamilton, driving for the Renault team. It was ironic that he had joined Renault as Alonso's replacement and was now joining McLaren under the same circumstances.

Hamilton was delighted with the decision, one that on paper appeared to make him de facto team number one. But this was something Hamilton was keen to dismiss, anxious not to repeat the mistake that Alonso had made with him a year earlier. 'I don't accept that,' he said. 'We expect to have exactly the same opportunity and I believe that is what we are going to be given. I'm sure as team-mates we are going to push to beat each other, push the team forward.'

But his ease with Kovalainen after the uneasy tension of his relationship with Alonso was plain to see. 'You know how it is with certain people,' he said in obvious reference to Alonso. 'Some people you ask questions and they give you one-word answers, and some people make the conversation and are just easy. With Heikki I don't need to make the conversation, he is happy to start it and we just can talk for ages. And I think he has very similar views to me. He loves the car without traction control, he loves racing wheel-to-wheel, he loves a real true spirit race. With that I think it just makes everything a little bit simpler.' The spaces between the lines of what he was saying were very small and didn't need much interpreting.

As the teams all commenced testing of their 2008 machines around the tracks of southern Spain, Hamilton expressed his satisfaction with the car. But no one missed the fact that consistently the fastest machine was the Ferrari of world champion Kimi Raikkonen. Lewis was going to have a challenge on his hands for '08. But he usually responds to those rather well.

INDEX